AURAL HISTORY

BEFORE YOU START TO READ THIS BOOK, TAKE THIS MOMENT to think about making a donation to punctum books, an independent non-profit press,

@ https://punctumbooks.com/support/

If you're reading the e-book, you can click on the image below to go directly to our donations site. Any amount, no matter the size, is appreciated and will help us to keep our ship of fools afloat. Contributions from dedicated readers will also help us to keep our commons open and to cultivate new work that can't find a welcoming port elsewhere. Our adventure is not possible without your support.
Vive la open access.

Fig. 1. Hieronymus Bosch, Ship of Fools (1490–1500)

Gila Ashtor

Aural History

Brainstorm Books
Santa Barbara, California

brainstorm books

First published in 2020 by Brainstorm Books
An imprint of punctum books, Earth, Milky Way
https://www.punctumbooks.com

ISBN-13: 978-1-950192-67-0 (print)
ISBN-13: 978-1-950192-68-7 (ePDF)

DOI: 10.21983/P3.0282.1.00

LCCN: 2019957788
Library of Congress Cataloging Data is available from the Library of Congress

Editorial team: Jasmine Vo and Karla Valverde
Book design: Vincent W.J. van Gerven Oei
Cover design: Karla Valverde and Vincent W.J. van Gerven Oei

Contents

Preface

I.

The protagonist is twelve years old when her father dies and twenty-seven when her younger brother runs away from home. Between these years the girl is functional, intelligent, reflective, amiable, engaging, serious, and often funny. She makes friends and gets scholarships and helps people, her family primarily, and often in unconventional ways. It is evident to some of the adults she encounters that she's working too much, and it might be a way of coping, but she does not speak emotionally about herself, and so in spite of how extroverted she can be in public, she is rather shy and self-effacing. She is not depressed or particularly withdrawn. She believes she's doing her best to make her dead beloved father proud. Everyone agrees that she is a good kid. The only rather unusual feature of these years is that, on three separate occasions, she falls in love with older, tougher, female teachers, but when invited to connect to them she cannot find a way to speak. Throughout these fifteen years, she has a vague, inarticulable sense of being "far away," but when asked *what from?* she has no clue and every attempt at therapeutic intervention ends up diagnosing her with "grief." It's only when the brother leaves that suddenly she falls apart, a world of needs and feelings exploding like a submarine that has been spit up on the beach. She did not know it at the time, but for fifteen years, the part of herself that told her what she wanted was totally submerged and inaccessible. Where had all these feelings been? Why hadn't there been any clues that some vital component of her psychic apparatus was mute and decommissioned?

II.

Sure, there is a burgeoning field of trauma research that tells us, fear affects our brain and freezes us – but really, *frozen*? For *fifteen* years?

Besides, she was not emotionally distant, detached, or unrelated. She could empathize with anyone, write stunning essays on her favorite books. She cried at night about how much she missed her dad. The brain cannot be feeling deeply and be deeply frozen at the same time.

Of course, if we turn to Lacan, we learn of misrecognition and that Language is fundamentally self-alienating, but tell me, does this seem like typical self-alienation to you? Lacan says we can't really "know" our own "desire," but perhaps we can acknowledge that, developmentally, "desire" is light years away from a more rudimentary self-relation. I think we can agree there is a meaningful distinction between knowing one's own deepest "desire" versus not knowing what discomfort feels like because you must believe that everything is fine.

In the world of psychotherapy, it has become so popular to talk about "dissociation," but that's describing a mechanism whereby parts of the self are split off from self-awareness, whereas what we're seeing in the girl is an entire psychic apparatus totally unplugged.

How do we understand the intractability of the inner signal's absolute deactivation? The systematic failure of talk-therapy to notice that some crucial feature of an affective and *reactive* self was gone?

This is the mystery *Aural History* sets out to recreate.

III.

It's likely that in spite of your most benevolent readerly intentions, you will not feel connected to the girl on the page. How could you?

Her primary mechanism of self-relation is fatally impaired.

Turns out, even though we tolerate a range of narrators, we still expect them to, at the very least, *narrate,* and, because narrative is driven by perspective on one's experience, and because it's precisely the loss of emotional reflexivity that destroys the girl's access to perspective, she cannot walk us through her own erasure.

Whereas traditionally memoir depends upon restoring and reconstructing feelings that we assume we must have *had* (even if at the time we didn't necessarily *know* precisely what our feelings were), *Aural History* reenacts what happens to a narrator when her feelings are neither known, nor even ever had.

What kind of experimental form can dramatize the self's evaporation?

Is it still technically a "memoir" if instead of getting closer to the self, we watch it bear its own repudiation?

When a memoir is a ghost story, what genre are we in?

IV.

As a thirty-something scholar of queer theory, I am trained to say there's really no such thing as a "true self." But as a practicing clinician, I hear wrenching stories centered on the pain of how a "truth" was breached, the mystery of moments when the "self" somehow submitted to its violation.

What is the injunction "know thyself" without the threat of self-betrayal?

V.

To explain the times we found ourselves endangered, we say: we had been motivated by hard feelings – of despair, anxiety, restlessness, devastation.

i.   That job we sabotaged without really remembering why;
ii. That year we drank ourselves to sleep each night even though we were sure we hated alcohol;
iii. That period of putting our bodies in conditions we would otherwise find reckless and enraging.

Later, we look back, and in some mix of horror and confusion, maybe compassion too, we say, it must have been depression driving us headlong toward that cliff, we must have been self-hating. With gratitude for our narrow escape, we insist that we were acting out of feelings that we had but couldn't appropriately handle.

There is something comforting about this explanation.

Even our peril is a tragedy that, by indirectly causing, we control.

What if instead we said: sometimes we lose ourselves without ever surrendering.

What if instead we said: it is not our feelings that are dangerous, but instead, the absence of a self-relation, the bewildering and temporary inability to *feel* what we are *feeling*.

What if we said: we are not always willfully destructive; sometimes we move as though under a spell, and then, somehow, we are awakened.

What makes the psyche fall asleep?

VI.

It is no longer scandalous to say that a vast majority of psychic life occurs unconsciously.

When in 1916, Freud reflected on the "wound" that his discovery of the "unconscious" would inflict on man's "naïve self-love," he compared his findings to the Copernican Revolution in which humankind was forced to recognize that, contrary to our grandiose presuppositions, "our earth was not the center of the universe."[1] Just as astronomical science dismissed the ancient myth of the earth's special centrality by demonstrating that it actually revolved around the sun, so too, Freud showed, the mind was not the pinnacle of sovereign self-control but actually the riven product of unseen and anarchic forces.

But if once upon a time this revelation of our limitations seemed it would irreparably "wound" us, today, we are so modern, we are so utterly enlightened, we don't so much as flinch to

1   Sigmund Freud, *A General Introduction to Psychoanalysis,* trans. G. Stanley Hall (New York: Boni and Liveright, 1920), 246–47.

hear that consciousness can be misleading, that we might really hate the friend we claim to love, crave the cruelty we feel torments us, keep secrets from ourselves, attach to people that we cannot want or shouldn't, be defensive.

Indeed, is it not an emblem of modernity to draw the shape of knowledge by the trace of its concessions, to say, alongside Freud, the "ego is not the master in his own house,"[2] that if consciousness is like an iceberg, we, as moderns, acquiesce to seeing nothing but the narrow tip?

VII.

So let us say we are Copernican and modest: does having a deep "unconscious" really explain the ease and speed with which we, somehow unaware, are susceptible to overriding our deepest needs and wishes?

i. I'm thinking of relationships that seemed okay while we were in them, and when they ended, it suddenly seemed clear that, in fact, all along some essential inner voice was missing that rendered us strangely muted and complicit.

ii. I'm thinking of encounters that seemed un-reckless when we did them, and only later recognized that even if "technically" we had "agreed," there were some basic signals of desire that were precluded, absent, mysteriously forbidden.

Is it really descriptively honest to keep insisting that even things we can't remember *willing* are actually expressions of a feeling that we *had* or *wanted*?

What about the difference between not-knowing our true feelings, and not having them at all?

The familiar philosophical claim that humankind is doomed to somber ignorance is oh so grand and transcendental that it for-

2   Sigmund Freud, "A Difficulty in the Path of Psycho-analysis," in *Standard Edition of the Complete Psychological Works of Sigmund Freud, Vol. XVII (1917–1919): An Infantile Neurosis and Other Works,* ed. and trans. James Strachey with Anna Freud (London: Hogarth Press, 1978–81), 134–44, at 143.

gets the fundamental difference between Absolutely Knowing your "Soul" and generally being able to *feel* what you're experiencing.

Put another way, you may not always know for sure whether you love or hate your mother. But your dynamic psychic functioning depends upon a voice that indicates to you the possible reactions that, in any given moment, you may be having.

VIII.

This is not a voice as in a "command" that you obey, but more like a private, internal signal that tells your somewhat conscious mind what you're affectively experiencing.

i. You run into someone and start talking and midway through, you start to think, "oh god I'm so annoyed, when can I plot my exit out of here."
ii. You're on a date and wondering, "I think I feel uncomfortable, maybe this person's not my type, or I'm just in a cranky mood, whatever."
iii. Or maybe you are yawning and you think, "I must be tired now, I didn't realize" or "I don't know why I'm sad but something isn't feeling right."

There is a channel between what we are *aware* of, on the one hand, and our *psycho-affective* life on the other, and every psyche has a messenger that ferries communications from our sensory experience to our conscious mind.

So if there is a signal, can't a signal be impaired? Can it disappear completely?

And what happens when – because it is a signal – you cannot recognize its absence until it's back to work again? And then you wonder: how could I not have *known* I was so miserable for all those anguished years? What was I *doing* every time I smiled and really *felt* it was okay?

Is it really incidental that the language used for this phenomena typically involves the phrase, "I lost myself," or was "untrue" to what I wanted?

IX.

Of course, once god is dead and the ego is dethroned, we are supposedly immune to the pathos of self-losing. Our well-honed postmodern scorn for the quaint promise of "true selfhood" – on the grounds that ideological interpellation is pervasive and the "self" is hopeless because so thoroughly "socially" *constructed* – provides us sexy abstract claims that stall in debates so vague and hyperbolic: the subject is or isn't dead? the subject is performing or divided? such that you'd almost (wrongly) think there is One, True, unit of measuring Selfhood that can represent the vast and complex range of what it means for the dynamic "self" to have a body/psyche in the context of interpersonal life.

After all, is it coincidental that so many examples of self-estrangement involve our relationship to other people, and if so, what does this indicate about how relationships structure and determine our elemental access to ourselves?

Do certain external conditions exacerbate our vulnerability to being self-abandoned?

Is sex a privileged scene of self-undoing?

What is the role of trauma in acute or systematic self-betrayal?

How do we represent a psychological phenomenon that – by definition – is not emotionally accessible until *after* the broken inner signal has been sufficiently restored?

X.

For all our supposed surrender to being Copernican and "decen-tered," we have, as yet, barely considered the implications of having a psychic system that revolves around the needs and dreams of *other* minds. What if we are susceptible therefore to pulls we can't feel moving us, to possible eclipse?

XI.

Aural History is an attempt to capture an event of self-annihilation that in the length of its duration and peculiar manner of manifestation, offers an extreme account of what it means to lose yourself, and have no way to know it.

I am a girl who did not want to be king

In the game we are playing, the king is my father and I am his daughter,

the prince.

My father is king and I am his prince.

My father, my king, in the game we are playing, you live forever and I'll stay your girlchild, adorable.

I am a child when he hands me the keys.

The game was not over.

The kingdom in flames.

And I said, father, can't you I see I'm burning?

My father, the king, answers nothing.

Why do we say when the king is dead, long live the king?

David was a shepherd boy appointed in the desert, first anointed in the dark.

I am the girl who is only a prince, who is only a girl.

I am the girl who once was a king.

D (David)

I know. It sounds ridiculous to say, *forgive me father*.

Weak, overwrought, even hysterical to say, *for I have sinned*.

I lost the voice of my dead dad as it sounded in my head.

So what?

I should be secular by now.

I should grow up. I should be free! I should be unapologetic about whatever uncontrolled developmental journey is happening to me.

It is grief. And, it's inevitable.

Independence. Self-possession.

Besides, I want to know: what kind of sin is it to say, I cannot hear your voice inside my head?

Forgive me father – how dramatic! Begging and confessing when it's not my fault, when there is no absolution.

But I can't help it, I am panicking.

I don't know what to do. Or, how to be. Or, who am I? Or, why, except it feels a sin to say, *I have forgotten the sound of your voice.*

Bless me father, I have fucked up.

That I lost you. That I had you? That I need you, still.

❦

I was nineteen when I suddenly noticed I could not summon what he sounded like.

At first, I meant the concrete sound of him. That tender mix of English, French and Hebrew that sounded elegant and hard to place. He called his accent "Belgian" because he didn't want the politics or desert heat of being born Israeli. And, anyway, "how many Belgians have you met?" He'd like to joke. "They're European but no one ever comes from there!" He said, "don't worry", when I said I'm worried that you'll be found out.

I was standing in the dining room of the house my mother bought with her tyrant lover in the summer after my first year of college, realizing I had no one to tell me what I should do.

Talk to me dad, I started begging the air.

I knew even then I was being symbolic.

I was twelve when he died. It had been years since we spoke. Who knew when the last time was I recalled his voice correctly.

But, now I heard actual silence where his companionship used to be.

Up until then, his words were a lake that I dipped my feet into when the sun was too hot and my mind couldn't find the comprehension it needed.

What do I do with the wreck of a boy that I'm raising? The baby brother that I treat as my son – when he again gets suspended for throwing his desk on the floor or looking high in the morning. Do I bargain with him for improvement or take away his electronic toys?

The woman who vies with the boy for parental attention, intervention, banging the furniture of every room she is in, whether she's happy or sad, spending money we need for the bakery business we're running, apologizing for not buying groceries or not signing forms on the counter or forgetting not to sign anything legally binding that I haven't first read. When my mother does another thing I think will finally sink us, does it make sense to sound judgmental as a self-righteous, smarter daughter would or pretend I am her husband telling her what to do? What will be more effective or effective at all?

Should I major in English literature or politics? Philosophy? Psychology? Every teacher tells me their own field is where I belong, but I find everything interesting and don't know how one is supposed to freely choose.

Based on his values and the things he said when I was little, I became adept at extrapolating an opinion he might give.

We talked this way for hours, he and I. I lived this way for years.

And then, all of a sudden, one day he was gone.

I am standing in the dining room in this decrepit creaking house they say they bought to fix, with its egg-yolk yellow wallpaper, gaudy golden antique table, and ghastly grand-cushioned chairs. The room is strewn with her old furniture and his, lit by the extravagant chandelier she opened a new credit card account to purchase. I'm thinking, should I go to this prestigious teaching internship in New York City, as planned. Or should I surrender to this overwhelming need I feel to be by myself for the first time and quiet.

So, I ask. Then, I ask again, as if he merely missed his cue. I say, it is your turn to remind me what I ought to do, but nothing comes back but an echo – the instantaneous awareness that no one's there.

I wear mostly bootcut, shapeless jeans, long-sleeve shirts, and hoodies in those days. I have short curly brown hair, no jewelry but a big silver heart on a necklace my mother gave me when I turned sixteen and fake diamond stud earrings that she says I should wear.

I am wider and fleshier than I should be for my narrow frame. Not overweight in a discernible way, just a generalized unfitness that I hope no one notices but, having been athletic, I know that I feel.

I see food as a logistical burden and every meal I eat makes me ill.

I smile often and widely.

I move briskly, talk quickly, never stand still long enough to seem tired.

There are girls in school who are always cajoling me to go out on the weekends with them. You're so funny, they tell me and giggle, c'mon. There are boys who feel sure that dating me will make them profound.

College is like being in a baby-proofed house after coming back from three tours in Iraq.

I have four majors, 2 minors, and four jobs, so that no one will ever notice how restless I am.

I don't want to notice how restless I am.
    I smother the shaking with errands and papers.

I am sufficiently enlightened to know that therapy is probably overdue, but also if someone tells me I should worry less and feel things deeply, I'll explode.

Besides, I'm not an idiot.
    I understand what a defense mechanism looks like.
    But I've only ever heard people talk about letting them go.

As I'm standing in the dining room, repeating I don't hear you, whispering *talk to me dad* the way you waken someone who is merely deeply sleeping, I can imagine, for a moment, how this could be a signal of healing as I've seen it advertised.

What a sign of maturation to finally renounce my stubborn colloquy with sonic ghosts.

But when the shrinks say this, I think they perceive attachment as something you can modulate freely to accommodate your changing needs, that you can journey from dependence to prideful autonomy by gradually getting to know yourself better.

How heroic the well-mourned adult must seem, putting away lovers, the next step from childish things.

At his funeral, I read a poem I had written called "daddy's little girl." I'm twelve and managed to rhyme girl with curl in a way that conveys how desperately I love him.

I cannot reach the microphone and everyone is crying.

I am adorable.

Afterward, people come up to me in a steady stream of pitying faces to tell me how proud my dead dad would be. People cry, pet my head, and say, "our father talked about you always. it wasn't just because you were his daughter that he was so crazy about you." They're telling stories to help themselves feel connected to my pain and it makes me want to comfort and reassure them.

I'll be okay, I fantasize saying.

Some of these mourners are so visibly heart-stricken I wonder if I should put an arm around their shoulder, say, now, now and gently pet their head. But, this would make plain the way I see them and, besides, I cannot reach them.

I have already checked.

Two years ago, when we moved back to Toronto after two years of his being sick in Boca Raton, he found an Israeli ex-commando with a judo club to teach me how to "defend myself." Since I would be "a girl growing up by myself in a dangerous world," he arranged for me to learn some moves from this steely-jawed veteran who was renowned for having trained his unit to kill the enemy without breaking a sweat.

I turned out to be a natural at judo, that art of dancing with and throwing other people. And, I find that as I'm seated in the front pews listening to mourners who are extra dramatic in their performative empathy, I am calculating if I have the necessary angles to bend myself into their torso, lift us back up quickly enough to fly into the air together, and land back down. My right arm still holds their lapels with them lying beneath me, too winded to keep saying they know how hard it is for me to lose a dad.

They think I lost my favorite person.

Because even from afar, it isn't hard to tell where temperamental affinities align in the kinship arrangement of our family life. The father and daughter are brainy, articulate and social. The mother and son are hyperactive, nonverbal, and difficult to reach.

They are thinking that I lost my playmate. Of the way I could be precocious on command when I was tagging along with him somewhere and he would say, "you'll never believe the question Gila asked me the other day – she's only 7! Tell them, Gila." And I could repeat it all bashfully while he laid his heavy hand on my shoulder, boasted, and beamed.

Maybe you could tell we were a duo: like two Tetris pieces who fell together, sidled up to each other and clicked.

We took long drives together to golf and resort country clubs – long hours out of town for cake deliveries and the schmoozing with chefs he was so fond of.

"Who's coming with me?" he would say on a Saturday morning, all of us scattered around the bakery business we owned.

He wore faded pale blue jeans, a thick cable knit wool sweater that pilled but could make his middle-age belly look like just another natural feature of the academic life, and a wool hat that he placed on the tip of his head so his curly, unkempt white hair was uncontained. He looked musty in the light grey leather jacket that was too old and small for him to close.

He smelled like moth balls and cheap aftershave and seemed completely unaware of the expanse separating the dashing 20 year old blond and blue-eyed smooth-talker who first bought these clothes and the bloated, bedraggled, uneasy small-business owner he had become.

When we heard him say "who's coming with me?" we took turns convincing him it was the other person's turn.

But, when he said, "if neither of you wants to come with your dad, that's ok, I'll go alone. Listen guys, I cannot force you." I ran to him and said, "I would love to go with you dad." His self-doubt didn't linger a single moment past the yes he heard and I glared and tried to squint with scorn at D, as I volunteered my hand to join his eager, sweaty palm.

We talked on those drives. Or, he talked and I listened.

I could tell when his logic was faulty or his insistences were weak, but I could see what my questions would do to him and so I stayed quiet while he told me what his dreams had been and ideas were – what he valued, wanted, thought.

Sometimes, he'd interrupt his meditations.
"I talk to you like you're an adult, okay?"

I would nod approvingly while he searched my face to find what he had put there before returning to the road and going on.

Often, he talked about his childhood. His years in an Israeli Kibbutz, where people participated according to their skills and everyone watched out for each other's interests. He talked about how loved he'd been, how his handsome Austrian looks were always teased and revered.

"I was allowed to be in the choir on the condition that I promised never to sing! This is how gorgeous I was and how bad my musical ear! Can you believe it, Gila? Imagine a teacher in North America telling a student to show up for performances but promising never to open his mouth. Ah," he would sigh, shaking his head from side to side vigorously in disbelief and pleasure and slapping his knee with whatever hand was not then on the wheel.

"You can't imagine it, can you? No, of course not. It was a different time, yes. That was the life though, not like here with everyone living separately, helping and worrying only about themselves."

"You would love the country, Gila. I don't know why you're not growing up there...huh? Did I make a mistake raising the two of you here? What do you think? But, you see it's not so simple. You have to understand. What would I do there, for example? I would have to have a designated profession, like one specific place that I went to and worked, like you guys in schools. But, I'm more creative than that, right? I couldn't just follow orders like the others.

"That's another good lesson to you, Gila. You have to know yourself!

"This way you don't have to ever depend on anyone. Except for me and your mother, no one will care about you in a real way. You have to expect this, understand?

"We're going to die one day and you'll have to learn how to take care of yourself – and D –, of course. Are you listening? It's going to be before you know it. Trust me. I lost my mother when I was young, early thirties, not a child, but you have to be ready.

"Are you following? I'm teaching you things you're going to need for the rest of your life."

While he drove, his talking shifted seamlessly between gears, exhortative, sometimes, plaintive, wistful, and fierce. The highways were narrow and sparsely populated, local routes to remote golf clubs hours outside of the city. He liked to keep his jacket on, and in the small patch of aisle between us lay his fraying leather gloves and khaki green wool hat. I didn't know when the driving would come to an end – only that every now and then the truck stopped and my dad would come around to the passenger door, put his hands firmly beneath my armpits, lift me out of the truck, and carry me down to the ground. He would announce the name of the resort we'd arrived at and give me his hand to hold onto. We were the delivery guys, he and I, and this was our route.

"This is my daughter," he'd say, as soon as we entered the fluorescent kitchens through the back door that said in bold letters "deliveries only."

It bustled with chefs cutting raw meat into cubes and putting them on metal skewers, assistants prepping potatoes for future roasting, cutting vegetables, loading industrial sized racks with stainless steel trays and zipping them into freezers the size of houses when they were done. When my father would lean down to say, "do you want something to eat? You're probably hungry," and I whispered, *French fries,* he got me grilled fish or spaghetti instead. Sometimes one of the men he was busy talking business with noticed I wasn't eating my food and said, "the kid probably prefers something from the children's menu instead," and when I nodded my father said, "yes, but they understand nothing, the kids these days only want to eat junk food." If the chef didn't get too distracted to follow through, I got freshly fried potato wedges and ate them quietly, pretending there was ketchup too.

These casual chats with hotel chefs excited him, and when we settled back into the truck, he was energized and boastful. "Ah," he would sigh, "such an interesting talk we just had! You see how important it is what I do? They liked me, didn't they, Gila? You can tell. It's amazing we have this account, amazing. It's because your father is charming! Eh? You should be proud of me. This is putting you through school! I'd like to see one of your parent's friends find something in common with an Italian hotel chef, huh? You see why I say that your schoolwork isn't everything? Because you have to be well-rounded. Having money isn't everything, believe me. You'll see when you get older what's important in life."

Everything in the truck was plastic and factory grey.

Because it was the driver's front section of a delivery truck, it was so narrow we sat with our backs to the rear metal wall and our knees to the window. When the hot air was on it blew steadily onto our faces. The classical music chimed as if from inside our ears.

"I loved my mother," he would tell me. "She was the gentlest person anyone knew. I'm not exaggerating. Her nickname in Yiddish was *guwtcha* for the 'good one.' Always smiling, always trying to make something better. Even when things were difficult – and Gila they were, don't get me wrong. This was Palestine before it was even a country! There were enemies everywhere. Difficulty getting food. Fights over everything. No one knew if we'd become independent or if the world would let us be wiped out again. Constant aggravation. Constant. You understand? Not like the way you kids grow up in North America, never worrying if there will be missiles over your head or a war the next day. Do you understand what I'm explaining to you? Are you listening? Is this too complicated for you, or are you following? I talk to you like you're an adult, okay. I'm sharing with you wisdom that you're going to use for the rest of your life. I know you're still young, but you can imagine the situations I'm describing, yes. Okay, so listen. Those were the conditions and people were bitter and worried but not my mother, never."

"She just smiled and made sure I had what I liked to eat. Always, she made sure I had what I liked to eat. Can you believe it? I loved chicken cutlets, and even when no one else had flour to bake with, she made me my favorite food to eat. I'm getting emotional even now."

"Ah, I wish that you could have met her."

"Gila, she died when I was still so young.

   "Brings me to tears to think how much you would have liked her. No?"

I nod and ask about the window. I cannot roll it down myself but want some air.

   "You'll catch a cold," he says.

"Do you see how important it is to be good like she was?"

"That's why you're named after her."

Gila means happiness.

"I know I've told you that before but you really need to appreciate how important it is to be good and to bring people joy like she did.

   I hope you're listening carefully to what I'm telling you.

   She was an amazing woman, my mother. She died so young."

I'm sorry that you're so sad, daddy.

"Thank you, Gila. It's good for me to talk like this. You understand me, I can tell. I don't know how I got so lucky to have such a daughter like you, huh? Your mother isn't able – well, it's ok. We both know what your mother's limitations are. She loves you though, the two of you. She's just not capable – let's not talk about her now, okay? We'll be back at the business soon anyway."

He sighed and drove and looked so wistful.

   He seemed so lonely sitting all dressed for the winter in his dessert delivery van.

I want to try to be good like you're telling me.

"That's good, Gila, that's good. That's what I like to hear."

I ask him to lower the heat because my skin is so itchy, but he says I'll get used to it, "no."

"As long as you take after her and don't become anything like your grandfather, you'll be okay."

I seized any occasion he mentioned his father to ask who this mysterious figure had been. I could never learn more than that he had been a world-renowned professor brought by the British to Palestine with other Viennese virtuosos to found the university there. I knew my father's face grew darker when he mentioned him.

"He was an awful man, okay. I wasn't good enough for him, not smart enough to be his son. What more is there to know? I don't want to talk about him, okay?"

"But dad," I would plead, "I just want to ask you one question."

"No," he would say, shaking his head, checking the rearview mirrors, suddenly anxious other cars were too close.

"There's nothing to know, okay? He was brilliant, but that's all he was. A typical intellectual who cares about his studies only. That's why I'm always telling you that being smart is not the most important thing. Take your mother – she can't understand what they're saying in the newspaper, right? Not in a sophisticated way like I can or even like you. Even though you're only in second grade, you can make sense of things, okay. Even without so much help you can piece things together okay, but she can't, right? But look how she can make the cakes we're selling. You see that different people have different skills? There's nothing wrong with that, Gila. And it's very important to remember that it's much more important to be a good person than to be brilliant. I know maybe you think that I'm exaggerating but these are life lessons I'm giving you here. He was –"

Why are you so angry, I kept wanting to ask him. *Did he hit you or starve you? Did he say cruel things? What did he do that made you hate him so much?*

He sounded like a boy yelling at a parent who had already left the room.

"There's nothing more to say about my father, okay? I wasn't good enough to be his son and, okay, so there's nothing you can do. But, if it's the last thing I do, I'll make sure that you turn out nothing like him. I don't care how much you like reading books or how smart your teachers say you are. I care about how you treat your mother and your brother. That's what matters. How you treat people who are less able than you, not how much you know about something or another.

No work is more important than being a good person, okay? Understand?

I will take away your books faster than you will have a chance to notice if I ever catch you being arrogant or thinking that you're special."

But dad –

"I hope you're listening carefully, Gila. Because there's nothing more important than family."

But dad –

"You're still little and you can still listen to me when I'm talking to you. I don't care how good you are in school. You understand? What matters is how you treat the ones that need you. Are you listening to me Gila?"

Yes, but dad I didn't do anything –

"Your brother is a good example. Obviously, he's nothing like you. The boy can't string two sentences together, ok, probably something's not exactly right with him but that never gives you the right not to help him when he needs you. Do you understand?"

I watched him work himself up into conviction.

Feel proud and accused.

Becoming wounded.

"That's why we have the business. It isn't fancy like your friends' parents who are lawyers and doctors, but I'm fed up with those people who have to think they know so much. That's not for me. I'm happy selling cakes."

I wanted desperately to reassure him. *You're not a failure daddy, I believe you.*

"What can I say to you, Gila? Being successful isn't everything! Look how happy those chefs were with the cakes we brought them, right? I'm building a business, damn it. You saw it for yourself, no? This is your business too. Remember that."

Can we open the window a little?
    I am gasping like I'm suffocating in this relentlessly hot blowing air.
    "You understand what I'm saying to you?
    I called it *Gateaux-Gil* because I named it after you! Don't ever let yourself forget that. This is your business too. One day it will be yours, okay? Are you listening? You see how much your father loves you."

The cold air slapped our faces when after hours of being cocooned in the overheated driver's quarters of the delivery truck the doors were opened and we put our feet on the ground. Our van was painted burgundy with our logo in gold because my father said he liked the royal connotations. But, maybe because regal paint colors aren't well absorbed by Toyota metal, our cake-mobile ended up looking less like a confectioner's chariot than a tacky truck begging unsubtly for admiration.

There was a huge "#47" painted in bright white on all three sides; this way people will think we have 46 other trucks! And our telephone number 905-709-CAKE broadcast in eager yellow.

As we waited for the industrial-sized garage door to rise up and open so we could park the truck inside the business and unload our empty trays, I wondered what was happening on the other side. Was my brother standing on stacked crates, splashing water in those metal sinks he couldn't reach, promising to wash bowls but watching bubbles overflow instead? Was our mom frosting a cake, impatiently, intently, her arm suspended in midair while the turntable exposed new angles to cover with cream, her olive skin polka dotted with chocolate, burly-bodied in an oversized t-shirt tightly stretched across her chest with the apron at half-mast around her waist?

I imagined running up to where she stood, inhaling the crisp fresh air and standing beside her while she worked. "Move!" she'd say, annoyed and push me. "Stupid girl, standing in my way."

She wouldn't ask me how the drive was or if I'd eaten. She didn't wonder if there was something I would like to say. It was obvious that any manifestation of the idea *I* existed aggravated and enraged her, and I could see that in how she shut me up and cut me off and shoved me, hard. What a fresh wound every trace of my *existing* causes that I can't repair.

"What do you want from me?" she'd bellow. "Standing like an idiot while I'm working. WHAT? MOVE! Always *looking,* huh, what do you think you see?"

She would be focused on cake-making motions, uncarefully but with all her strength, and might say, "Nu, pass the piping jelly. What are you *standing* there." Then she might say, "How does it look?" And, she would flash a grimace cracked with pride at those crooked sponge cake tiers held together by overbeaten cream and wipe her bangs away with the backside of the hand that still held tightly to the palette knife and say, "It's not so bad, you see? While you do *nothing,* how *hard* I work?" And, I could tell that she was tired then, her breathing heavy with fatigue, defeat, her face uncurious, satisfied, and not-minding I was there.

She is the baker and my father is the businessman, but she always says how much she *hates* making those *stupid* cakes! When my father walks in to see her throwing slabs of Belgian chocolate onto the table or slamming metal bowls into the sink he says, "Rough day, my favorite baker? The chocolate bother you today?" and tries to put his arm around her overweight and over-heating frame. After too many instances of reassuring customers, "trust me, the chocolate mousse only looks like it's missing the correct number of rosettes! We like to change up the décor every now and then, eh? To be *original!*" He hires a professional pastry chef to make most of the cakes. There are still certain things she's stuck having to do and when he hears a lot of banging from his office he comes out and says, "Is it time for coffee, Alla? Looks like the meringue is getting on your nerves today? Let's give it some peace and quiet, maybe you'll be in a different mood later?"

Most of the time, when the metal door finally rose high enough off the ground, it was as if we deplaned from a spacecraft and were light years away. There was screaming and commotion. Air bursting with cold and loud shrieking.

Mother and son were usually mid-chase: her running after him with a spatula aiming for his backside and him laughing uproariously while squeezing his six-year-old body behind pails of sugar that were taller and wider than him. She would scream and wave her metal sabre while he zigzagged his skinny exuberant frame between the cylindrical columns of powders and flours that filled the space like reeds.

"I'm going to kill your son!" she'd say when the industrial garage door opens and sees us standing there wide-eyed and stunned like refugees from somewhere far away and quiet.

"Get him, Alex, or I swear to God I'm going...I don't even *know* what I'm going to do to him yet! He is...he is...a *monster*! He really is! *Alex,* I hate him. I *hate* him! Animal! That's what he is, an *animal*! Gila, what are you staring at? Can't you see the syrup your stupid brother spilled across the floor? How useless and stupid can you be? Go! Now! Get a mop and start cleaning! Now! What the hell are you waiting for? Move! Now! Alex, she is a waste of space, a *waste,* you understand? Look at these disgusting children, nu, you *tell* me? How can someone *live* with them? They are monsters, *both* of them. At least he is wild, *hyper,* a boy, but *her,* look at her, Alex, *look,* standing there like a useless *idiot*. What are you looking at already, stupid girl? I said to go and clean!"

Immediately, I want to get back in the truck where it is so overstuffed with heat. I cannot breathe and think I will not breathe ever again.

His every word was clinging, pleading for agreement. *Yes, I see you're hurting. Yes, you're right. You're wronged.*

I want to drive back to Blue Mountain Golf Club and listen again and again to how clever he is.

I see this is chaos and I have been spared. That every moment I'm still standing makes her madder – that I'm standing? That I'm still? My transfixed face infuriates.

I see how hard you're working, dad.
    I see we are alike.

There is motion and commotion here. The mother and son will be like this for hours.

Maybe I could inch away until it's over. If I could make it to the office without them noticing, I could read.

I was afraid that drive would never end.

Afraid he'd want me next to him forever.

I won't be a professor, dad, I promise.

I promise I'll be nice to you when I grow up.

The business has my name on it.

"I leave people with a good taste in their mouths, that's what you say to strangers who ask what you do."

You ask me, "do I see what you have made?"

Gateaux-Gil, "the first word is for 'cakes' in French. The second is for my daughter."

"My mother was nicknamed 'the good one.'"

Gila means happiness.

In Hebrew.
   Gateaux means cakes in French.

He says "call me Belgian," no one ever comes from there anyway.

I'm named after the good one, the business is named after me.
   But I don't want your baby, daddy, please.

ꙡ

He'd been dead seven years when I suddenly noticed I couldn't conjure the sound of his talking.

And I wonder, should I add it to the pile?

After all, there is a heap of cherished things I can't retain.

The way he laughed or walked, for instance.
The way he playfully elongated my name to coax me out of bed some mornings. I hated the nickname enough to wake up shouting, *stop it dad! You're so annoying.*

As I strain to recall his professorial lilt, I notice how ugly this kitchen is, how inhospitable.

On the phone, Ms. Tobin keeps telling me to go to therapy. "I know it won't change *every*thing," she whispers and I bark back, "What's to change?"
I imagine how she cocks her head and looks at me exasperatedly.

It's something about my "running so much," and she keeps telling me, "you have to stop it" and "admit."
She even says, "You'll crash one day, you'll see, you can't keep running like you do from everything that happened. You can't keep trying to *do* everything, keep everything intact." But, I have no idea what she means by "stopping" doing what I never *started.*

She says, "go to therapy" and then "come over, afterward." *Come over.* Sit at the table where her children eat, it's warm there and so quiet.
What is she thinking? Come over afterward.
Where her family eats.
I need to *be* in this kitchen, *liking* this kitchen, smiling,
do you need help *cleaning* this kitchen?
I can talk to the dead in my head, to the living I smile
let me help you with those dishes
let me decorate that cake

let me tell you what I know of tortes, meringues, and petits fours.

"You're a good kid," Ms. Tobin she says to me sometimes and I picture how she wants to stroke my face, if it wasn't so awkward. If I wasn't so tough or don't-touch-me untouchable.

"You're only seventeen," she says to me often, "your mother's an adult, you can't control –"

She understands nothing. *I'm not listening, promise.*

She's only a teacher who thinks I'm a helper.

What the fuck is she thinking, *come over?*

Before I went away to college, I helped devise a budget so our mother could balance the books in the bakery while I was in school, but a week after I left she bought this huge, expensive house instead.

I knew better than to shriek *what have you done?*

So I only said, "Mum please tell me that you're paying half-and-half with him? You know we can't afford the whole thing?" To which she slammed the phone back into the wall-mounted receiver and when – after many hours of calling her back and begging her to listen, she finally agreed to answer – said, it's none of your business! You are a selfish, ungrateful bitch. I owe you *nothing*! NOTHING! Understand?!"

I understand. Of course, I understand.

She needs me when the mess she's made becomes too scary. But when she sees me running after her, gathering the debris of what she's blown to shreds, each piece still glowing with the heat it still harbors, she hates me, screams, "You selfish creature, how dare you try to make things neat?"

I hear you say forgive them, just forgive them, for they know not – and they can't.

I said, "This means we're going to lose the business." But, my threat, of course, just makes her hiss back "so?"

"So *what*? What are you going to DO about it? –"

She's laughing, eyes wide, eager, "it's *your* problem, don't you understand? I don't give a *shit* what happens to this stupid business. It was your father's and then he left me so *go*, you stupid girl, leave me *alone*! Who wants a fucking life of making cakes? Go" – she thunders, shoves me – "go! You were his favorite, always crying to him, and he thought you were so sweet, go see if you can stop me!"

When you said take care, you meant forgive? *Always* there is another cheek to give.

"Go!" the mother says, "I dare you."

"Come over," says Ms. Tobin, "I'll be here."

Where are you, dad? I need to know. This kitchen she just bought and can't afford is so ugly and I'm tired.

❦

The day after he died, she sobbed and chanted, "What will I do? We'll end up homeless without your father taking care of us. Homeless! Oh my god, what's going to happen to us? Oh my god, we're going to die, we're going to *die*."

D buried his ten-year old body into her heaving chest. He was chubby from four years of the macaroni and cheese dinners I made him and she whimpered and moaned into the ringlets of his hair – I can't do the things he did, I *can't*, it's a matter of time before we're going to be homeless – and then she became listless and leaden, the louder and harder he shook.

She didn't notice I was there until I promised I would do whatever was needed to keep us all afloat.

Then she nodded blankly into a barren space. As if to show me the abyss that was there no matter what I offered.

I said, "I will take two buses after school to get to the business every afternoon."

I said, "we'll start by cleaning out the office."

I said, "do you know where the accounting books are?"

When she nodded, I said, "That's great! See how well we are doing already?"

I said, "Is it too much to ask if you know what his sales pitch was," and when she shook her head ferociously, I said, "you know, who needs it anyway? It's not like we're going to be able to do exactly what he did anyway."

When I then realized I had no idea how we would avoid going bankrupt, I said, "let's just start with filling the showcase with cakes. Can you get into the routine of making the same dozen tortes every week?"

When she nodded, I thought, *okay, good, then you will do what you do best and I will help the customers.*

Like an ocean a pebble has been thrown into, her face expanded into minor ripples, then swallowed whole whatever paltry rock disturbed her placid stare.

You can sink into but can't dent the impassive, stolid sea.

I said, "We're going to be okay." I said, "We don't need much and I'll repeat the things dad did." I said, "Please mum, don't be upset, I'll be helpful, really helpful."

For once, my talking didn't make her angry and I could see that she didn't hate me after all. Maybe all this time she was only helpless. Now I knew if I could do the things she needed, she would see that I wasn't trying to ruin her life, that I was really always on her side.

I watched her vacantly cry onto D and recognized this as the lostness I could feel was always underneath her fury.

It wouldn't be so hard to help her.
    I could take charge of things she couldn't handle.
    She would see how much I loved her when she saw how hard I worked.

This only means I get up early. And help make cakes and copy what I saw him do.

I couldn't reach the counters.

And, I couldn't do the math.

I said, "mum, if I'm going to run a business, I need a cash register that calculates $20 minus $13.95 quickly."
    She turned to me, incredulous – "you're not *embarrassed* to be so stupid?" –

But, *wait!* I thought, *I'm trying to help you.*
    Wait, no, remember, *I'm on your side.*

She pet D's curls and shook her head.

The doe-eyed boy peeked out from her embrace. Because he doesn't have the language even to ask this, the entire weight of *what the fuck's going to happen* resides in his watery, bottomless eyes.

While she glared, disgusted with me, I said I'm just not good at math.

I won't be stupid with the other things, you'll see.

Her gold-hooped earrings swooshed back and forth, her blond-brown hair moving slightly from the wind her movements made.

Customers can be so forgiving it hurts.

ૐ

I came home from college and I sat against the kitchen cabinets and wept.

I said, I just can't go, *I can't.*

Knowing I was home from school, Ms. Tobin called and said, "Gila, I can tell over the phone you're crying. What I don't understand is what you mean when you say you can't leave."

Her voice so soft, I closed my eyes and tucked into her question.

"Gila," she said, "talk to me. You keep saying you can't leave. Tell me why. *Why* can't you leave?"

Each question like a blanket she spread beneath my knees.

"Talk to me, Gila. You know I get worried when I hear you that quiet. I can hear that you're upset. College is a big transition, but it's an appropriate one. You need to say something to me. You need to say more than just you *can't.*"

The receiver breathing near my ear, I feel her questions stroke the sound waves.

As if she's skipping over me to ask my skin instead.

You are an angel, Ms. Tobin, in all-black attire and pin-straight grey hair.
    I want to yield you everything.
    Keep talking and I'll rest my head.

"Are you worried about your mother and D? Is that why you say you can't go away? But Gila, it's *not* your job to take care of them for the rest of your life. You *deserve* to go away to school, okay? Do you hear me? You got a full scholarship, for god's sake."

She thinks I'm scared of my first day of school.

She thinks I'm prone to overcomplicate my wishes, and now she's coaxing me to recognize – admit – a Bachelor of Arts can't augur real-life doom.

I hear her tenderness, I do, but my mind is stuck in a room with his dying a decade away.

❦

When possible, I pretended I was sleeping, my back to his chest, holding my breathing.

When his chemo made him too enfeebled for long-distance drives, he lay down next to me at nights in bed and talked and wept to me from there, my twin mattress with ninja turtle sheets the new venue for our private congress.

I pretended I was sleeping, my back to his chest, holding my breathing.

I was becoming immune to doomsday pontifications and felt myself shrug when he said I would need to be strong because any day now things would get worse. *How much worse could things get?* I sometimes wanted to scream.

The other day, I rushed to find you when you cried for help and soon D and I were lifting you from having fallen near the toilet, your pants stuck at the knees, your vegetative weight too dense for our nine- and ten-year-old bodies to carry. I don't see how it could get worse than seeing your blood cancer lesions bespeckle your freckly skin or watching you wither before us, coughing your lungs into a cup or a pillow, choking on air until every room everywhere resounds with your rattle.

I tell myself I've learned to navigate the scenes of his decay.

I wind myself around the wheelchair, close my eyes to unhear his cough.

When he points with a shaking finger at a glass of old orange juice encrusted with residual pulp, the straw so mangled there's no way liquid could pass through, and says he's thirsty: "Hold the glass under my chin so I can drink." I am obedient but turn my eyes myopic. I do not see the glass I'm holding, the food stuck in the beard he's too immune-deficient to shave, or the stench of bedriddenness his every minor movement exhales.

I curl up with my knees to my chin and my back to his talking.

Sometimes, I lay flat and pretend to sleep.

I know I'm callous and ungiving.

I want to tell him I don't care about his going. *Can your exit take another route?*

I won't keep crumbling every time you come in here and spill your grief and say, "come closer, and say, please hug me, please, Gila, it hurts so much, forgive me Gila, please, you understand."

I want to say, *I won't keep lying here, just waiting for you to crawl in here and decompose.*

His agony like a sack of heavy bones I can't wiggle out from under.

I want to say, *can you just die already?* if that will mean at night I fall asleep without your heaving chest against my neck.

Except, sometimes he cries from a well so deep and disbelieving, I then worry he's already gone. "I don't want to die!" he shrieks and repeats. "Gila, I don't want to die!"

"No, don't say that, daddy, no, please no," I suddenly say, and turn and fling my arms around his neck.

No more pretending things I'd say to him, pretending I'm asleep.

"I finally found what I wanted! You and D and the business. No! Gila, no."

No, I cry, *don't say that, daddy,* no, my crying catching up to his, joining his, until together we're howling from the same bottom of bereft.

I want to say, *stop begging, stop saying that we're dying, stop saying there's nothing we can do.*

I say, "I will do anything. Just tell me what to do."

"I don't want to die!" He keeps screaming and begging.

There is not enough air for these gasps of despair.

"I am finally settled, you and D, your mother. It took me so long to find what I wanted. I was lost and kept looking for something. I didn't know what, until you, and the business. And mum and the boy. I want to see you grow up! You are everything to me. If I die now, I won't see you grow up?! How...Gila, no!"

Dad, I will do anything you ask me.
Yes, I'll come closer, keep holding your head in my hands.

His need is tremendous, my body was small.

I try, when I hug him, to secure a pocket of air for my head so I can keep breathing.

No, I won't leave you, I promise. Yes, I'll forget how weak you became but hold onto everything else like you asked me.
I'll make it like you never left.

I promise.

When he finally leaves, I turn my face toward the pillow and cry where no one hears me. I tell God, *you have to save him.*
You who never sleeps and never rests, come down and intervene with me.
You see that I am good deep down.
You see that I need help.
You who makes the earth and heaven, don't take away my father, *please.*
You came to David in the wilderness. Alone, in hiding, with his harp. Can't you see I'm also desperate? Come now and make his going stop.
Our Father who protects his children, it's me who's calling out. *Mi ma'amakim.*
You have to save him, we can't without him, please.

❧

He was more sober in the daytime.

Propped up by several pillows, he held court at his bedside, patting with his veiny, spotted hand a space of sweat-soaked sheets for me to sit on while I awaited my assignment on what to do after he died.

There were pill bottles strewn across the bed, thick medical textbooks in piles on the grey carpeted floor.

He presided over this urine-drenched kingdom with such authoritative splendor it looked as though this was a mess that military strategizing made. As if the sheets were crumpled and distressed because he was knee deep in oversized maps of enemy territory. As if outstretched ambition had caused this disarray and not leukemia.

"Let's be honest," he'd begin each time. "We both know this disease is going to kill me".

When these meetings started, he was still strong enough to pick me up and hoist me on the bed. My legs in tomboy jeans dangling, half-wanting to kick the IV machine to see what would happen, mostly wanting to look serious enough to deserve being in this war room consulting with the general.

I am his deputy and we have a mission.

I think of stories that I learned in Hebrew School. God pulls aside a humble, unsuspecting soul and says, *I've chosen you to be my special helper. Come forward, make your father-maker proud.*

I nodded earnestly as the commandments floated.

Take care of them, the both of them.
He's wild, I know, but he looks up to you. She is – what can I say to you? She's...
She loves you, but it's hard for her.
We both know she can't do what it takes.
You don't have a choice.

It's not your fault this is happening, but do you think I want it either?

He looks up to you.

Don't get angry with her.

I'm counting on you, Gila.

But *wait!* I want to interject immediately, *what if they don't listen?*

Like when I ask her what time she's coming home and she laughs and says "when you *see* me, *that's* when I'm home! ASKING like I *owe* you something. So selfish, so *pathetic,* it's unbelievable! What right have you to know when I'll be home?"

When I call her after school and say, "It's been an hour, me and D are worried, are you coming? Will you pick us up today?" she yells into the phone, "how *dare* you be so selfish? Maybe I will *never* pick you up, did that *occur* to you? Huh? You're so *smart,* yes? Your *teachers* think you're smart? So, go, *find* yourself a way to get home. I have had enough of such an ugly voice asking all the time these selfish questions. Is that you *crying?* You're not *ashamed* to be such a baby at *ten years old?* Get it through your head, you stupid girl. I'm not your *father* who *cares* about you when you cry. Poor Gila, always trying to protect you like you can't be hurt! How manipulative you are, *daddy, daddy* always what I hear. You are *disgusting,* don't you *see* that? ACTING like a *victim* when *I'm* the one who should be taken care of. *Me!* Oh, how *much* I hate you! I can't *stand* you, nu, *get* that through your *head.* Hang up the phone *right now* and *pray* or *do* whatever you want, *cry* to someone else. I don't *care,* just go to *hell!* Your teachers love you? Maybe they can bring you and your brother home."

She puts my questions in her mouth to make me taste their gross offense.

She has an accent but not of any language spoken.

She is from Belarus, but says she thinks in English now. People always ask her where she's from and she giggles as if inscrutable is a compliment, not a sign of their confusion.

She has a screaming voice and flirting voice and sometimes she sounds as though she isn't there.

It's mostly gruffness, heat for emphasis, words too narrow for her feeling, sentences too late for thought.

I notice other mothers ask their children how school was or if they're cold or if they're hungry, but if I start to say something I learned that day, or thought, or want, she cuts me off, abruptly, says with fury "I *burned* my hand today, *okay*? in the *oven,* stupid, *shitty* oven."

If my father boasts of a smart thing I said or did, she looks restless and increasingly annoyed, then bangs and breaks a plate or kicks a door. She shouts, "This *chair,* this *shelf,* this whole *house* is in my way, I can't do *anything*! *Stupid* furniture! I *hate* this house! Why am I standing here when *she* is doing *nothing*? Entitled brat!"

I know he'll worry if I scratch my knee (*It could be broken! You never know!*), but if she sees me limping, wincing, holding my stomach, shaking, she starts to push me, glare, silent and enraged. "Why are you walking slowly? Stupid girl. *Nu?* You think you're *special*? Something wrong with you? *Move!* Who do you *think* you *are*? You think *anyone* except your father *cares* how you are *feeling*?"

As soon as he gets sick, there are no more doctor visits or teacher meetings.

"To hell with *everyone!*" she shouts a few times daily, while swerving the car and smashing vases. "It's not *my* problem, understand? Who *wants* you anyway, you tell me, you disgusting waste of space."

When she puts me in a dress she bought, she glows excitedly at what she's made, but if I squirm or whine, *Please, I like my corduroy pants better,* she lunges at me to rip the outfit off herself, swears. "No more clothes for *you,* ungrateful bitch! It's not my job to serve you what you like, *okay*? Who do you think you are, having PREFERENCES? Who do you think you *are*? What does it *matter* what you *like*? You stupid spoiled piece of shit, you're getting nothing from now on, I promise! Absolutely *nothing –*"

If I cry and then apologize, she yells to, "save your tears for some-one else! *I* would let you cry yourself to *death,* what do I *care*? Maybe you'd *learn* something. You give me absolutely nothing, *nothing,* do you understand? Maybe your father thinks you're innocent but *I* know better. Manipulative little bitch! Don't let me hear another cry from you or I swear to god, you better *run,* now, *go,* always asking for attention. What about *me*? Did it *occur* to you that *I* need things? Who do you *think* you *are*? *Crying* like a baby when you're *eight* years *old*?"

Once he dies, she's always saying, "Now, it's time for *war*! You stupid girl! You don't know *anything,* understand? You're always *looking, trying* to understand, but you're *such* a *waste,* such a *rot-ten* and retarded girl. What can you offer? *Nothing*! Your father loved me, only he did, the rest of you are *horrible*! Now *look* at you! *Looking* scared. How *darrre* you act like such a disgusting baby! What are you crying about? *Huh*? Your life is easy! I'm too *good* to you, *that's* the problem, *nu.* You *spoiled* piece of *shit.* You are how old? *Eleven* now? *Twelve*? You have no *clue. No clue* how much I still can hurt you. You think because you're smart. Because your *teachers* like you. Don't let me *see* your *face* or I'm going to throw you out, I *promise*! *Looking* scared! Yeah? You should! Get out! Now! *Out!*"

Her eyes are shining brightly in these moments, daring and sure.

As if she knows something of chaos I am unwilling, still, to learn.

As if this world is what her world feels like, always.

As if to say, we are *all* in total chaos now, *see*? Let's see how many smart ideas you're having now, when you don't know the next time you'll eat.

Welcome to my world, you spoiled, sheltered-talking thing who always wants *to know.* I dare you to keep bothering me with stupid questions.

He knows that she is like this, right? Sometimes, I'm sure he has to overhear her say, "You're lucky your father walked in because I can't *stand* to see your ugly crying face ," and sometimes he even says to her, "Enough, Alla, okay? The kids need to eat, even though you are fed up with them. I don't blame you. It's hard to make so many cakes, okay? But make them something simple, please. They're starving, okay, can you do that?"

When she roars back, "Let them go to hell! Those *rotten* creatures, if it wasn't for you, I'd like to see how long they'd last! Ha! I want to *see*. Nu Alex, don't defend them! I want to see how long they'd last without you always taking their side!" He whispers gently that he knows how awful kids can be and he will lecture us. Gila understands what she's done wrong. He says, "You're right, they need to be more independent. She didn't mean to make you angry. In her mind, maybe she wasn't talking back to you, she was just trying to *explain* herself."

What does he mean, "*take care of them?*"

There is a small dog I tell my friend I can take care of. We are ten years old. The dog is white and black and very small. Although, when I checked if we could babysit my school friend's dog, she said, "Why are you *bothering* me with *nonsense* about your stupid friends? I don't know or *care* about your friends. I'm *tired,* can't you *see* that?" "But my father says it's only for three days, we'll make it work."

He's away that day making deliveries to golf clubs out of town. We have keys to their house, the tiny dog is in a locked plastic crate, and we are supposed to pick it up early in the morning. I wake her up, excited. "Why are you *bothering* me? *I'm* not leaving the house so early, *why* would I do *that?*"

"Because," I start to panic-whine, "because we said we'd pick up Freddie and –"

"Who is this *Freddie*?"

"Mum, I *told* you. The girl from school that I'm friends with? Karen? Her dog. Dad said –"

"I don't know *what* you're talking about –"

"But, mum, we promised. The dog is –"

"You stop whining now or I'm going to smack you. I don't know who this Karen is. Or her dog and I don't care. I have errands to run, I'm going –"

"But, wait –"

"No! I'm getting dressed and going. You think your stupid friend is more important than everything else?"

"No, I wasn't saying that. *Please*. But the dog is there all by himself."

"Where is her house?"

"I don't know. You drove me there before. I don't know directions anywhere. Maybe I can find the address in the school book or something."

"Well, you better find it quick. I'm leaving. I'm not going to stand around here waiting for *you*."

"But mum, you took me there before, remember? For her birthday party and –"

"No!"

"But then, what if I can't find it? Please. The dog is all by himself."

"What a *baby* you are. *Ten* years old and starting to get so *emotional*. And for what? A stupid animal somewhere? I want to see you care so much for anyone but yourself. Huh? You think it's possible? I don't think so, no –"

"But mum, maybe if I find out where she lives we can go together and get him?"

"*I'm* not driving you there –"

"But dad is gone all day."

"Well, then I guess that stupid dog, whatever his name is, can stay there by himself!"

Hours go by. She leaves the house while I'm hysterical, comes back, leaves again and says the dog is not her problem – neither am I.

When it's nighttime, my father returns and I beg him to go and get the dog.

He says, "What happened here, can't you see the child's upset? Do I have to go myself?"

She glares at me and wordless, livid, knocks a side table over and grabs the keys.

When she returns half an hour later, she hurls the small cage to where I'm waiting and says, "Don't let me see your face or I will kill you. You take your fucking dog and *run* where I don't find you –"

The dog is covered in its own vomit and feces, shaking, starved.

What does he mean, *take care of them*?

Get up and go forth from your homeland, from your father's house, your birthplace, unto a land that I will show you.

Every year, I win the school-wide contest of who can memorize more of the Bible.

David was out-sized by his opponent.

Is there a word for being put against something too huge? Not outnumbered or outdone. Not outmanned, exactly. Not overwhelmed, not overtaken. Not a *feeling* about a differential, not the act *after* it's done. No – more like the knowledge slowly dawning of being disproportionately matched.

I imagine David had one gasp of panic before he went to find a rock and sling.

One "oh no no no no."

One "no, I *can't. Don't* make me. *No.*"

From the depths I cried to you, he wrote while running from the king.

But prayer comes while running, not the no of standing still, standing dumbly, stiffly standing. Saying *no* is not to someone. Not only to someone. But to a knowledge you don't want to know, *no* to knowing that the world is ending while you're standing still just knowing. That the world is ending. While you are small and it is big and you are without something you can do. And your knowing keeps you standing and the knowing keeps you still.

Oh no no no no no.

Don't make me. *No.*

From the depths I cried to you, oh lord, he wrote in hiding from the king. The same king who was his father once.

Lord of mine, will you please hear my voice. Bring your ear toward my cries.

I repeat the orphan-warrior's fugitive *please* in my nighttime bedroom sky.

I think maybe he takes aside each one of them, like he does with me, and says, "When I'm gone, this is your task. You have to do the things I'm laying out before you on this day. Gila is in charge. You have to listen when she tells you what to do."

We must be each bequeathed our wartime assignations. He has some other way he talks to them, I'm sure.

He has figured out where each one of us belongs. When the time comes and we're on our own, we'll go directly to the space marked x and get into position.

I nod to show I understand the mission.

He doesn't know there is this game I play where I pretend that someone asks me which one of them I'd rather lose.

I sometimes tell the world to take him, I want to be with her instead.

Sometimes, when it's a Sunday and she's in a happy mood, she'll say, "Gila, let's go buy some drapes, I feel like sewing something for the house!" or, "there's a sale at *off the rack,* let's see what we can find!"

The velocity in her movement makes her every gleeful enterprise contagious. "Come, let's go! *Nu!* I'm going to make a drape-thing, so perrty, to hang up in the house!" With sentences mangled by word choice and order and vivacity that makes anyone standing stably look dead, she swoops into a room and you can almost hear her gold hoop earrings flapping at her neck while she gesticulates her plans.

She never seems to know whether it's too late or still early and she giggles while her eyes sparkle brightly as, in a flurry, she hatches a scheme. "Let's go to the mall, stop to get a haircut on the way and then pick up a movie near the house before we leave because it closes later! Yes? Nu! Let's go! It's going to be fun!" And she isn't wrong, it is. I swear sometimes I see the sparks that fly above her head while she is moving. She huffs and puffs when some mundane detail from reality causes her bustling stunt to stall, as if the limits of space and language don't actually belong to her. "*Nu!,*" she says, "What is this traffic?" and swerves the car in fury off the road.

Sometimes, I feel so sure her happiness cannot be ruined, I even ask her "can you hold my hand?" But then she stops abruptly and hisses with repulsion, "*What?* What do you *want?* Why would I *do* something like *that*? Why do you *always* have to *bother* me?"

I say, "I don't know, just *can you*?" And so she does, but her hand is so listless when we interlock that I protest and whine, "That doesn't *count,* Mum. Can you hold my hand *for real*?" And then she squeezes hard until it hurts.

She asks, "That better?" I see her irritation metamorphose into pleasure, as I squirm and try to pry her fingers loose.

"No," I say, "Forget it." "Good," she says, "let's go," and wrests her arm away and laughs.

Our limbs go back where they belong and I wait and hope she will not say, "You *see*?" This misstep proves I still don't disappear my self enough to be good company.

"Let's check that store" is how I'll know I am forgiven.

I yell inside myself, *why don't I ever learn?* I keep wanting her to see that I'm okay but okay is only when she doesn't have to notice me. I never learn. There's no such thing as *I'm okay*.

I'm not supposed to take up *any* space, and any space is too much space. I'm not supposed to betray any sign there is a *person* there.

Eventually, she'll see something to buy and I will nod so eagerly when she asks me if I like it.

When she fetches a sparkly, fluorescent peach outfit, I twist my unease into wonder because I know she's happy stuffing my body into dresses, telling me to turn around, and matching it with this hat and what about these shoes.

"I always wanted my own little girl!" she exuberantly announces, "before you, I had only boys and I hated it! *Hated* your two half-brothers!" When we find exciting outfits she tells me how the other sons she had with a man before my dad "don't count, you know? Because boys, they only take and take and give you *nothing* in return!"

In these moments, it is so clear there is no such thing as a well-behaved child when a dressed-up doll is what she really wants.

People say I look like dad, with our pale white skin and blue-green eyes, while she is hazel-eyed and olive colored with hair that's blond or brown or reddish, and how overweight depends on if the diet's working. She wears tight-fitting rayon blouses with frills along the neckline and big "PRADA" sequined letters sloping in and out across her breasts. There are leopard-print pants she likes to wear with a cheetah patterned turtleneck because she says, "It's classy to mix and match the colors, and you can't tell these are designer knock-offs if you wear them with high leather heels and a purse that has another big designer name in gold metal."

Her face is hopeful while it scans the racks for bright new outfits, yet fragile like what's cracked inside will break without more shiny clothes to put inside a closet that, like a mobile hanging above a crib, swirls around and around her head to soothe her.

I like to say *you're pretty* to the pink shirt she's trying on because when she feels that way, her hard face softens, her head bends gently, and for a moment she smiles a little less tersely. For a moment, her fear and bewilderment give way to rest.

Once, when she was at her most expansive, she told a story of something that happened when she was my age.

I knew that she had parents, a mother who was so mean she didn't hesitate to hit her. Whenever she finally caught up with D to smack him, she'd cry immediately afterward that she didn't mean to go that far. Sometimes, when my father wanted to insult her, he would calmly say, "It's not your fault you're rough sometimes. From where would you know any better? You didn't have a warm mother like mine to teach you how to behave." And, finding recognition in the condescension, she'd always cry and say, "I didn't, Alex, see? It's not my fault I am this way."

My ears always perked at the prospect of a story. I always knew there was a hidden cause, a forest she got lost in, a basement she got left in, some awful, unimaginable deed that would explain how she got broken.

"Do you want to hear about how when I was your age, I once had rabbits?"

"You had a farm?" I say, intrigued.

"Sure!" she says excitedly. "Where the rabbits were when I was younger. Your age now, maybe seven or eight."

"But, I didn't know you grew up on a farm?" I ask, trying to picture the scene.

"Maybe it wasn't a farm, exactly, I don't know. We had animals, that's what I know."

"Like cows?"

"Sure. Maybe some cows."

"Horses?"

"No horses."

"Then, what other animals?"

"Gila, I don't know, okay? We had chickens that my father used to cook for dinner."

"Ew! Mum, that's horrible!"

"What? Where do you think your meat comes from? It was a chicken once!"

"I didn't know your father was a farmer."

"He wasn't a farmer. I didn't say he was a farmer."

"But you just said –"

"I don't know what you want from me. We had chickens and rabbits –"

"Was there hay?"

"Of course!"

"Wow, so it probably was a farm, mum."

"That's what I'm trying to tell you!"

"And did you live on it?"

"Yes. No. It was part of the house. I don't know. Why does it matter?"

"I don't know. Because I wanted to see what it was – "

"There were chickens. Maybe roosters. Are those the same thing? Who knows or cares. The point is I used to like to play there by myself. I had a brother seven years younger but I wasn't good to him the way you are to D. I used to torture him. I feel guilty thinking about the things I did to him then. Oh, well. It's ok. But I liked to be there by myself and play with the rabbits after school. They were so cute. Yeah –"

"And so? Why did you stop?"

"Stop what?"

"You were telling me about the rabbits and then the story stopped."

"Oh. I didn't notice. Ha! I feel bad, that's probably why."

"But why do you feel bad? About your brother?"

"Who?"

"Your brother who you said that you were mean to?"

"Him, no. He deserved it. Everyone was always saying how gorgeous he was. I couldn't take it anymore. I wanted him to suffer for once. Like I did – always being screamed at by our mother. Still, he had it so easy, it made me sick."

"But your daddy loved you, right?"

"Yeah, sure. I was everything to him. But, it didn't protect me from the way my mother used to beat me. But what would have? It was the days when parents did that. And in Russia, try getting involved in human rights or bullshit like that. Ha! Anyway, he was an angel and I hated him for it."

"And that's why you stopped talking about the farm?"

"What farm? Gila, what the hell are you talking about?"

"I don't know. You were telling me about the rabbits you were playing with and that you did mean things to your brother and then you stopped talking."

"Oh, yeah, okay, the rabbits. Yeah. There were two of them. These little white ones. What do you call them in English, the little ones?"

"Bunnies?"

"Yes, exactly! You see, you can be good for something! Bunnies. They were white and so small and I loved playing with them. And then – I don't know what happened, they just died."

"Wait, what? How?"

"I know, that's it. Just like that. I don't really know. First one, then...." She's shaking her head dramatically as if seeing them before her now – dead. "Horrible, I know."

"But, mum, how did they just die all of a sudden? Were they sick?"

"No. They were healthy."

"Are you sure?"

"Yes, absolutely. They were healthy. Only healthy rabbits. What did you call them?"

"Bunnies."

"Bunnies. Only healthy ones. Plus, they were so young. What could have been wrong with them? Nothing."

"But then what happened?"

"I don't know." She shakes her head again and looks dolorous.

"Who can tell?" she says with a smirk ever so faintly bubbling beneath an anguished face. "They are rabbits after all. Animals."

"Maybe they were hungry?"

"I fed them."

"Maybe they got hurt when you weren't looking?"

"I was the one playing with them when they died."

"Wait, what do you mean?"

"Just that! I was playing with them and then, before I knew it, they were dead."

"Oh no, mum, that's so bad, mum. What happened?"

"Yeah," she says, staring forward into nowhere, blankly.

"I was playing with both of them. I wanted them to kiss."

"And then what?"

"I don't know. I just held one rabbit in one hand and the other in the other hand and I tried to bring them together so they could kiss and then I noticed one of them wasn't playing anymore."

"But – "

"I probably was too rough with them. Who knows?" She shrugs and performs the imaginary scene of one hand holding something it wants to shove into the other.

"Just like this," she says with animated hands and bright, excited eyes.

"It was so funny because I didn't know and I kept playing and playing. Then I noticed the rabbit in my hand wasn't moving anymore."

"And what about the other one?" I say, trying to stifle the horror radiating slowly.

"Huh? I don't know. I think it died also."

"What?! Both rabbits died?"

"I think so." She faces downward with her childlike somber face.

"I didn't mean to!" she proclaims. "I was just *playing,* and then I don't know. Before I know it, they were dead."

I wipe the look of mine that says, *you killed those baby rabbits.*

I can hear my questions bouncing off her Teflon brain, echoing in my own ears without ever touching down for a single moment in her mind.

"It's not your fault, mum. You were just playing, probably wanting to have fun."

"Of course! Exactly. I didn't *mean* to. I just wanted them to kiss. Stupid creatures. And I remember how small they were, too small for me to hold them. I knew it would be so nice if they could kiss each other. That's all I tried to do. But they didn't listen. You understand? Besides, I didn't know they were so – what's the word?"

"Small?"

"No, something else, when it can break so easily."

"Delicate?"

"Yes! Exactly."

"Fragile?"

"Huh? Yes, Nu, so tiny and pathetic!"

"Were you very sorry afterward?"

"Yes, of course I was! I'm not a monster!"

"I know, I know. It's just...was your dad upset?"

"Yes, of course."

"Were you punished?"

"No, because he knew I didn't do it on purpose. I just wanted them to kiss."

"And how did you become okay after?"

"What do you mean?"

"Like, after you told your father and you didn't have the rabbits anymore, did you feel horrible? Did you still go to school?"

"Sure! Why not? I don't understand your question."

"How did you feel better after you saw what happened to them?"

"Yeah. I told you I was upset. But then, I don't know. It's so funny, isn't it? That I was trying to make them kiss and instead I killed them!"

"But you must have been so sad then, when it happened? Right, mum?"

"What?! I don't know what you mean."

"That you were feeling sorry. I just mean that you must have felt really bad for what you did to them by accident."

"Okay."

"What?"

"Okay, so what?"

"I don't know. Didn't you feel very bad? I just don't understand."

"Gila! I don't know what you want from me, okay?"

What I want? I'm looking for the feeling pulsing behind her eyes. It doesn't have to be remorse or sadness, just anything other than this hollowness and pleasure.

"Mum, why are you staring at me in that way? I didn't mean to hurt you and you look like you're confused. I didn't mean to be confusing."

"Because I don't know what you *want from me,* that's all. I hit one into the other and they were too little, I guess, *okay.* Or, I was too rough, and what is there to understand except your mother is so silly sometimes? It's such a funny thing that happened, Gila, no?" She's irritated, agitated, angry, then dismissive and relieved.

No, I say inside, while nodding yes.

She laughs and laughs and, looking sheepish and coquettish, waits for me to join her.

❦

How am I supposed to watch them when he's gone?

He can't mean really *watch* them, like he does with us.

Maybe what he means is be a helper, since he won't be here to do the things in person. Covering for him while he's away, until they're fine again or he comes back. Kind of like his messenger.

God is always saying, trust me, never mind that you are weak and they are strong.

Trust me, go up to the sea and it will open. Go.

Except it isn't only *they won't listen* but this look she has that says she isn't feeling anything – isn't *there*.

Even when she smashes dishes, throws chairs against the wall, tells me she will kill the neighbor's dog next time it runs too near the car, it isn't really malice in her eyes, but hollow calmness where it's impossible to tell how much it burns inside.

I am five or six and he isn't home. She takes my stuffed toy tiger and shows me what it looks like emerging soaking wet, disfigured from the washing machine, holding it with two fingers by its ear. "He doesn't look so nice to sleep with now!" she booms, smiling and staring while I plunge to retrieve it from her grasp.

"Always such a crying baby," she taunts and laughs and pulls the tiger higher, "you think you're going to tell your father? If this is what I do to him, your precious favorite tiger while you are sleeping, just think what I can do to you, huh? You stupid, sensitive, little girl. Just think before you tell your *daddy*."

I know from how she's smirking that she wants me to keep wailing, jumping up to reach my friend, only hungry for the pleasure of seeing something burning.

I say through my sobs, "I'll be good from now on," and, she slams the wet tiger with frustrated fury into the ground. "You will never be good, stupid girl, no matter what your silly father tells you: rotten to the core, you understand?"

There is a bonfire crackling, dancing across her brown eyes.

He can't mean really *watch* them, like he does with us.

God is always saying, trust me. I only choose men that are able.
I am chosen. I am able.

There's no such thing as an unready prophet.

Moses had a stutter. Jonah said, *you're kidding!* Sarah laughed.
I will memorize his way of talking, calm and in control, laying out what everyone will do, offering to answer questions.
Repeat after me: You shall engrave God's word upon the inner tablet of your soul.

I'll say, mum and D, this is what we have before us. Let's discuss how we'll proceed.

ع

When I say I won't survive the absence of his soothing, measured, Belgian voice, I am not being sentimental.

I mean: thought is a sound that tethers me to language, sense.

I mean: without words to bring another being near, it is a senseless, barren, ashen place.

Like being told, behold! You're naked.

In a garden rated R.

And you aren't nine and curly-headed, naming the stuffed animals.

And now you *know* nothing is there.

And no one's coming, ever, later.

And I'm not Adam – knowing there's a maker.

I can't do it, dad, all by myself.

You were dead two days. She bought me dresses.

"Here," she said, "to make you feel better, okay?"

I could feel my shock vie with my rage and tie with incomprehension.

What?

What do you mean, *you bought me dresses?*

Is this some kind of evil joke?

What will I do with dresses?

Dresses? As I prep my speech to welcome mourners since it's my job – s*tarting today!* – to be a father, husband, grown-up man.

I train my outrage to scorch the earth her eyes are fastened on, but then I look and see the soil's already bleached, blinded, and vacant.

How do you scream at a mind already broken?

She looks so lost, so fatally unknowing.

And on the other hand, she's telling me *this* is what she needs to like me.

Even she won't kill her favorite dressed-up doll.

Wild, wilfull and bewildered.

She's giving me a uniform for my deployment to your absence.

It's not a garden, it's a jungle and these dresses are fatigues to camouflage my difference.

"Here," she said, "I bought you dresses."

Dresses?
Just when I noticed I was naked.
In a wasteland.
With no chance you'll walk in later, ever.
"Here," she said, "I bought you dresses."
In a flash I see: this is a gift, protective,
as maternal as she'll ever get.
I want to lay my tomboy body at her feet
and then destroy my arms for ever not being angled to her chest in prayer,
for not being yet
already the doll-playing girl-doll this woman deserves.
The boys they take and take and never give.
"I always wanted a little girl," she says, self-soothingly, "is that so much to fucking ask?"
"Here," she said. "Put on these dresses."
"Here," she said. "No talking but I give you dresses."
Forget Adam *naming* all the animals. Think Mowgli in his toga *taming* them.
I'll need them to survive, *won't I?*
I'm going to lose my mind not-talking, getting dressed in dresses to be the girl-doll she needs and the prodigal son you wanted.
I'm going to lose my mind not-talking.

The angel that rescues me, *come!*

I don't care, dad, what you're saying, only *that* you're saying.
Tell me anything.
Things I know already, barely hear
your talking in my ear
is how I know I'm not
alone.

These fragments I have –
Dad?

Don't leave me in a land without you –
Dad!

We had a deal, I thought. *I let you die as long as you stay with me in my head.*

Dad?

Forgive me father, please.

I don't know where your talking went?

Come back, dad, I can't lose you.

Tell me anything.

I close my eyes and search for how you'd tell me what to do.

You'd say – ?

Come back, dad! I can't lose you.

Are you listening?

I can't lose you. Not the part of you that kept me going.

In a garden rated R.

In a wasteland, it's a wasteland. Don't leave me here, not-talking. Do you hear me?

Shhh.

I'm listening?

I can't, dad. I can't lose you, not like that, dad, not right now.

Not when realizing I can't lose you is how I know no no no, know –

you're gone already,

aren't you?

☙

P (Prince)

You scramble eggs for him, make toast for her, tell them how hungry they will be if they don't eat.

They still don't get their bodies out of bed.

You're thirteen, almost, scrawny still. He's ten and you can poke him still, annoy him, without him hitting back too hard.

With her it's harder. She gets angry, can bolt up suddenly and promise to make your day hell later. She can hurl her toast at the kitchen wall.

You walk back and forth between their rooms, "c'mon you guys," you coax them, mostly gently, beg them to wake up, "it's time."

You get yourself up extra early so there's a moment to strategize before the running, bargaining, frenzied averting and diffusing starts.

Your mind runs through the checklist: breakfast first, get them up, make sure they get to school and work on time. He will refuse to go and so will she. it sucks, he says, it's stupid / I'm not going / I'm not going! Fuck it. They hate me there. I hate it / I'm not going / I'm not learning anything.

But the trick is to say something before he gets to "you can't make me," because he's right of course. You can't. And, by the time you're there, it's in another realm.
   He's small still, smaller than you, and wants to feel like a good boy and listen, but if it is one of those days where he doesn't feel like trying, you are screwed. You have to get in front of that potential feeling *fast*.

Get him to sit down and eat the eggs you made him.
   Don't ask or tell him *anything*.
   If he says he isn't hungry / why am I here? / I want to be sleeping! I don't know what you want from me, I'm tired still, I hate the morning! I hate this day already! /

Remind him, gently, slowly, look him in the eyes. They are only eggs, I promise. You say, there is nothing else to do right now but eat them and move on. When he forgets or in frustration bangs the fork back down and the table shakes, says I don't know what I'm doing / I'm not hungry! / I don't want to eat, repeat that these are only eggs. There's nothing else to think about but sitting, staying here with you in the kitchen, eating what's already there.

You know how delicate the mornings are. Every new day a fresh shock to him, I hate this food! / what am I doing? / what do you want from me? I'm tired, I don't know what you want from me / this morning sucks / my teacher sucks / I have to leave and run away / I have to go / I'm going back upstairs.

You must never let yourself respond to this, not in the morning. You learned that early. Let him let it out. He wakes up agitated and confused. Just put the food in front of him and say it's warm, why not try it while the eggs are warm, you made him toast, he likes this bread. If he says I don't! / I hate this bread! You never make me what I like, I'm always hungry / I hate this / I can't do it anymore / I can't, I can't, you say, you do? Oh no, that's my mistake. Tell me what bread you like and I will get it for next time. This is an opportunity to organize his anger and you don't let it slip by. The bread is wrong; the bread can be corrected.

When he's restless and darts his eyes around the room, you know he's finished eating. You tell him what he should be doing next.
    Go downstairs and get your shoes on, get your jacket, sit and wait until I come and if the timing works and he can get there before he gets distracted, you are halfway through this morning battle. If there have been moments where he isn't hot and frantic, there's a greater chance he'll make it to the school without a total meltdown. If he's downstairs, you are almost at the finish line. It is a ten-mile marathon and you'll have passed the first round. "I'm coming," you holler to remind him. We're almost at the part where we're at the classroom door and you're reminding him that *being good is easy* because you *know* he's good, inside, if he didn't get so overwhelmed with anger he would do so well

in school. Today is a day to show the world how good he is, how smart he is when he's okay.

Of course, if she comes down to the kitchen first, you start again from zero, *behind* zero, off the race course, or outside the track. Because as soon as the sonic boom of yelling hits his shoulders, back, the yelling in her voice slamming down some internal keyboard in his head, it's like an alarm is pulled and you have to move, you have to run, diffuse it quickly.

She'll see you in the kitchen and yell, "D will you move your things from the back of the car instead of sitting there, eating, doing nothing? You rotten spoiled boy! Don't leave your stuff around!"

He gets pale and lit up in an instant.

It doesn't matter how every night you tell her, please don't scream at him in the morning. His nerves are fragile and when he flips out here, he's hyper and discouraged everywhere, at school and later on tonight. I cannot always bring him back from that before he gets in trouble, please mum, just ignore him in the morning so I can have at least one single early round where he doesn't explode. It increases his chances of making it through the day.

I didn't leave my bag! / It's not my fault / I'm going back to bed, I hate this here, I fucking hate it, hate you all / I'm going upstairs / why am I here? This stupid food, I don't want food! / I said I'm not hungry in the morning! She screams back and soon he's storming off and banging things and she is smiling at you, shrugging, "what?! Don't look at me like that!" – guilty and mischievous, coquettish, coy, smiling and shrugging – "it's not my fault, I promise. Yell at *him*, not me! The boy is *wild*! It's only in the *morning* I remember certain things I have to tell him."

You say okay and change your face because if you so much as entertain a reprimand, she'll turn from playful, guilty, goading, to injured fury quick.

You say okay. Say, "I'm going to talk to him but for now I made you toast before you go to work." You hope she's feeling far enough away from anger to launch into a story about someone who enraged her, that will distract her from launching into why she will not go to work today.

The sugar supplier who keeps demanding a check.

The mechanic who says he fixed what you paid for but everyone's a liar, *everyone*.

Her hairdresser. "My color is horrible, isn't it? Isn't it? There is grey popping out, probably he's using cheap coloring, *bastard*! how I hate them all! I hope he rots in hell before I go back again." The r's are made to bear the entire weight of her fury so they are rolling, crashing against the air. "I hope he rrrrots!" she hollers.

The customers are horrible too.

"Gila, do you see what I have to put up with? Better to be dead than go through with this day."

You must distract her from this rolling indignation before it grows bigger from the reaction it creates. You have to tell her something from the news you read that morning, try to redirect her anger where it will burn and gradually taper off.

But if it's too late for that because either you were too slow to intercept the escalating fury or didn't choose a topic fast enough or wisely, then just match her outrage with your own. "The customer said what?!" you say, exclaiming unequivocally that she is right and the world is bad. "The mechanic *did* that to you?! of course you are upset, it is upsetting." "People are disgusting!, she will say, "they are disgusting and the motherfuckers *screw* you any chance you get," you nod, you look afflicted, you show her that you understand that she is hurting, which she is. She is hurting. You understand that she is hurting.

This fury is still better than when she says she's sick of putting up with everything and the business can fuck itself, "I'm not going to do it, I'm done, fuck the orders I have, the cakes can make themselves for all I care, what do I care? I don't give a shit what happens!"

You know that if she bangs something on her way downstairs, can't fit into her clothes, is screaming to the world the diet isn't working!, that it will take more than gentle listening to help her go to work today. After you tell her she's right to be *so* fed-up, her life is not fair *at all*, the business *is* awful, her life is the *worst*, you say, as if for the first time, "I'll help you. Remember? I said I'll run the business with you?" You go through all the things you'll do when you get there later, after school. You'll look into the account book Dad was using. You will figure out how much money you need to make. How hard can that math really be? You have a calculator. Dad wasn't that good at math either, you don't think.

If she senses even a whiff of exasperation, she will pounce on you and say you're selfish and you're just trying to get what you want. You reassure her that this isn't true, you love her and you want to help. Her life is so impossible, unfair.

If it's frustration that she hears, she'll storm upstairs and slam the doors until the hinges loosen and when you come, she'll scream in a deep voice, booming, "I HATE you, piece of shit you are, you only care about the stupid business!"

You can't get close or she will whack you with her pent-up limbs.

Stay at the door and quietly just tell her that you're sorry, you know "life's been unfair," she can come back down to the kitchen. You will help her with whatever she can't do, you promise.

If she settles down, you say you're sorry she has to go to work today, you know how hard it is but you will be there later. Your eighth-grade teacher lets you out as soon as you're done with the homework and class is so easy, you're always done early.

If D is watching this or hearing it, her threats to give up on the business freak him out; he will vibrate, quietly, and intermittently ask you, "what's going on? I don't understand / I don't understand! / I'm too stupid is she leaving like Dad left and it will be just us? / I don't want mum to leave us it's because of me / Gila what's going to happen? Is she going to stay in her room forever, Gila? / it's all my fault / I'm such a rotten boy / no good / no good / no good / I deserve to be dead instead of dad / I am so bad / the teachers hate me too / I'm not going to school today I'm going to stay with mum upstairs / I'm going to stay with her / I'm not going."

When you see him look at you like this, you know for him the day is over. If you can't find a way to calm him down before he gets to school, you know there is only a tiny chance you can still retrieve him. Take out the shrapnel he's absorbed and put band-aids on the lacerations he's inflicted. You know that when he goes to school like this, he'll hit another student, stand on his desk in class, be angry then devastated later, not know how he got there when he promised to be good.

On the school days that don't go like this (there are a few) you walk together and talk to him. You say, you have to get through school somehow. We have to find a way for that to happen.

He listens while you say you know how much he hates it, that it isn't the right fit for someone with his brain.

You say you know that he is brilliant, the way he fixes the radio, knows how the transmission works in a car. Even though he's not very verbal, there is more than one way to be smart. You say, "D, I know how smart you are, okay? Today, let's show your teachers how smart a boy you can be."

One day there might be a school for him, but for now he has to manage. You tell him a dead father is no excuse for misbehaving.

He's silent while you two are walking.

He never talks but he seems peaceful while you're talking to him. At the classroom door, you send him off. Remind him what you talked about, today let's show everyone how good you are inside. He nods. The teacher looks at you, skeptical or pitiful, depending on the teacher.

You have talked to all of them, many, many times. You explain that he isn't trying to misbehave. He just can't help it. He really can't. His misbehavior is a problem you are working on with him. He knows it's wrong to throw toys and desks and hurt people. His father died. He's very sweet inside and you have seen that he can be very calm if the things around him are kept quiet, reassuring.

When you do his homework with him, you can tell he has no clue what any of the language means. He isn't reading properly. He gets confused. He doesn't understand when people talk to him either. He doesn't watch TV or play any game. He only seems to like to take apart a machine and then try putting it back together. He's quiet then, the only time the electric wiring running through him seems held together in a syncopated peace.

You used to say he could watch movies with you, thinking it would help him learn to sound like other kids his age but then he'd look so confused when it was done. You asked him what was wrong and he just stared at you, so tender and bewildered, I don't know who the bad guy or the good guy is? Was that a happy ending Gila? I don't understand. It was Batman or it had aliens, didn't matter. Is something wrong with me? He'd ask you and you always reassured him no. No, nothing's wrong with you, D, the movies aren't for everyone.

You translate what you see for him, break big ideas into small pieces that you can give him one by one to chew.

You try to tell this to his teachers but still they look at you and say, so patronizingly, that's sweet that he can get along with you but in the real world...

You tune out after that, but maybe you should listen.

You can't stand the way they talk about him, as if he's a deviant, or retarded even. Even though it's crystal fucking clear the kid just cannot function in the world the way it's built. He isn't bad or stupid. You mean it when you tell him you think he's smarter than you, if only the world had a way for him to show it. Good grades mean nothing, you assure him, and you mean that too. So what that you get A's, that teachers think you're gifted, it means nothing, really nothing.

You see that he's like a raw wire, exposed to the elements, can't process like you do, using language, argument.

He sees it all, feels everything. You're sure, you can see it in his big brown eyes, the way when dad was in the hospital, he curled up next to him like a small puppy would and said I'm staying here, I'm sick with cancer too.

You couldn't face him when he asked if dad was dead, how long would it be before he came back.

For years when you all piled into the hospital room, he ran right to the IV stand to check if it was working, taught himself to fix it when the fluid wasn't dripping, said proudly that he would take care of dad even better than the nurses! He didn't seem to mind the stench of moist bed-ridden bodies and decay. He'd curl up next to him and report how many times he farted yesterday, he thinks he beat Dad's world record. "Are you keeping track in here like I do when you're not at home?"

You don't want to admit that you prefer it when he's hyper.

Easier to regulate a shaking body than when he doesn't talk at all. Just watches and you know he must feel all the same pain you do, he sees everything, only without the words to turn it into sense.

You tell yourself he trusts you. He looks as though he trusts you.

This means that even if he spins out of control, there will always be a way to intercede.

There is a rope that you can throw for him to climb back up on.

He will not be like her other son, that gorgeous, troublemaking twenty-two-year-old from a marriage she had before your dad. He comes by every few months and asks for money. He's out of jail, he's done with drugs, the lines don't change. His crooked smile always so inviting, his sadness always something you wish that you could reach. He lived with you when you were born then moved away right after. Now when he comes, he pets you on the head, not listening for what you say after he high-fives you with "what's up, little G?"

You know that D is different, more innocent, less mischievous, more antagonized by all the rules than restless for a way to break them.

He is not your older-brother kind of dangerous. He couldn't steal or lie or coerce someone – you're sure he doesn't have that kind of fluency, that kind of ease. You watch his every single movement, the gap between his moods, the things he may be thinking but doesn't have the words to ask. When the teacher says what's the homework, can you write down what she's saying? When the boys outside are playing, do you think that you could join them? Do you understand the kinds of games they play?

When you see those watery eyes refract your question, you quickly say, you don't need to play if you don't want to, D let's think about something else that you can do. But maybe it's not fast enough to spare the shame he feels, maybe you should avoid the corners where his confusion gets caught.

You must be more careful not to embarrass him.
    The world is bustling in a language he doesn't understand. You must stop thinking that he can *tell* you what or why a thing upsets him. Get it through your head: he doesn't know.
    If he doesn't understand something, it's because you haven't put it in a form that he can recognize and reach. It is so cruel to put in front of him a sound that he can only hear as clanking. That you're calling words, but he only hears noise he doesn't comprehend.

Frustration turns into despair so quickly. If he says he doesn't get it more than twice, soon it's I can't do it, I'm too dumb / retarded / mum says I'm not good at things like you are and I shouldn't try / I won't try no more! / I'm finished, Gila finished

I'm / done I / can't can't can't and I'm going to be a retarded person when I'm older I just / know / I know it.

You have to get ahead of this.

Dad always said he isn't like you. But sometimes he said ignore the boy, he is an idiot, thank god I have you to talk with. And, other times, don't think only about yourself, it is your job to watch him. You wonder what is it that he would do? For you, there aren't questions, except how, how to reach a boy that no one understands.

When you've said to her there is a problem, "D isn't getting any better, I'm worried what will…," she looks at you, a storm of indignation growing forceful in her eyes. "He's fine. Stop being so dramatic. Poor-little-baby he'll be *fine*! What about me? You selfish, stupid girl, it's *me* who's stuck with these disgusting cakes and the two of *you*! Imagine *my* life, how horrible it is!"

You don't push her anymore because the once or twice you said, why don't you care? Or, mum, this is serious about the school, they're going to expel the child, she roared back – you know what? *I'm* not going to work today! "*YOU* make the cakes and tell me how you like it. You think D is such a poor baby, huh? That spoiled little brother of yours is all you care about, huh? *That's* what you think? He doesn't know how good he has it! The two of you *revolt* me. One day, I'm going to leave this shitty life for good and then we'll see how smart you are and how much you worry about that brother of yours, okay? You like that? You piece of shit, you happy now?"

You don't know how he pulled it off. She never yelled like this at him. She was enraged for sure, but other times coquettish, even sweet. And when he'd come upon her screaming, he would diffuse the moment quickly, saying something like "what's going on?" or "what'd they do?" He controlled her fury peacefully, but how, you ask him, "tell me how?"

Your mother gets impatient, he would tell you. She has a lot to do, she's warm inside, she loves you, in her way.

You're such a feeble substitute.
You're such a pitiful, impotent king.

You ask too many questions. The point must be to govern things without her knowing.
"Be humble!" He always implored you.
Maybe you are flaunting power and that's why she fights you when you say you're helping? Don't say that you are helping.
Stop sounding like you're powerful.
You are not superior.
"Be humble," he said, learn that others know something *no matter* how much you read. Your reading isn't everything. Don't you dare be self-important.

When she's threatened, she looks as though she'll kill you, but you remind yourself *she's warm inside.* This heat you feel beneath you burning is just intensity you don't know how to master.

Are you saying that my asking her for help with D could feel like boasting to her?
You can find a way to help the boy discreetly.

Eventually, you don't mention D at all, if you can help it.

She signs the forms you give her and when principals ask how come they never meet the mom you say, she wanted to be here, she's busy, trying her best to do everything since your dad died, and they nod their heads empathically. Such a strong mother you have they say always with amazement, teary eyed and hollow, it must be so hard to have to do everything she has to do. What a good girl you must be for helping.

You wanted to say, father, can you see I'm helping?

You sit with him when she's still driving home. Windows of time when the townhouse is quiet and your thirteen and ten-year-old bodies can huddle together at the head of the long kitchen table.

You think, *if we could do this everyday, he might even pass a class or two.*

Maybe next year, he'll learn to do this on his own. Maybe it's only this attention that he needs. He's smart enough. He'll learn from this. It just takes practice. It just takes time.

You're feeling, *this isn't so hopeless.*

You're daydreaming about the day he does his homework by himself, one day he even graduates, he gets a job all by himself and then – "What are you doing?" She barks and glares at you directly.

"Come, D, let's go buy a computer for you! I saw one on sale when I stopped at the mall on my way home. You want to go and buy it?"

You look at her, stricken, shocked and almost shriek "we had a deal!"

Remember? We don't agree to buy him more things until he tries to do a bit better at school.

We are reinforcing bad behavior.

We are sending him mixed messages, confusing him, telling him no matter what he does that we'll reward him...

But, one look again at her and you can see she's daring you to utter this response.

If you fight with her, you'll put him in between you.

This is a battle you will lose by waging. A battle you've already lost.

You just sit there speechless while she flings her arms into the air, her earrings dangling in the wind her motion's creating. Disbelieving when she hollers, "come let's go! what is she bothering you with here? huh, D? wouldn't you rather go buy a computer with me? She's annoying you, isn't she? Trying to tell you what to do? Making you sit and listen to what *she* thinks is so important! Come! I'll buy you a burger while we are driving and she can eat dinner here alone, what do you think?"

Sometimes he looks back to you while he is rising and sometimes, he doesn't.

Better just to let him go. Don't say a word to her while she glares at you triumphantly and nonchalantly.

You know that she can't help herself.

You tell yourself she can't resist the sight of something fragile. As if its weakness is a provocation.

If it is breakable, she wants to break it. Flimsy, frail or flammable, she wants to watch it burn.

If you showed up dressed to put out fires, she will set the entire kingdom, made of straw, ablaze.

You must camouflage the fact that you are helping.

He told you to *be humble.* And you still don't get it, do you?

You cannot shove the answers in their faces.

You cannot make them come to you. *Stop being self-important.* Go to them.

Besides, it's not like he passed you the scepter and said you're in charge.

That urine-soaked "take care of them" more fact than coronation.

"Be quiet and effacing."

Repeat, *you know how horrible her life is, and you're so sorry that you're useless.*

When every evening at the business, they sit and swear about the people who pissed them off and screwed them, don't stay in the office with your homework, hiding. Go to where they are and join them. Show them that you're like them, that you're not so stiff and rigid. Be humble. You can do your homework later. What is it anyway, a book report? You know that is a joke compared to what you need to learn out here.

It's an industrial space, the bakery. Pale, cheap grey linoleum floors, thirty-foot ceilings, always so cold because – "You cannot heat a place this size!" she screams to you when she sees you shaking. You wear so many layers that they bunch at the wrist and your hands eventually get swollen and blue.

The place is always messy, discarded cake boxes stacked neglected on counters that shine metallic and bright under harsh fluorescent lights.

The "front" is supposed to be for retail; that was the idea you had when she said she would never be able to set foot in the golf clubs and restaurants, chatting with chefs like he did. You knew it was true, asked if we could just sell cakes to regular people, directly?

"Retail?" she said, in her gruff, frustrated tone, "is that what you say?"

You never heard the word before but then she said that since it wouldn't change what cakes she made, whatever, maybe it would work. You'd be the one to help the customers, after school, and on weekends.

Since the business had no money, the difference between an industrial factory with triple decker ovens and walk-in freezers was a door you put up that blocked off the "back" and some tables D found somewhere that you assembled near the window to call it a café.

Whatever decorative things there were she brought from home: a lampshade here, a plant and Monet poster there. The place looked like a guestroom made up of incoherent, leftover parts, unwelcoming, uncomfortable, not knowing what it offered except the cakes it once only sold from the backdoor of a truck.

Every day when things are finished, the two of them are sitting at a table, self-righteous and united. She tells him his teachers are stupid and cows. He says she's right to have sent the new electrician to hell.

D comes in at the end of the day from the mechanic shop next door. When a year ago you first arrived here together after school, he noticed the scrappy Harry's Best Auto Body before you did and begged to go and spend an hour there. An hour turned into afternoons and weekends and soon he didn't even come to the business when you arrived off the bus. And really, this was just as well, they loved him there, told you how talented he was at fixing cars. *He's talented!* You repeated to yourself. He could, maybe, go to school for that. There are programs and careers.

D comes in after the day is over. His oversized t-shirts stained with grease from lying under a car, his jeans hanging so low on his backside you see the blue boxers you bought. The thin white stripe, a sudden glimpse of how skinny and young he still is, his hands black from spending day after day reassembling metal parts.

She lights up and yells to you, "Gila! D is here! Go and make him something to eat, okay? he looks so hungry! poor baby. come! working all day. let's sit and eat."

They sit and are at ease with each other; like construction workers when the sun has set, their hard hats on the table, empty soda bottles between them, commiserating, too tired to be upright still but then too tired to get up.

You're running back and forth from the kitchen to his plate, to feed him.

You're one of them, you want to say.

Forget the big words and big questions.

Forget needing to make sense of things.

Laugh with them, he's older now and funny, cruder too you think, maybe from working in that shop all day. Every second word he's swearing but no point correcting. This will squander any chance you have of learning to be easygoing.

"Stop being self-important," he would say.

Where does it get you to read Dumas? When instead there is the *real,* common man?

I'd rather you be decent than be brilliant, *do you understand?*

Your teachers say you're gifted but that means *nothing* if you aren't humble. Get your priorities straight. School means nothing compared to the hard work of running a business. Take me for instance, I am *happy* making cakes. I am happy doing simple things. So what your grandfather was a genius, look where that got him, okay? So what he was a famous professor? It's *me* who knows how to be successful in life. Your mother is so warm and real. She is a treasure! I took her to Europe and she tried the pastries and could figure out how to make them. She didn't need these pastry chefs or culinary schools, you see? This business puts you kids through school and it's because I saw that potential in her right away. Only a ticket to Paris it cost me to start Gateaux Gil! None of this nonsense with the years of finding someone trained, a real chef with his pretensions, ideas of his own. Forget it. This is a *family* business. We use what we have. No fancy education *here!* Now *that's* what I call brilliant! Forget about the PhD, schmee-h-D! So she's a little rough around the edges, okay? But she means well, she's just...and D, he's such a special boy. Don't think because you're smart, Gila, you're special. I am teaching you what *really* counts. You see what a successful business I built with your mother in charge of the cakes? When I met her, she was a waitress and I was just a salesman and look now. I pay for Hebrew school for the two of you. If even *once* I hear you, even once Gila, you think you're smart, even once I catch that you are losing sight of what's important, I will pull you out of school so fast I promise you won't know what hit you, *understand*?

Father, can you see I'm helping?

The cakes are made, one by one, each day. *You're right,* you think, the books can wait.

You see the wisdom of his message now.

Your learning gets you nowhere in a world inflammable, uncertain, *what is it that you're trying to know?* You think you're better than this business? This is your business. Built by hand. There is more virtue in these simple tasks than all the wisdom you can find in books. She makes the cakes, I sell them. If you are quiet when they're laughing, it is you who doesn't understand. It doesn't matter if you're so-called "brilliant." Who are you to ever feel unequal? If there's a difference when you talk to them, it is on you to make it disappear.

❧

Dad? I am assuming that you are in heaven,
    which means you know
    our older brother died today.

Kevin, twenty-four, six feet high and always rapping, with his broken smile, no shortage of excuses, twenty-four, was out of jail, was over here last night to wish me happy birthday, shot himself, he had a gun?
    I am assuming you already know all this, but I'm talking now not to report but to
    beg you, please, for intervention.
    D is small but already he is so much like him.
    You used to say as much when you were angry.
    Those dark brown eyes, unreachability. That look that says he doesn't hear me sometimes when I say, "you know what look I mean?"
    But you didn't talk about this possibility.
    You never said, and by the way, the boy could die.
    He was so charming, always, sad and trouble-making
    but benign? I thought.
    You never said take care he doesn't *kill* himself
    How am I supposed to stop the kid from giving up?
    He's getting older, taller, says, don't tuck me in, it's cool, see you tomorrow, and through the door I hear Slim Shady blaring.
    I sometimes say, those lyrics sound so interesting, what do you think that rapper's saying? And he shrugs those bony shoulders while his eyes glaze over, says dismissively, as gently as he can I think, *who gives a shit? It's fucking wicked! This shit is – yo, don't be such a tightass teacher all the time? Ok?*

I bought myself some CDs and I listened.

The rage is stunning, absolute, inspiring.

"I get it, D!" I want to yell, but then he'll start to put on headphones and I won't know the voices cooing in his ears.
    Kevin was into reggae lately. Came by bedecked in bling and stolen sneakers, said he was practicing Rastafarian, the language of his new true self, might even rename himself after his inner

Ethiopian prince. "What about Lex-us yah," he said, "for my album when I come back from Jamaica."

My first thought when she said he's dead was: the idiot ate too many patties.

I can't believe that it can even *be* that easy,

    Like,

I'm fed up so I'm going?

It took you four long years to almost die then die for good, but here it's just, *yo, fuck it guys, I'm out* –

    Dad, he says that *all the time*

    Go fuck yourself, he tells me when it's early and I say no matter what he goes to school,

    He doesn't seem the violent type except when he's about to be enraged, explode,

    I guess he is the violent type?

    I have to be much gentler, don't I?

    Tell me what you're seeing that I'm missing, dad. Forgive me, I'm failing you, I know this never would have happened on your watch.

    I worry he won't always listen.

    What if he just up and says one day, *G, I'm done* and *you can't help me,*

    I never thought that was an option.

    Seriously.

    Is this a fucking joke?

    Like, for your birthday thought we'd show you that there's more than sudden death to be afraid of, there are moments that are fine until you find out later

    you have no fucking clue what someone else will do.

    Did you know that this could happen?

    Kevin said, *you're my only half-sister! Of course I came by to celebrate your turning fifteen!* I only have one sister!

    I said that neon yellow Adidas sweatshirt, if you really want to know what gift to get, that's what I want.

    "A boy's shirt!" mum said. "Always with those stupid sporty hoodies, tssk!" she hissed exasperatedly. "Why can't you ask for something purrty like a *normal* girl!"

    I am disgusting, aren't I? Say it.

You always told me I was selfish.

I missed the clues because I said that neon yellow sweatshirt, I did. I wanted it, and so I let him die instead of thinking, hmm, it's kind of strange you're here to "celebrate" when I only see you barely twice in a *good* year.

I have to be more careful, don't I? It's not only that D can fall if I'm not watching, he can *jump* if I don't stop him. Just up and say, *I'm done now, so I'm going.*

I'm in the kitchen sweeping, we'll have guests again, you know.

I will smarten up, I promise. And, by the way, my stupid birthday sucked without you anyway. Now it's done for good, whatever, doesn't matter.

Nothing matters. God can fuck himself, for good now. I am unafraid, except about what D can do, help me to keep him out? And keep him safe, dad. Find a way to send me down your wisdom, or whatever else it takes. I don't hear any bass-thumping lullabies blasting from his room. He's smart enough to get ideas from a thing like this. Dad it scares me shitless when he's quiet.

ṽ

She strode into the room, unsmiling.

Black trousers, black turtleneck, boots, black blazer, pin-straight bob of bright white hair. Brown tortoise glasses, a little oversized, silver bangles that clanked every time she moved her wrists. She had a black leather bag in tow that she dumped impatiently on the desk when she entered the classroom and a black cashmere coat that trailed her with such devotion it might as well have been a cape. She discarded these accessories annoyedly, as if they were a burden, she couldn't wait a moment longer to escape. She had olive skin, brown eyes and a long nose with an elegant bump. Her frame was thin, her movements were brusque, and she seemed to be in enough private commotion to make her entrance that morning intriguing and untouchable, elaborate and austere.

"So, this is world literature?" she said suddenly, looking up from her glasses for the first time at all of us sitting wide-eyed, collectively watching her.

"I'm assuming at least *one* of you knows how to answer that question?"

Her way of measuring the room felt like an accusation, teasing but already exasperated.

"You're so quiet!" she continued, as she walked around to the front of the desk and got ready to perch herself on its edge.

"Do I *know* any of you?" she asked, scanning the room full of seventeen-year-old girls for someone she had taught before.

"No familiar faces, huh?" she said, as if simultaneously offended and daring. "I guess that means they know something *you* don't. Oh, well," she said, feigning a wound and waving the air away with her hands. "We should start already, shouldn't we?"

Since my last name was always the first name to be called, I frantically tried to prepare for whatever caustic thing I thought she'd say but she had even less patience for the class list than the protocol of welcoming new students to their first day of a course. So, by the time I steadied myself for my name to be called, she was already on to Berger, Cooper, Davidson, Goldberg, Goldstein, Ennis.

"I'm not going to bother memorizing your names," she said, her hands again shooing away the air in front of her, as if it, like us, was yet another obstacle she couldn't wait to eschew. She dumped the class list on the desk she was sitting on and narrowed her eyes at the class.

"I'll bet that many of you won't be back here for class number two, so I'll wait a little while before figuring out who is who. This isn't a typical high school literature class. I don't know how many of you have heard, but I don't give A's for effort or ever give A's at all for that matter. So, if that's what you're looking for, I suggest you save us all a future headache and take another course." She scanned the room again, measuring our shock and trepidation.

"Got it?" she said abruptly and with satisfaction.
　"Who wants to start by telling me what they know of Isabel Allende? Or, Latin American literature generally? I'm assuming we can cut the administrative crap and start with what we're reading – unless that's a problem for anyone?" She gingerly rolled up her thin cashmere sleeves. "I don't hear an objection, so good. You're either too shy or too scared, either one works *fine* for me." She licked her lips. It was a performance well done. "Let's start with what you know. I'm assuming you're not *all* completely ignorant?"

And Gila sat there, transfixed.

When the class had ended, her peers were eagerly gathering their backpacks to head to the next installment of their senior year high school schedules, but Gila sat there frozen.

"Is there a reason you're still sitting there?" Ms. Tobin asked, half-laughing and a little amused by the ridiculousness of a seventeen-year-old refraining from the desperate post-class rush out the door.

When Gila didn't respond, Ms. Tobin, while continuing the busy motions of repacking her bags with the books and class lists she unloaded, said, this time somewhat less mischievously, "Is there a reason you're not heading to your next class, whatever it is? You don't want to be late on the first day, hardly makes a good impression. You aren't new here, are you? We don't get new students in the senior year. What with all the Jewish studies, it's impossible for anyone to come in from somewhere else and just catch up. So be it then. But then you must know your way around these halls, yes? An answer would be nice, you know?"

Gila looked at the ground and said, "Is there another class you're teaching?"

"What?" Ms. Tobin said immediately and heatedly, "*already* you are trying to make a change? From what to what? I teach the regular English Literature class in addition to this course on World Literature. I probably lost a good few students here today. Happens every time. Without fail really. You kids want easy grades and I make absolutely clear I will *not* give them. That's as it should be. I don't want to be teaching students who only care about grades anyway, so it always works out. But that's not what this is about, I take it?"

"I need to be in your other English class as well," Gila mumbled, her eyes still fastened to the painted concrete floor.

"You need to *what*?" Ms. Tobin repeated, with exaggerated disbelief. "But that's ridiculous. You already have a class and god knows I am not exactly interested in having another paper to grade."

"But," Gila retorted right away, "but please...I will be a good student, I promise. I will do anything. Please, I need to be in your... please."

"What's all this about?" Ms. Tobin said, maintaining her annoyance but also, for the first time, a little intrigued. "Do you hate your other class or something? It isn't usually the case that people are fighting to get into *two* of my classes. What is this all about?"

Ms. Tobin was electrifying, swapping back and forth between British mannered stoicism and reversed Yiddish intonations, depending on the effect she was seeking.

"I don't hate the other class, no. It's fine, it's easy. I shouldn't say easy, but it isn't that I'm trying to get out of something, it's..."

"Well, if you were, this wouldn't be the wisest move, you realize that, I presume? I very rarely give A's to students. Did you not listen to what I said today in class? So, if you care about your transcript, I would stay where you are. Besides, who wants the same teacher for more than one course?"

"I do," Gila's eyes jumped up from the floor, "please."

"Who are you? Do I know you from somewhere or something? I don't understand why all of a sudden you want to be in *both* of my classes? Strange. Anyway, it isn't really up to me. You would need to get permission from the administration. You'll have to tell them why, and you might want to think about giving them a better answer than you're giving me. It's a little bizarre, all of this, but if they are fine with it – which I should warn you, they may *not* be – then I guess it's fine with me. I need to run. And you need to go to your next class." Whatever momentary interest had made the teacher soft had closed up and made her tone sharp and hard again. "I suggest you go and speak to someone in the office. They can decide. I have to run. I have already spent too much time here talking with you. Are you going to get up and go to your next class? I think it's about time you started moving in that direction." With that last instruction-admonition, Ms. Tobin turned from the desk toward the door.

Gila was still sitting, eyes fastened to the ground, when Ms. Tobin left and the room was empty.

Ms. Tobin opened each class with a provocative taunt. After a minute or two surveying her flock, she sat atop the desk, legs folded elegantly in front of her with her all-black pants and sweater contrasting sharply with her straight grey hair, and launched a run-on rhetorical question.

"I am assuming you've all done the readings. Now, someone tell me, will you, what causes Gatsby's downfall? What precipitated his eventual demise? I mean, when we start the book, he seems wealthy, powerful, so glamorous, doesn't he? Like he has everything. He throws these magnificent parties. He is mysterious. But, then by the end of the novel, there is no one even to come to his funeral. That's quite the fall from grace, wouldn't you say? Rather *humbling,* don't you think?"

She is smirking, scanning the faces of these suburban Hebrew day school students to see whether, past their kippahs, zippered ski fleeces and shining braces, any glimmer of existential angst is beginning to show.

"No one has anything to say about Gatsby? This is a man who had everything, or so we thought. Tells you something about the power of denial, wouldn't you say so? He tries to run away from who he is and where he comes from, but does he succeed? Come on, guys, would you say his self-delusion succeeds?"

The turns students take to redeem him propel the engine of her sermon further.

"What are we learning here about denial? What are we learning about money? Now some of you might think that money is important, perhaps even the most important measure of success, but is that true in Gatsby's case? Now it's true that he throws glamorous parties, but does he have what he's looking for? I know you guys aren't used to asking these questions, but I need you to think about this novel."

When a scrawny boy mounts a defense of Gatsby, saying the man had everything he wanted because he was wealthy and powerful, Ms. Tobin jumps up from the desk and starts pacing, elated.

"So, are you telling me that money is the most important thing in life? Shawn, is that what you're saying?"

Her austere all-black designer attire is a brisk thunderbolt amidst the rows of scrawny, non-athletic teenagers in their baggy sweat-pants, Tiffany bat mitzvah bracelets, pony tails. Every student here is a child of doctors, bankers and trust funds. They are greeted with snacks and live-in nannies when they come home from school. Christmas at Whistler, summer overnight camps, family tours of Israel. The mix of wealth and unenlightenment makes them insular, focused at all times on making sure the next generation reproduces their own.

Ms. Tobin circles the room exaltedly, like the class is both audi-ence and prey. She is going to ruffle these sheltered lives, one hoodied Josh/Amanda at a time.

"Shawn, if as you say, *money* is the most important thing in life, then why is it that Gatsby ends up all alone? Surely, his ending is not a fate you'd like for yourself? Or, would you?" She looks around the room for other students nodding. "What about com-panionship? You think this man is happy? For all the parties he throws and the lavish lifestyle he achieves?"

When Shawn tries to answer, she says again, "Is that the kind of funeral you'd want? This is a man who preferred denial to facing the truth. And you know what that tells you: that there are more important things in life than being *successful*. Like, say, *self-knowledge,* for example?"

Shawn is undeterred and tries to say something but, as soon as she hears him start to talk about how money leads to affording things, which leads to having things you want and causes hap-piness, Ms. Tobin pounces. "And, will money keep you warm at night!" she nearly shouts. It isn't easy to tell whether this is mock-outrage or authentic shock, but so as to capitalize on this ambiguity, Ms. Tobin, this time standing in the back of the class where every head must turn to see her, continues, "I know you're still young Shawn, but when you get older and it's your own life, you tell me how it feels to have money instead of everything else. Okay? Because you might be *fooled* into thinking that financial success is the only thing that matters but I assure you, I *assure* you, that it isn't. There is a lot of suffering out there and sooner or later it is going to catch up with you. Maybe not now and maybe not until you're a hell of a lot older okay, but no one, mark my words, *no* one, gets through this life unscathed. Got it? So, when we talk about money and what is *valuable,* I want you to think about this: will money keep you warm at night? Can you sleep with it? Will it comfort you? You think about that for a moment, okay? Because I don't think it will, Shawn. And, you know what? By the time you realize that, it's going to be too late for you. You are going to make decisions about what's important to you and what you want and if you think that money is the most important thing, then let me tell you – you are in for *quite* the surprise." As she gesticulated to the beat of this impassioned philippic, the Cartier bangles on her arms clanked against each other, adding to the moment's overall dramatic effect. Where other prophet-preachers might have sanded down the edges of their imputations out of reluctance or misgiving about the potential irony of lambasting materialism in a three-hundred-dollar haircut, Ms. Tobin acted like the austere wealth she exuded conferred credibility upon her ideas somehow. There was authority in saying that you *had* something but didn't ever need it. After all, confronting privilege by rolling up cozy, sensuous sleeves meant she wasn't speaking out of resentment but from within knowingness and plenty. She would not be caught dead wanting something, and this scene was no exception.

Gila was still there after all the other students left.

She was taking as long as possible to put her books in her backpack and get up from her seat.

"So, what do *you* think of Gatsby?" Ms. Tobin asked aloud without addressing her directly.

"You don't say much in class but you certainly look like you're paying attention. What did *you* think of class today?"

While Ms. Tobin talked, Gila could not take her eyes off her, but at the sudden prompt for her to answer, she froze and trained her eyes to the floor.

"Amazing," she said, quietly. "I don't know what else to say. I'm sorry."

For one brief moment, Ms. Tobin abruptly stopped what she was doing. "Your name is Gila, right? Aren't you the kid who asked to be in both my classes?"

Gila nodded.

"What did you think was so great about the class? I'm not sure they really understood what I was trying to get at. It's easy to delude yourself is all, but that's a difficult pill to swallow and most people would prefer to run than confront who they are. Oh well." Ms. Tobin resumed to organize her books and pivoted to leave the class. "It's time for me to go. Don't you have another class to go to?"

"No."

"Really? But there's another period after this one, I'm sure of it."

"Yeah, but I can be late."

"Well *I'm* certainly not holding you back. Maybe you'll say a word or two in class next time?" Ms. Tobin was walking out gracefully, her big purse brimming with books, about to shut the classroom light. When she noticed that Gila wasn't next to her, she stopped and turned around. "Is there a reason that you're still standing there?" she asked, surprised and annoyed.

"I don't know," Gila whispered, "I just, I'm sorry, I don't –"

"Listen, I can't keep standing here all day, I have errands to run and you have another class to go to. If you have something to say, why don't you walk with me and you can say it, okay? Let's go."

Gila caught up to her, elated, and they left the classroom for the hallway.

"So, what is it that felt so important to ask?"

"I don't know," Gila said, her downcast eyes affixed to the moving floor. She was accustomed to studying the teacher from afar, a seat in the back of the class, but here she was, walking right alongside her. She tried not to be visibly shaking. "I just, I guess, I don't know, it's just –"

"You're going to have to do better than that. What is it you're trying to say?"

"I don't know, just something about Gatsby, I guess. I don't know, just..."

"Yes, what about him? Can you speak a little more quickly? I really have errands to run."

"Yes, sorry, yes of course. I don't know, it's just, maybe it wasn't his fault?"

"*What* wasn't his fault? That he was running away from who he is? Whose fault *is* that? And don't you see, it's not really about whether or not it was his fault but about the fact that there are consequences for the choices we make, especially when it comes to running away from our *selves*."

"I know, no, I know. I guess, no. I don't know. I guess you're right."

"You don't sound convinced."

"I don't know, maybe not everyone is able –"

"Able to do *what*?"

"To confront themselves or whatever it is. Maybe he wasn't ready, but he would be one day, or something. I don't know."

"You need to speak more clearly, you know that? You have a lot of ideas but you're practically stuttering. Clearly, you have a brain in your head, so god knows why the hell you're falling all over yourself. Anyway," she said, rather abruptly, "I have errands I need to run and you have a class to go to."

Gila waited for Ms. Tobin's shoes to disappear from the spot on the floor she was staring at.

"You have to go to class, you know. You can't just stand *here,* looking at the ground."

"I know."

"This isn't your first year here, is it? You're not new?"

"No."

"But you're not exactly like the other students in your class. What do your parents do?"

"We own a bakery that my father started when I was born. He started it but now I run it with my mother."

"Well that's not the clearest sentence I ever heard but it'll do, I guess."

"Sorry. My father isn't running it anymore. It's just me and my mother. And I have a little brother too. My father, he, well, he got sick and died a few years ago, so yeah, sorry. I'm sorry for not being clear."

"It's fine. Stop apologizing so much, will you? A bakery is certainly not what most kids in this school are used to. Interesting. Well, I really do have to go now. And you are going to get in trouble if you don't get yourself to class."

Ms. Tobin waited for some signal that Gila registered what she was saying, then tightened her grip on the bag she was carrying and turned to walk away.

Gila forced her legs to walk again.

You must go to class. Snap out of this.

That was your chance to talk. Get her attention. Now, you'll be lucky if she ever talks to you again.

She is incredible, isn't she, dad?

You'd like her, I think. She reminds me of you.

When I listen to her, it's the only time since you left there is quiet again, a moment of peace.

Now that you're old enough to drive, you buy food to make, something to grab when you walk in at night or for D when he suddenly arrives demanding to be fed. She says she's on a diet, doesn't need a meal and, although she's overweight, is trying this time, minus gluten, minus carbs, only protein, it changes. Doesn't matter because you three are never home at the same time. It's yearbook, school wide assemblies, you have to just keep doing what there is to do, just keep it going and it all makes sense. As soon as D got old enough to drive there was no stopping him from going places. You don't know where. You can't ask when he walks in at the early hours of the morning where he's coming from, because if he lies, then he can lie about other things and it's a snowball after that, not worth the risk. He's brasher, tougher, gets in different kinds of trouble but you weigh it very carefully. What are the incidents that require a reproach or a response. This has become a battlefield or always was a battlefield, doesn't matter. Now, it's you and him, trying very frantically to keep the world from crumbling once and for all. You play it cool. You have to just stay steady.

He is fourteen, fifteen, sixteen. You explain to officers, judges. He is a boy who only has you. Be gentle or he'll disappear. This is a battlefield, and landmines blow up daily. Just yesterday she said she lost the savings that were in the bank. Bought a diet plan that cost more than it advertised on tv. Sometimes, she says she's giving up for good, running away. Her every explosive moment of outrage triggers him and the spiral is unstoppable, you just extinguish fires one by one. You can hear him screaming that he's burning what the fuck am I gonna do / she's going / Gila make her stop / it's my fault fuck / fuck no / tell her she can't leave us Gila! / I'm gonna kill myself tell her / Gila / I'll find a way for us to have more money, yeah? Tell her that, she hung up on me! / I can't get through she just says that she's done with us I'm gonna / smash something / I'm gonna I don't know / care / fuck it Gila / I'm gonna go with her if she leaves us here / is she / gonna go? / you watch I'm gonna leave I swear to you / I fucking swear bullshit! / this is / bullshit!

Have mercy, you tell the teachers and police who say they'll punish him for drugs they think he used or trouble he is linked to. This is about surviving. Whatever law and order justice you may *think* applies, it doesn't. You will beg on his behalf. A rap sheet is a slippery slope and already he is barely not in jail. *Please* you always ask them, this is no time for any holy ideas about what wayward children need. Things have to keep on moving and they will get better. They will get older, independent.

You have a system. It isn't perfect but it keeps things on *this* side of Armageddon.

He always calls you when he's freaking out. Five, ten times a day you talk him down from the edge of the cliff he is on. The fucking teacher pissed me off! / I'm fucking done I hate her / hate them all I'm gonna show them all / they want to see fucked up? I'm gonna fucking show them / I didn't do anything but no one / stupid bitch / no one listens / they're fucking out to get me Gila I swear / I swear to you I didn't / they are out to get me / I'm gonna fucking –

First, you have to stop the bleeding, find out where is the wound. You have to find it, put a bandage on. No big questions or explaining, just stabilize him so he doesn't hurl the phone into a wall before you have a chance to calm him down. You say the world isn't a horrible place, even though it seems that way right now. It isn't out to get him. He doesn't need to drive his car into a wall to show how angry he is inside. You're listening. They fucked him over. It was a misunderstanding. Let's figure it out. D? Stay on the phone and we're going to figure it out. You figure you have a few minutes at the beginning to meet this rage correctly or you worry that you'll lose the boy for good. You never know.

My arm's blown off! / My leg's on fire! / Those fucking pricks at school they fucking / fucked me over Gila / fucked me over! Yelling in your ear, he says I'm gonna smash something / to make it stop my / fucking head –

But you have language that can organize his feelings and you use it. Talk him down. Tell him this feeling that you have it isn't fatal. It only looks like that from a certain angle. Listen to me and I'll show you what is really going on. The guy at the mechanic shop was *joking* when he said you seem like you aren't social. Your teacher didn't say you're stupid – you aren't stupid, you are brilliant. She said you're *struggling* in class, which is true D. That's not *supposed* to be offensive. The barista didn't fuck you over, he really probably *did* forget what kind of drink you ordered, does that make sense? You make it all make sense to him. He isn't stupid.

But, for now, he can't go through the day without a few hours of your suturing the wounds he has inflicted or endured.

You feel how hot his rage is, burning, but as long as you're together, you won't let the flames devour him, won't let the boy combust.

As long as he is calling, you are grateful.

You worry most about the day he doesn't call. You are the only one that calms him down and brings him back. You know that he could end it all. He threatens it. You don't say it would kill you if he did. He doesn't register when you talk about yourself. You have to just keep being there and showing him you're in this war together.

You're here until he's old enough to do this on his own.

You can bring him back, talk until he's calmer fine / I'm gonna go now see you / bye. Hangs up. *Is this enough,* you wonder? He needs to be airlifted from a warzone to stand a chance at all at being better but *how*? She'd never let him. Never let you help the boy so blatantly.

She is mostly at the house of tyrant lover; she says, "Because of the two of you, he can't come here! Don't you judge me or I swear to god –" But you never say a single word to her about the man. You know your job is to stay silent. "I am a grown woman," she has yelled at you, "And I am entitled to find my own happiness! Don't *talk* to me about responsibility to those goddamn fucking cakes! They can rrott in hell for all I care!" Sometimes asking when or if she's coming back or going directly to the business is enough to trigger this tirade. But you don't mind it when she's at his house. It is better than when he's over here.

On the weekends, she insists on dinner. She dresses up with something she has been fighting with for hours; on evenings such as these, the closet is her enemy. "Nothing fits!" she wails and smacks the air. "It doesn't matter what I do. I'm fat and it's not my fault. It is the fucking business, that's what it is. Who can work with cakes and not pick at them sometimes? Even your father said it wasn't my fault! Now look at me – He's going to say I'm ugly, isn't he? Nu? Tell me, don't you lie!"

You sit on the edge of the bed and say she looks okay. "But, I'm *horrible*!" she says and then sometimes she turns on you. "I gave everything I had to having children and this is what I get. An ugly figure that no man will love. Oh my god!" she cries and sometimes you get really worried because it's fine when it stays depressed like this but if it gets too close to the edge of anger and recrimination she will say, "How dare you try to help me when you are the reason I'm in this position!"

He'll come over in jeans and a t-shirt and in an instant make whatever she's wearing seem ridiculous. Too colorful, too tight, too much perfume. Overeager. You want to run over and reassure her, but once he's here you go from being her adjutant to the daughter it is his job to educate.

"Your hair is too long!" he'll bark at you when you open the door. Or, "your hair is too short!" Or, "what ugly jeans are you wearing? Do you really not have any sense of what a woman should wear?"

His Russian accent is so thick you struggle to make sense of his sentences and you're always a few minutes behind by the time you've translated the insult.

"Gila! I thought you were a girl and yet you wear these baggy, ugly t-shirts with these jeans! What is this? What's wrong with you? All that studying and you think it's okay to look like such a dog? No man will care how smart you are, you trust me now, okay? You look hideous. You understand? Sweetie, explain it to your daughter, that she looks disgusting and no man will want her. Understand?"

When he cannot find the word he's looking for, she helps him and sometimes says "okay, okay, I think she gets the picture, don't you Gila? You'll smarten up in what you wear? You'll *try* at least not to look so ugly?"

He talks about his week at work. It's a menial factory job but he says he was an educated engineer in Russia before he left. You listen for the part where it will turn to school and while his beer belly exhales and he spreads his legs to get comfortable. She strokes his arm and neck, whispers in his ear and giggles, telling him how kind he is for helping her wretched kid make decisions.

No matter how it ever starts, it ends up with him telling you to go be a pharmacist. "Do you think your mother should support you all your life? Huh, you spoiled little brat? Is that what you're expecting?"

If you say, but you're not good at science, he says, "You're lazy! If you're actually as smart as everyone says, you should be good at everything you study."

If you say, but you actually like English and maybe you could do something with that he calls her from her dishwashing and says, "Do you hear the kind of spoiled creature you've raised?! Literature she wants to study! Nice to be rich!" He laughs at this for many long minutes, incredulous and indignant.

You used to try to argue back because he seemed like underneath the bluster and attacking, he might listen, but now you understand that this is how the evening goes. One day, after you do more of the things he advises you to do, he will be more pleased by your appearance and decisions and this vitriol might change to praise. You just have to find a way to do the things he's telling you to do, but it's so hard to see how you could go into science. Also, just get over whatever makes it hard to just look like a girl.

"You are good at *nothing,* understand? I see the way you cook when I am here. You're not a natural like your mother. You think that I can't tell the difference? *Everyone* can tell the difference. You have no talent in that department. It is obvious. And, you don't really have any other domestic skills either. What do you do? You help out here and there every so often. *Nothing* compared to what you owe this woman! She is your *mother,* do you understand? Do you even know the meaning of responsibility? Someone so spoiled and entitled like *you,* I'm not sure they teach that word to you in the books you read."

It is only when he mentions D that you break down and cry.

He says, "You are too selfish even to make sure your brother is okay? What kind of person could be so disgusting as that?"

"No," you whisper, "no, it isn't true." You start to list the things you do but he's not listening. When he asks her for confirmation, she nods her head flirtatiously and says, "it's true, the girl was always selfish. Even her father thought so! Ha! It's about time someone put her in her place. Continue baby, don't worry if she seems upset, she just doesn't like someone telling her she's wrong, go on!"

You tell yourself this isn't happening.

Say something! You know it can't be true, it just can't be right to say that you're not doing everything you can.

"But, then why is your brother so fucked up? If you were helping, why is he not doing better? Huh, you tell me *that*? You wretched creature, answer that! Stop crying and start fucking paying attention."

She sometimes interjects to say, "it's true, why *isn't* he doing any better if you say you care so much about him? Huh? Nu? Answer him, my sweet lover is talking to you! He's helping you see your mistakes so you can *correct* them, understand? You are lucky that someone is willing to do this in the place of your father! And, instead you're sitting there sniveling, crying, like a baby! Gila, you should be ashamed of your behavior. *Ashamed.* How disappointed your father would be with you right now!"

One minute she is coquettish, begging you to bail her out of her financial messes, telling you that you'd all drown without your taking care of things and, at another turn, she's adding final touches to the speech he's making about your faults.

I am begging you to tell me what you really think.

Dad, please, if you can send a sign from heaven, please, I just can't tell. At first, I think there's no way that he's right because I'm doing everything you asked me to. They are my life, this, the business, everything. There's nothing else I'm doing, nothing else I want.

But then, you also warned me I was selfish, that I had a tendency to read instead of helping. There are more important things in life than books.

I had a tendency to think that I was better.

But dad you have to hear me, please.

I was a child then. I am your helper now.

❧

It's *Death of a Salesman* time.

"Someone talk to me about Willy Loman. Let's hear it, go. This play is a masterpiece; I want to hear you thinking. Rachel? Jared? What have we learned so far? Who is this man? What is he after? What does he want? What *motivates* him? I don't see any hands. Why is that? Your papers last time were mostly terrible so you could all use the chance to improve your grade, which I'm assuming all of you care about, and class participation is one of those ways." Ms. Tobin ran her fingers through her pin straight short grey hair and then folded her arms around her chest to indicate she was impatiently waiting.

She paced around the class and encouraged students who were making an effort. She defended Willy when they said he was pathetic and excoriated him when they said he was aggrieved. There was a sweet spot in between these choices that, even after months of analyzing Willy's tragic ancestors, the class was not equipped to ascertain.

"Everyone turn to page thirty-three. This is Willy talking to his sons. Ready?

"That's just what I mean. Bernard can get the best marks in school, y'understand, but when he gets out in the business world, y'understand, you are going to be five times ahead of him. That's why I thank Almighty God you're both built like Adonises. Because the man who makes an appearance in the business world, the man who creates personal interest, is the man who gets ahead. Be liked and you will never want. You take me, for instance. I never have to wait in line to see a buyer. 'Willy Loman is here!' That's all they have to know, and I go right through."

When Josh tries to suggest that Willy is religious because he mentions the Almighty, Ms. Tobin dramatically uses her right hand as a shade for her eyes and shakes her head emphatically. "Can we branch out a little, please? I know we are at Hebrew School but can we *try* to think bigger when we are analyzing a text? Okay? This is not your Talmud class. I want you to be thinking in terms of motivation. Voice. Character. Psychology. Okay? Let's forget about the Almighty for a second. What do we learn here about Willy Loman's sense of the world around him?"

"That appearance is important to him?" someone says and Ms. Tobin, aware that she is pulling teeth, barely concealing her irritation, answers, "and *what* about appearance is important? Is this a man who is successful? Is this a man who did what he wanted to do in life? Is he proud of himself? Is he *happy* in these scenes? Come on, guys. We have been talking about Hamlet and Gatsby for weeks now. You can do better than this. Think about the power of self-delusion. We talked about this. What does it mean to deny who you are? Do they succeed? Michael? Shira? C'mon guys. Forget about your grades or comfortable family vacations for a moment. Just *think* about this character."

I see you when we lived in Florida, your curly white hair stuck to your forehead. The air is so humid. For the first time, you have a small belly that hangs over your belt. Your blue eyes still piercing but there's no way to hide desperation in this climate, the heat forces everything out.

We drive to the hotels together to sell them our cakes. We are new here. 1991 and you said there's a recession in Canada, so we're going to move here for a little while before you make enough money to move back to Ha'aretz, where you decided you might really belong. Many people come to Florida to make money you say. It is proven.

Wait until they see the cakes we make. Overnight we're going to make it here! Forget about Toronto. They are too conservative there, not enough willingness to try new things. But this is America, Gil., This is where we're going to make our name.

Your accent was charming in Canada where everyone is from somewhere else, but here it was just strange and foreign and, when you did your "the accent's Belgian" shtick, they only looked more confused. You cultivated a kind of strangeness you thought of as distinction but here you were a silly man peddling unfamiliar wares.

I see you sweating, unaccustomed to a belly or this heat, and insisting to chefs who are happy to eat cheesecakes why your sacher-torte is so unique.

They can't pronounce the French-Semitic name of our business (Gaytex-Guyle they say when they read Gateaux-Gil on the business card), but they will come around, you'll see, you say.

You promise to match whatever wholesale price they're paying, you say the cake is so good they won't go back to key lime pie. But, when we meet with them on the sunny, sticky patios of their sprawling, tacky, flamingo pink hotels they'll tell you, loudly, in that friendly all-American way, 'Buddy, save the pitch. We don't give two whits what Count of Austria this cake is named after or if the chocolate's Belgian or fake, so long as it's like what we're used to and we can serve it with ice cream or put it in a doggy bag if the customer wants.'

I see you trying to show these uncultured North Americans the light, one fancy non-pronounceable mille-feuille at a time. And then I see you as a child, blond hair and cherubic, your father an Austrian refugee in this backwater called Palestine – a man with a German name and German training who was in Birkenau before the British government took him out to be amongst the "saved" that would build a university in the holy desert. I see that nothing would be good enough for him, he who has been exiled from Vienna to a place where oranges are a delicacy and the people are proud to work the land with their hands. Where the language, ancient, is missing all the words for a cultured mind to speak in. He is a renowned professor when no one cares about a department of history, when war is what's real. I see how he must have found everything to be a diminution of his worth and measure. I see him with his sharp, aristocratic nose, Edward Strauss, a prodigy, student of the gymnasium, three PhDs, and here you are: a lad born in Jerusalem, a father who isn't like the other struggling, laboring, Zionist men.

When every dad wore maple leaf sweatshirts and talked about the hockey game, synagogue fundraisers, or the new ski slopes and whether they'd be open in time for the family trip, you showed up in your knitted Nordic sweaters and elbow patches soliciting their ideas on the issues in the news. They put their arms on your shoulders and teasingly called you "intellectual" and I see you, how much sense this made, how dear to you this designation. Even though you eschewed the value of intellection when it came to me or came to "real life." Even when the European's anguished battle *with the philistines was not really true for you, who was Israeli, who had a home that you were from and did belong to.*

Ms. Tobin looks to Gila periodically in these moments of exasperation and sees longing and the faintest smile. Gila never raises her hand but they have a silent understanding.

Before each paper is due, the other students clamor for her help because everyone knows she understands what Tobin's saying. She's only interjected in these discussions a handful of times, but everyone catches how Ms. Tobin's tone shifts when they are talking. It isn't the teacher chiding a student into enlightenment but a public moment of another, private conversation.

Each day they walk together after class. It is never formal, never official. If Ms. Tobin is tied up answering students' questions, Gila takes longer at her desk so she isn't standing there visibly waiting. The first few times, Gila felt sure Ms. Tobin would be annoyed to see her waiting and took the interruption of their nascent routine as a signal that Ms. Tobin was a teacher who had other students to attend to. But when she got to the door she could hear Ms. Tobin ask, her voice climbing over the student in front of her, "Didn't you have a question for me, Gila? Just wait there, or outside if you prefer. And, when I'm done here, I can answer it."

From then on Gila understood that no matter how disrupted their post-class ritual could be, Ms. Tobin expected them to do their rounds together down the halls.

These conversations don't start or end with any acknowledgement of what they were doing. As if any terms for this encounter would crumble something fragile, force into representation something as yet too urgent and delicate for form. What rules exist are clear, unspoken.

Often Ms. Tobin begins where she left off in class. "That scene's incredible, isn't it?" she'll say, her face lit up, impassioned. "That moment when Willy has to face what he's done, what he's been avoiding? What do you think?"

If Gila says, "It is so haunting to see him fall apart," Ms. Tobin responds, "But it was inevitable, you see that, don't you?"

Once there is a launching point, Ms. Tobin talks about how hard it is to be courageous. "People think that it's good enough in life to do the things that are expected of you, but it rarely is. It's rarely what is going to make you happy. Do you know what makes you happy? In fact, who am I kidding? I don't even really care about happy, who's happy? No one's *happy*. The god-damn idea is overrated, but fulfillment means something to me and you can't get there if you're always running away. Believe me when I say it doesn't work. It really doesn't even if you think it does, even if you have yourself a decent run. It catches up eventually. Everything you think you're outsmarting and escaping, I promise you, you're *not*."

Gila walked in silence next to her, provided questions when there was something that could be asked. She was always barely audible, eyes always trained on the ground. She nodded to the beat of Ms. Tobin's conclusions. Sometimes she said, "Maybe there is another reason people run away? Maybe they're scared and just can't find a way..." but Ms. Tobin wasn't altogether sympathetic to exculpating sinners.

"There's nothing easy about striving for fulfillment, believe me, *I* know. I have had my fight and I would do it again but if you think you're going to get somewhere without fighting, then you're simply deluding yourself, that's all. You think my life's been easy? I'm not going to talk about my life. I *assure* you of that, but what I mean to say is that I know firsthand you simply cannot take a shortcut and expect that everything you want will all work out. There are sacrifices to be made. And Willy Loman doesn't want to make sacrifices, and you know what? Gatsby doesn't either."

The severity of Ms. Tobin's message is accentuated by the sight of her all-black-clad thin figure, gesticulating zealously in these mundane adolescent-filled halls. It is not a glittering pulpit but when she's been asked if she wouldn't be more compelled by college students or a boarding school somewhere, she says, amusedly, and in the name of modestly, "I want to turn some lights on. I don't need the pomp and circumstance, thank you very much. No sir, that's not for me, not plain ole' me who isn't hungry for the recognition." As if becoming professorial is too fancy for her impromptu wisdom, this Jewish day school's elementariness a kind of street cred for her activist gig.

Gila always looks up from the floor at even the most fleeting indication Ms. Tobin might, in some small and powerful way, talk about her personal life, but she never lets anything slip she doesn't mean to share.

She has five children and her husband is a banker.

This information is common knowledge at the school but when a student accidentally writes "Mrs." on a paper, Ms. Tobin roars back, "That's my mother-in-law, thank you very much. Be more careful or I'll dock a grade." This feisty feminism sits alongside judgments about the foolishness of artists who insist on having domesticity as well. There are mentions every now and then of her wanting, once, to have been a writer or a painter of some kind. "But you can't have it all," she'll say with a knowingness that belies the tentativeness of these lines; wistfully shake her head, suggesting rather than resisting any intimations of regret.

When they walk together down the high school corridors, Ms. Tobin often retells stories of peoples' shock at discovering she has so many children (with *that* leather jacket? to which Ms. Tobin replies, "What? You think they need to fit underneath it?") or shock that she is married and lives in a big house (don't seem the Betty Crocker type? she quips and grimaces). She seems pleased to hear that she is, in fact, mysterious, and even to people who know her, stubbornly enigmatic. "We are all alone anyway," she muses to Gila, and when Gila shakes her head, struggling, feebly, to refute these layers of self-imposed limitation, Ms. Tobin shoots back, "Don't you worry about me. I know how to take care of myself and I know perfectly well what I can and cannot do. If I am alone, it is by my own choosing. You make choices and then you have to live with them. And there isn't any way around that. Not for you or for me or for anyone, believe me." Gila stares directly at her, looking anguished and confused; sometimes she even whispers "no," or, "maybe you just haven't found someone yet who understands you." And, once or twice, she says, "but you could leave teaching and try your hand at art?" But, by the time the teacher hears the word "dream," her response is fierce and swift and non-negotiable. While Gila scrambles to find a flaw in Ms. Tobin's tragic-as-realist cloak, desperate to show her that it *isn't* too late to actualize whatever secret ambitions are hinted at, if not disclosed even, every now and then, suggesting lightly that Tobin is too talented to resign herself to pushing others forward while refusing aspiration for herself, Ms. Tobin listens, smiles, and when the moment is right, brushes Gila's pleading efforts away, her bangles clanking against each other while she announces, circumspectly, "Focus on yourself, my dear. It's far too late for me. Not everything that's broken can be fixed and that's the fact of it. I can accept that and so should you." When these interchanges happen, Ms. Tobin smiles at the coveted reflection in Gila's heartbroken eyes. In Gila's yearning, she locates confirmation that, even if her appetite for recognition (as a would-have-been-artist) must be tempered by "reality," she has at least mastered a formula for turning the "self" into an aesthetic achievement. As with her style of dress, the sharp edges on blazers and haircuts and bold metal glasses, alongside the smoothness of fine cashmere sweaters and soft-silken words elegantly spoken, Ms. Tobin brought austerity and sensuality together in every gesture, as if to say that it was always and only *constraint* that made knowledge, or closeness, precious and irresistible. Always decisive and never confused, she tended to her persona meticulously, playing only at the edges that she had put there. By turn provoking intimacy and forbidding it, she was ardent, impassioned, single-minded about sustaining desire at just the right temperature. She treated her own depths as the source of a constant, inextinguishable fire and cultivated a heated detachment that invited and withheld at the same moment, always and only baring her wounds by tracing, with a single lightly pressured finger, the shape of her scars.

Once when they were walking, Ms. Tobin abruptly stopped amidst their stroll and said, "Well, *you* should know something about running away from yourself? No one hangs around after class to talk about tragic heroes if they aren't trying to figure something out for themselves. I'm right, aren't I? Maybe you can look up at me for once while I am talking? Not ready yet, I see. Well, that's fine. But tell me this: what is it that you're escaping from?"

"I'm not, I'm..." Gila whispered, under her breath.

"You're not what? Running? Of course you are. The only question is from *what*?"

"But I'm...I'm just...I like these books."

"Oh please, Gila. Spare me this bullshit, please. You are on every committee this school has to offer. You are at the top of every class you're in, from what I've heard. The principal practically calls you at home when he needs something organized in this place. Not to mention that you run the yearbook and god only knows what else. Now no one, and I mean *no one,* does that unless there's something they are desperately trying to avoid. So, what is it? Talk."

Gila squirmed. It was clear she had not expected this. She looked like she was desperate to disappear. She struggled to breathe.

"I get that you are going through something. It doesn't take a genius to figure that out, but why don't you talk to me instead of always deflecting to one of these fictional characters. I know you said your father died. I'm sure that has something to do with it, yes? You're still pretty young for something like that to happen."

There was a new softness in Ms. Tobin's tone that brought Gila to tears.

Dad, make it stop. I can't.

"I can't, Ms. Tobin. Everything is fine."

"Then why are you crying as soon as I ask what's going on in your life? That is not the response of someone who's fine."

"I'm sorry, I just –"

"And what in god's name are you *apologizing* for? You're not doing anything wrong. For god's sake I'm just asking you to talk to me. I don't bite, you know."

"I know."

"Then what is it? You said you help out in the bakery? Your mother is managing okay?"

"Yes."

"Do you have siblings?"

"A brother, yes. And we're okay, we really are. We're managing."

"Then why are you falling apart when I ask how you're doing?"

"I don't know, I'm sorry. I guess I'm not that used to talking."

"Well, that's for sure! I'd say that's quite the understatement. I have heard a handful from you in months of talking about these books and never *once* about yourself, you know that?"

"No. I'm sorry, I can try."

"Enough already. I'm not *blaming* you. I'm just trying to get you to open up a little."

"What does that mean?"

"What do I mean by *open up*? I mean, get you to be a little less scared all the time, maybe even suggest that you breathe? You know, that kind of thing. You should try it sometime."

"But I don't think –"

"Don't think so much, for a change, okay? I'm not asking you a *question*. I'm just making a suggestion, that's all. What you end up doing with it is your business. So, don't worry about what I'm saying. I just think you might consider what I'm suggesting. If you ever want to talk, I understand a thing or two, I –"

"No. No, it's okay. Please, it's fine. I don't need anything. I'm okay –"

Ms. Tobin stood still, surprised by this degree of terror and restraint.

"I have errands to run so I can't keep standing here and talking like this. But I said what I had to and the rest is up to you."

Gila didn't move and Ms. Tobin said again, "I need to go, okay, and you need to go back to class. We'll continue this, okay?"

"You're not upset with me?"

"Why would I be upset with you?"

"I don't know."

"Well, then I don't know what you're asking."

"I'm sorry. It's nothing. I'm sorry."

"Listen, I can see that you're worried but there's nothing to be worried about. I have things I need to do, and you have a class to go to, so that's all. Okay? Look at me, and I can go, okay? Can you do that?"

When Gila didn't move, Ms. Tobin exhaled her frustration and Gila finally made her neck rise and glance in Ms. Tobin's direction.

"Good, that's good. Thank you. You had me worried for a moment. Go to French class."

With that Ms. Tobin turned around and walked toward her minivan, which was always a strange sight when Gila got a glimpse of it from the doorway window. A woman in a black blazer and bracing grey hair climbing into an SUV, the ultimate accoutrement of domestic life and children, grocery shopping, carpool, even a pet.

Dad, I would do anything to keep her talking. It's the only time since you that there is quiet inside my head. I feel peaceful when I listen. What if she gets fed up and stops these conversations? It would destroy me, dad, because there's no one else who notices anything, knows me at all. Except you, I know.

You two would get along, I think. I wouldn't need her in this way if you were here but for now at least. Forgive me, dad. Is it ok? To talk like this? I'm trying to be good, I think she understands that I'm your helper.

I know you wanted me to grow up to be decent and I think she wants that too.

I've never had anyone talk to me the way she just did. So gentle. It is unbearable.

I wish I didn't know it was an option. Open up? What if...I can't imagine.

No one is looking out for me as you have done and do. I won't talk to her, I promise.

The only voice I listen to is yours and only yours and indivisible. Don't stop talking, ever, tell me what to do. She is a stranger. I am your prince.

You are my father and there is only one father and my father is king.

It wasn't long before Gila was the character whose denial was the subject of their perambulatory examinations.

"Don't you see you're running from your feelings?" Ms. Tobin would exclaim as soon as they were past the threshold of the classroom door. No prefatory friendliness, no break from where they last left off.

Gila tried to ask "what feelings?" but there never was a chance to slow the momentum of this emancipation crusade with a question like that.

Gila wanted to ask what experience "overworking" was protecting her from, but it was clear that any challenge to the basic terms of Ms. Tobin's interpretation would have disturbed the entire endeavor's narrative and emotional scheme.

Ms. Tobin led the way, assailing, overriding Gila's tentative protestations.

When Gila meekly said, "No, I'm not running, I don't think." Ms. Tobin laughed and said, "You have to be kidding me, right? You're the goddamn class president, *in addition* to whatever else you do to take care of your family. You're going to have to do better than *that*!"

When Gila said, "It isn't hard, the things you say I do. It's just my job to do –" Ms. Tobin cut her off, "Your *job*?" she'd say incredulously. "What seventeen-year-old is responsible for running a bakery and raising their brother? Not to mention whatever else you do that you don't say anything about. Even finding *that* out about you was like pulling teeth."

"My mother helps, sometimes."

"Oh yeah?", Ms. Tobin would retort, "Then how come I see a teenager who doesn't look like she ever has lunch with her, or like she has slept that much, or like she ever does anything social? You're popular, I see that. People like you, but that isn't the same as being social like the other students in your class. Have you once gone out on a Saturday night? Tell me the truth."

Ms. Tobin saw this line of questioning embarrassed Gila but did not relent.

"I didn't think so, and why *is* that? If your life is so *normal,* then why do I see the permanent look of worry on your face? Huh, Gila? Why don't you think about that for a minute. Why don't you stop, for just a minute, trying to defend your mother and your father and just admit the situation you're in."

"Stop, please. My father is innocent. It's not his fault he died. He got sick. My mother is...helpless. She can't do things better. You have to understand, it's not that simple. Please –"

When this line of cross-examination arrived at the familiar impasse, Gila tried to say how "things were better now. They're not so bad. Maybe before when I was smaller but now, I have things under control."

She wanted to explain how much progress she'd made. Wouldn't Ms. Tobin be proud? Take a break from her scorching tough-love indignation to appreciate that running the bakery had become a more functional enterprise? She even tried, "the business is my baby." But Ms. Tobin balked and said, "you must be kidding! Nothing I know about you suggests to me that you would find making cakes a compelling activity. Reading, maybe. Doing something with children, teaching maybe. But a retail business, really Gila? I don't think so."

Gila stared at the floor and almost said, *but they are my customers.* I have become attached to my Balkan flock. I know their cravings and their tastes, what they want when they dump their fake designer purses and flashy key chains on the counter and gruffly mutter, "Nu? What's new today?" I know they don't want mousse or tarts or sponge cakes (too boring, not enough layers, too many layers of dough). I have learned how to deliver cakes on the weekends, in the evenings, to the Russian nightclubs with their Slavic techno blaring without letting my cakes disappear (= letting the kitchen staff eat them) because I have taught myself to say in Russian, Sergei, *eeydee sudah, pazhalosta.* I even bring them extra pastries, so they have some to eat instead of what the wedding party paid for. They talk to me in Russian and I answer back in English and we have an understanding. I am facilitating their celebrations. It is rewarding work. When the day is done, I think about Ludmila who asked for extra hazelnuts on the top of her cake, or Dimitri who said our meringues are the best of their kind in all of our Toronto suburb! I am proud of what I'm doing. It is an easy thing to nourish people who want something that's not too sweet, very crunchy, goes with vodka. And, we are doing better. There's still no money because mom spends it on clothes for parties with her tyrant lover or other things. I do not ask, but she's better now that I deal with the customers. Being patient with them isn't hard. For the moments when I'm helping them find just the right size of the cake for their anniversary party (two pieces per person if they are my Russians, half for my Canadians who are always on a diet!) or decide whether white or dark chocolate dacquoise is better, I see what is meant about finding purpose where others see inconsequential tasks.

Gila tried to say, "I'm learning things I wouldn't learn in school." But, Ms. Tobin smacked her lips and found this counter-argument ridiculous.

Ms. Tobin flat out refused to see grey areas. "There's right and wrong when it comes to what a child should be expected to do, okay? And, from what I gather, although getting information from you is virtually impossible, still, from the little you *have* reluctantly said, I would think anyone could agree that whatever is going on in your house is completely outrageous. Need I remind you that last week your mother got remarried and you didn't even tell me? I happened to notice that you were extra quiet – which, by the way, the fact that I can even detect the differences between these states of yours is pretty incredible, wouldn't you say? I should do this for a living. I should stop being a teacher and be a therapist instead. Anyway, that's beside the point. Where was I? Oh yeah, you're going to tell me your father would have wanted this for you? You are running yourself *ragged*. Absolutely ragged. I say this as someone who has raised five children. Listen to me. They will manage without you, they always do. Go to a movie one night on the weekend. What about that? How is that as an idea for you? Will you try that? I see that you're not really listening to a word that I'm saying, are you?

You're too polite to just outright tell me you won't follow my advice, but I think I know you well enough by now to guess that you *ain't* going to any movie any time soon, are you? Am I right about that?"

What Gila tried to say, but couldn't, was that it was her job, she couldn't leave it. That even if she "left," where would she go? She was in charge of things and while they burned, she was a fireman. She tried to say, "But maybe, later," meaning, even if there really was a screaming other person underneath the frantic son holding a hose and fetching water, it wasn't time to let her out.

Maybe when the buildings were no longer burning?

She tried to say, "Ms. Tobin, I promised I would watch them, I –"

Father, can you see I'm burning?

Gila tried to say, "I know there are things I'm not addressing, but maybe when they're safe and settled, later. I will come out later, talk more later." *When the buildings are no longer burning.* When the kingdom he built can stand on its own.

She didn't dare repeat the terms of the deathbed covenant that bound her to this current situation. She knew Ms. Tobin would declare it null and void, say decisively, "That was then and this is now," say, "You were only twelve!", offer any number of rational arguments that did not take into account that fealty was not the simple cause of her oppression. There is no one else to watch them. And no one else to be if I am not his faithful son.

When the vice-principal rabbi was asked to recommend a student for recruitment by an American school, he found Gila and instructed her to get ready to apply. And, when Gila asked Ms. Tobin whether or not she should go ahead, Ms. Tobin said, "You're kidding, right? *Of course,* you are applying!"

Gila tried to vocalize the other side. She'd be leaving D, responsibilities, the school's expenses, but there was a scholarship no student from Canada had ever gotten and Ms. Tobin said to worry about everything else later if she actually got in. She always dreamed of studying in Boston and it was only four years and he would have agreed that a liberal education was the kind of thing, if done unpretentiously, that mattered.

When Gila got in, she drove over to Ms. Tobin's house, elated and in shock. She called first, a number that she had but until then had never used. And, when the husband answered the phone, she could hear Ms. Tobin in the background saying, "Just tell her to come over! Don't bother passing me the phone. Just tell her to get into the car and bring the letter over."

When Gila said, "I can't go, but I have to." Ms. Tobin didn't miss a beat. "You're going, Gila, whether you like it or not. This is the opportunity of a lifetime and you are getting on that plane, you mark my words, you understand?"

When Gila got back home that night, there was a new boyfriend who had just moved in. There was, although there shouldn't have been, some expectation that someone would be home to celebrate the good news but there was only this stranger who didn't speak English and the fleeting sight of her mother grasping for a robe.

I need to talk to you, we have a problem, dad.

The question of what it meant to move away was all they talked about these days. Ms. Tobin kept saying, "I understand your reservations. It is scary for anyone your age to move away, although surely, you'll be more independent than most. But, it's time and it's the right thing to do. Go find yourself. You deserve some freedom. Nothing is going to happen here, I promise you. Your mother can take care of herself and so can your brother. You'll see. You're scared and it makes sense to be scared. But you have earned this, you need to remember that. Do you hear me? You deserve it. And, besides, it would be more expensive at this point for you to stay in Toronto and go to school here. That's just a fact, by the way."

The sound of Ms. Tobin's voice insisting, explaining, assuring, assailing was like a blanket Gila crawled into and she found some kind of quiet there.

He would have wanted her to go. He would have wanted her to stay.

When Gila said, "Okay," she knew there wasn't any other option. He had always been so proud of her accomplishments, and she wagered this would be no exception. Besides, D was never home anymore and she could talk to him by phone as many times as usual. She wouldn't do less to keep him safe.

I won't forget my place or allow myself to feel important.

I will take care of them from far away. It's not that far. Ms. Tobin is right; I can't stay here.

Forgive me father, if I have sinned?

For saying yes, I'm going,
   I am your servant but
   Not only or
   Not solely, or
   I may also be a student, dad.

Ms. Tobin says this is normal mourning and I agree, I think. Not that I will ever be okay, but that it won't replace the loss of you to live outside my head, that it won't send you away if I am once again, also, a child, and once again as I had been before, your prince who also had these things I wanted.

Ms. Tobin says I'll never reach the end of grief.

Even if I do, sometimes I'll feel you're far away.

You're far away, dad, that's the truth.

You're far away, and she says that isn't ever going to change. But, I am here and I need to find a way to stay.

I will always be your helper, but let me be allowed to speak.

Oh dad, forgive me if I am surrendering. I am, I think, surrendering. There's a quiet when she talks to me, and it feels like there is someone there, shh, if you're silent, can you hear a sound?

Not much to say or think but *some*thing and it's been nothing, only nothing, saying nothing, since you left.

While you were in my head, I prayed to bring you back.

I thought my cries would reach the heavens and bring you here, to where I need you near,

but now that part of things is over, father.

You're not coming back.

And, I don't see the point in weeping, fasting, bending air to hold my pleading, there is nothing I can say to move you, nothing I can do to make you speak. Can't you see?

I go to you, but still you don't come back to me.

And, although I've done all that you wanted –

There is silence still and no one there.

And I am here, still, do you understand? I am here. I have to live. I have to fucking live.

If I have sinned, forgive me dad.

If I forget thee oh – *please,*
don't be ridiculous, I won't forget.
But if I do, my right hand will forget its function.
And if I do – dad, *please,*
I can't forget, just understand, I'm only coping,
yours will ever be the one voice in my head.
Don't worry, dad. Forgive me, dad. What else am I supposed
to do?
The ground is cold, the night withholding,
how can I leave while you're still here? You are not here.
you're in my head, you are my head – how can I stay?
It has been years. I see:
I am going to him; he will not come back to me.
For years, I exhort but he is not revived. I beg and he does not
awaken. And so, I listen when she says, "It's time to go." I see:
talking is between the living.

I wanted to say *forgive me father.*
  I almost said *for I have sinned.*

[But, you should have seen how magical she looked
  So all-black-clad, short grey-white hair

A stark sharp-angled angel
  Fiery gestures, then talking whisper-thin]

I wanted to say *forgive me dad*
  [For I wanted every word she says.]

Besides my writing suffers when the only ones I talk to are the dead.

[Because the pen she points with becomes a wand to scold with, bring you near.]

Besides [her poise, her certainty, how unafraid she was to speak]
  what kind of sin is it to say, *I have forgotten the sound of your voice?*

༄

K (King)

It is an office on Manhattan's Upper West Side. Modern, massive, all glass windows, family-friendly. Doorman. Foyer. In the office, there is African Art, masks on the bookshelves, sculptures of bodies or gods. The therapist, Dr. Peters, is tall and lean, wearing tight pants and a slim fitting blouse. A high-waisted belt divides them. She has long brown hair. When the door opens onto the waiting room, she smiles a little uneasily toward the new patient, motioning her in. She has a very deep voice. She looks delicate and mischievous. The room is small but one wall is a window. Gila, twenty-five, wears jeans and a loose-fitting dress shirt, loafers, a messenger bag. She has short curly hair. It is October.

Gila: "So. Hi. You should know, I'm not good at being a patient."

Dr. Peters: "Hm. That's an interesting way to begin."

Gila: "Oh, really? What's so interesting about that? I'm being honest."

Dr. Peters: "I didn't say you weren't. It's just, well…How shall I put this…not that typical for a new patient to introduce themselves that way. That's all. Did you hear it as a condemnation?"

Gila: "That *would* be interesting wouldn't it? Then we could talk about *why* I heard it as a condemnation. Thank you but no. I heard it as you saying you're surprised. But I'm not typical. And, I don't have time. To waste. I don't want to spend week after week just analyzing *why* I feel something or what it *means,* that kind of thing."

Dr. Peters: "That kind of thing?"

Gila: "Oh, seriously, are we going to do *this* the whole time?"

Dr. Peters: "When you say *this,* what do you *mean*?"

Gila: "Oh my god. Is this a joke?"

Dr. Peters: "I'm afraid I don't know what you're talking about. What would be a *joke* in what I asked you?"

Gila: "I think we should start this again."

Dr. Peters: "Oh-kay. I suppose. What did you have in mind?"

Gila: "I don't know."

Dr. Peters: "Shall we start with you telling me a little bit about yourself?"

Gila: "Sure. What I'm doing now or the whole personal-biography thing?"

Dr. Peters: [chuckles] "Anything you like."

Gila: "I just finished a graduate degree in Literature and Philosophy at Chicago. It was amazing. I worked on theory and psychoanalysis. And, yeah. I don't know, fascinating. I want to do more of it, but I don't know how yet. I need to figure that out."

Dr. Peters: "So, you studied psychoanalysis?"

Gila: "Yeah. I guess that's kind of why I want to skip all the micro-analysis of my every word and manner of expression. I can kind of do that myself. Although, it's not because of studying psychoanalysis so much that I am a close-reader of literature. It's kind of the same thing."

Dr. Peters: "Is that so?"

Gila: "Yes. When you ask that I can't tell if you're surprised or skeptical."

Dr. Peters: "Hm. Is it important to you to know what it is I'm feeling?"

Gila: "No. Yes. This again?"

Dr. Peters: "By *this,* what is it that you mean?"

Gila: "Oh god. I thought we said we'd start again. I just explained that I don't want to do this micro-analysis of my every word routine."

Dr. Peters: "Yes, I suppose you *did* say something about what you *didn't* want to do, but I guess I don't quite understand it. Perhaps you're trying to insinuate that I'm not intelligent enough for you?"

Gila: "No, it's nothing like that. If I wanted to say that, I would. I wouldn't *insinuate* it. What I'm trying to say is different than that. I don't know. I don't want to talk about irrelevant stuff that I can figure out on my own."

Dr. Peters: "And, is it important for you to figure stuff out on your own?"

Gila: "Not in and of itself it isn't, no. But, I can't help that it comes pretty naturally to me. My point is that isn't what I need your help with."

Dr. Peters: [silence]

Gila: "Does that make sense?"

Dr. Peters: "I don't know yet. It sounds like you're saying you don't need anyone's help to analyze yourself. So, I'm wondering what brings you here."

Gila: [silence] "Yes."

Dr. Peters: "I am assuming you're not here against your will?"

Gila: [laughs] "No, no. Not really. Which doesn't really mean I want to be here but I think I see that I have no choice."

Dr. Peters: "You have no choice? Really? Did something happen to force you to come here?"

Gila: "No. Yes. I don't know. I'm holding back when I need to speak. When I want to say something, like in my writing or when it is important. Or, talking to someone who is important. I get totally silent. It's like I freeze or something. I don't know."

Dr. Peters: "I'm not sure I fully understand. You seem to have no problem expressing your opinions here with me?"

Gila: "That sounded a little sarcastic."

Dr. Peters: [smirking] "Was it? I didn't exactly mean to be sarcastic. I was just letting you know what I've observed so far."

Gila: "Whatever. Yes. I have no problem speaking my mind here, but this is silly. This is easy. What I'm saying here doesn't even qualify as thinking. It's just responding to the stupid questions you're asking. It's just impatience talking. What I'm referring to is when it comes to something meaningful. It's like...I don't know how to explain it. I don't mean to be withholding but then I cannot talk. This came up in a paper I was writing. In Chicago. On a book. There was so much I was trying to talk about but when it came time to talking I couldn't say what I was *actually* thinking. Am I making any sense? I don't know how to explain it."

Dr. Peters: [silence]

Gila: "Is something wrong? That last question wasn't rhetorical."

Dr. Peters: "I'm not sure yet, I'm afraid. It seems like you experience my questions as *nonsense*?

Gila: "Actually, I think I said they were stupid. Are you still stuck at that part? I said so much since then. Did I offend you somehow? Is that why you take us back there?"

Dr. Peters: "Well, no, Gila. I'm not *offended*. But, I am surprised that you would think it's not important to talk about why you experience my questions as – *stupid,* did you call them?"

Gila: "Because they are. Listen, I really am not trying to be offensive. You're smiling like this is amusing. I am not usually such an obnoxious kid but I'm trying to focus on something and you're getting distracted."

Dr. Peters: [laughs]

Gila: "Is that funny somehow?"

Dr. Peters: "Didn't you mean it to be?"

Gila: "Not at all, no. I have no idea what's funny to you."

Dr. Peters: "Really?"

Gila: "Yes."

Dr. Peters: "Well, you're – what shall we call it? – style is unusual to say the least."

Gila: "Okay?"

Dr. Peters: "And I'm not used to someone talking that way to me, telling me my questions are dumb. Perhaps, you can appreciate that that is a little insulting?"

Gila: "Not really, no. I'm not insulting at all. I'm just trying to be clear about what's relevant and what isn't. I was trying to tell you a story about what brings me here. Your questions were distracting. And irrelevant. And, you get insulted easily. Why is that? I don't really care. It's not my business. The point is there was something I was trying to say and that's all I really want to focus on. Can I go back to outlining the issue, so you can understand what I'm trying to talk about?"

Dr. Peters: "Um, yes. But perhaps, if you don't mind, of course, you can give me a little background about your life, like where you were born and grew up and your parents, things like that? Perhaps it would help me to understand you better."

Gila: "I don't think it would. But fine. Toronto. I was born there. Parents had a bakery business that they started when I was born. Dad got sick when I was eight, died when I was 12. I took care of my mother and brother after that. My older brother died too when I was 14. Otherwise, nothing much else. I got a scholarship to study in Boston and went, and then Chicago for graduate school after that. Now, I'm here in New York City trying to figure out if I should apply to PhD programs or do something else instead. I don't know what. Psychoanalysis is interesting to me too, maybe one day."

Dr. Peters: "Wow, well, you said you wanted to study psycho-analysis? Do you mean therapy?"

Gila: "You sound surprised."

Dr. Peters: "Well, naturally, yes, I am a little since you seem to rather *detest* the experience of being a patient. I guess I'm wondering what your interest in this is, but –"

Gila: "I am not always like this."

Dr. Peters: "Oh?"

Gila: "I mean, I'm usually the one that everyone talks to and I help them figure things out. I'm actually very gentle. I like feelings – other people's. What you're seeing now is different. It's because it has to do with me, I think. I could do what you're doing, no problem. It's the being a *patient* part that gives me a hard time."

Dr. Peters: "Uh huh, if you say so. Can we go back to your biography for a moment, please, if you don't mind?"

Gila: "You have a lot of books here on relational psychoanalysis. Is that your particular orientation?" [looking around the room] "It's certainly a compelling critique of classical analytic technique, but I'm not sure that I'm convinced. It claims to be more modern but there are blind spots too in its theorization of technique. Don't you think?"

Dr. Peters: [silence]

Gila: "Are you not going to answer that?"

Dr. Peters: "I think it was *your* turn to talk about your biographical history?"

Gila: "Whatever."

Dr. Peters: "You said your father died?"

Gila: "Yeah. Got sick and died."

Dr. Peters: "Don't you think that would be important to this work?"

Gila: "Not really, no."

Dr. Peters: "Care to explain?"

Gila: "More than I have already?"

Dr. Peters: "You didn't."

Gila: "Really? Okay. What do you need to know?"

Dr. Peters: "Um, well, maybe you can start by telling me a little bit about what that's been like for you?"

Gila: "Watching my father die? It fucking sucked. He was the parent I was closest to. He was a parent, period. My mother, she, well, she can be difficult to deal with. My dad and I were very close. Then he got blood cancer, some rare and incurable kind, and died four and a half years later. What else is it you *need* to know?"

Dr. Peters: "You imply that your mother is difficult? Difficult how?"

Gila: "I didn't *imply* anything, I said it outright. She's kind of more like a teenager, so it's like raising a teenager, if that makes any sense? But she's better now. She's...outrageous still but older. It's like there's a little less crazy stuff she can pull. She takes me shopping. Or, sends me clothes. I don't mind. It's a way we can relate. My brother is my baby. He is not very high-functioning in the world or anything, but he's brilliant in his own way. Does all this information help you? Can we move on now?"

Dr. Peters: "Well, just one moment there, if you don't mind? You say your mother is like a *teenager,* if I'm understanding this right, but you have a good relationship with her?"

Gila: "Is that hard to understand? It's complicated. Obviously. But she's older now and she doesn't yell or anything, not from far away. She's lonely. Calls to tell me what new outfit she's bought me. We go shopping together. I don't mind. I don't care much about what I wear and, at least this way, we have something in common."

Dr. Peters: "Oh-kay. Do you like shopping with your mother?"

Gila: "What? I don't understand. It's what works."

Dr. Peters: "Yes, but I'm wondering if you enjoy –"

Gila: "I don't know what you're getting at. It works. She buys clothes she thinks I should wear and it's fine. What aren't you understanding?"

Dr. Peters: [pauses] "I don't know. And then you say your brother is your baby? Is he much younger than you?"

Gila: "No, not really, only two years younger, but he's always struggled more. With everything. I wouldn't know how to explain it. It's like...he just can't navigate the world. Language, dealing with people, school, traffic, stuff like that. I guess that's everything? Everything is hard for him but...so, it sometimes takes a lot of talking. Before and after he goes to work. Before and after he needs to eat dinner. Before he goes to sleep. In the morning when he gets up. I don't know if that makes sense. I *think* he's getting better, but the truth is I don't know. I worry."

Dr. Peters: "You feel responsible for him?"

Gila: "I *am* responsible for him."

Dr. Peters: "Uh-huh [she exhales loudly]. What I mean is that you're only two years older yourself. That makes him what, about twenty-three years old? He's not, properly speaking, a *baby,* as you called him."

Gila: "Is there a question there? Or, are you just proving you can do arithmetic?"

Dr. Peters: [laughs] "Wow, okay, *no.* I wasn't just proving my math skills [laughs a little more]. Although, they are rather impressive, aren't they? [leans back in her chair]. No. I was trying to understand why, if there was so little of an age difference between you, it somehow made sense that you had to take care of him."

Gila: "I don't understand your question."

Dr. Peters: "Well, it's actually pretty straightforward –"

Gila: "Apparently not straightforward enough."

Dr. Peters: "Or, in your case, *too* straightforward?"

Gila: "Whatever."

Dr. Peters: "What I mean is, you have no problem seeing that he has difficulty with certain things, but when it comes to your own life everything is fine and you don't need help."

Gila: "You're kidding me. Is that what I said? I'm *here,* aren't I? I never said I didn't need help. But, it's different, what he needs and what I need. He can't manage in the world, but that's never been difficult for me. Managing. In the world. You can't compare. Why are you comparing? You didn't get what I just said about D, did you? Don't bother answering that, I'm not actually asking. Just shocked that's all."

Dr. Peters: "I'm sorry that you feel I didn't –"

Gila: "And don't give me this, *I feel you didn't understand me crap.* Please. It isn't *subjective.* You *didn't* understand. You think my taking care of him is some *deflection* of my own suffering?"

Dr. Peters: "I didn't say that. I was –"

Gila: "You didn't need to. You just don't get the stakes, that's all. The *situation.*"

Dr. Peters: "Which is that you feel he is your baby."

Gila: "He *is.* Forget it."

Dr. Peters: "That you're a very generous sister who is helping him out?"

Gila: "Really. Just forget it. You don't have the terms –"

Dr. Peters: "I don't have the terms for what?"

Gila: "To understand that it's my *job*."

Dr. Peters: "I understand you feel very responsible for him. That you care about him a great deal."

Gila: "Okay, we're really done having this conversation. It's fine. It is unusual. I get it. You can only think in very familiar terms. It's fine. You tried. Can we move on now? It's time to move on."

Dr. Peters: "Well, Gila, yes. I suppose we can move on if you'd like to, but –"

Gila: "Good, yes, I'd like to."

Dr. Peters: "But, it's just, well, I can't believe you wouldn't think this isn't important to talk about with someone?"

Gila: "I didn't say it isn't important to talk about with someone. I said it isn't important to talk about right now with *you*. Or, at least not in the way you're approaching it. I had a teacher in high school. We're still very close. Ms. Tobin. I think she understands this stuff. I talk to her."

Dr. Peters: "Oh? Can you tell me a little bit about her, then?"

Gila: "No, not really, not now. I don't *know* you at all. Talking about a dead parent is one thing. But, Ms. Tobin, I wouldn't know how to talk about her. She takes care of me. Like, Gila you-need-to-eat-dinner-takes-care-of-me, you need to sleep-once-in-awhile-takes-care-of-me. I wouldn't be here if she didn't help me when she did."

Dr. Peters: [silence]

Gila: "Are you going to say anything?"

Dr. Peters: "Your voice changes when you talk about your teacher. I am struck by that, that's all."

Gila: "She is the closest person to me."

Dr. Peters: "Hm. And friends your age?"

Gila: "They're children, unfortunately. No offense to them. They like me. They are always asking to be closer, but what am I supposed to talk about? How to get my brother out of jail? How to convince my mother not to sign away the business the next time she's furious or falls in love? They worry about who to date and what their parents did that annoyed them. There isn't a tremendous amount of common ground. Which is fine. It's been that way for most of my life."

Dr. Peters: "It must be hard to be so alone with all of this experience."

Gila: "I don't know."

Dr. Peters: "Well it is certainly hard to lose a parent when you were so young, wouldn't you say?"

Gila: "I guess. But I worry you're not really paying attention. I survived whatever happened. Yes, it sucked, and maybe I wished that things had gone another way but they didn't and it's over now. I'm more or less okay."

Dr. Peters: "Well –"

Gila: "Please, spare me the part where you tell me that my life is hard. That's really not the point. The –"

Dr. Peters: "What is the point?"

Gila: "The point is that I got away. I'm here now – on my own. I'm free. I get to read. I used to think...I don't know. Maybe that I wouldn't? I'd be too busy with the business, with D. But then, after I met Tobin, I accepted that I didn't need to be there all the time. I could still do the things I needed to. But I could leave. Have my own life. That kind of thing. That *that's* what grieving meant or something. Moving on."

Dr. Peters: "And?"

Gila: "So, I did that. I opened up a little. I know that's funny to you, but I said *nothing* before. *Actually* nothing. There was a shrink or two in high school that, after my brother died, thought, hey, maybe this kid should talk to someone? But that didn't...basically when my mother found out, she lost it. What's wrong with you? How dare you make yourself a problem? That kind of thing. Fine. I didn't ask for it and had nothing to say anyway. But after Tobin and then Raynite, I talked more. Or, talked to *them*. Or, just talked to all those ghosts *less*. So, things are normal, more or less. Does that make sense?"

Dr. Peters: "I'm not quite sure. It's hard for me to see how you can say you're not affected by the things that happened. Or, say with such conviction that you do not need to talk about them. But, even if that was the case, what is it that brings you here right now? I'm not sure I fully understand that."

Gila: "I don't know. Whatever. Maybe it's too hard to explain. It's that when I went to Chicago, I finally got to read things I had always been so desperate to study; human psychology, literature, philosophy, loss and grief, gender, all that fun stuff. I wrote papers on these things and did well enough by other people's standards. Got nominated, best thesis stuff. Except my professor, Raynite, she was incredible. She knew the work wasn't complete. That I was holding back what I really thought and meant to say. 'Stop being so withholding!' she always told me. 'Come out and say what it is you think!' She said that I was too defensive or self-protective. I can't keep track. It's kind of complicated. She said I need to grow up, let go, stop hiding and being so quiet."

Dr. Peters: "So, you want help trying to say what's on your mind?"

Gila: "It sounds simple when you say it that way. That isn't what I mean. I mean, I *couldn't* say what I was actually thinking. When I tried to, it's like, I don't know, like my mind is underwater. Or, my brain is. No, my brain is fine. I read a few books every day. That's easy. It's my mind or what I think. When we walked and talked, Prof. Raynite would say to me, 'It's *your* turn now. Tell me what you think of theory x or of this concept,' and I would completely freeze. It drove her crazy. I don't blame her. She said, 'Stop being coy. It's clear your mind is thinking a bunch of things.' But, the problem was I *wasn't* being coy. Or, *doing* anything. My thoughts were there, I guess. But, it's like I couldn't reach them. Something holds me back, but I don't know what. I am trying not to. I want to speak. I need to practice talking more, I think. Maybe saying what I think will loosen up whatever grip I have or something like that. I don't mean to be coy or withholding now either. It's just so hard to explain."

Dr. Peters: "It sounds like you have a lot you're trying to figure out."

Gila: "Sure. I guess. And then what?"

Dr. Peters: "Then what? What?"

Gila: "Do you have any insight into what I'm talking about?"

Dr. Peters: "Well. Hm. I think I have a way of understanding what you're saying but, of course, I imagine that you'll find what I say to be *simplistic*."

Gila: "If it is simplistic, then I'll find it that way, you're right. But, can you worry less about your own feelings for just a moment and tell me what you think?"

Dr. Peters: "You really are a rather difficult patient, you know that?"

Gila: "I'm not trying to be, I'm sorry. This isn't personal, of course. I just need you to focus on what's important and not get distracted by your own sensitivities and bad listening habits that you've developed while becoming a shrink."

Dr. Peters: "Wow! Well, that's quite the damning assessment, isn't it?"

Gila: "Really? I didn't mean it to be that way. I'm just trying to encourage you to listen for what I'm *actually* saying and not the things you're trained to listen for. That's all. Sorry if that's hurtful. I'm really not trying to be that way at all. I like you, I –"

Dr. Peters: "Ha!"

Gila: "Is that funny for some reason?"

Dr. Peters: "I'm just a little shocked to hear you say that. It seems like you can't tolerate anything I say."

Gila: "Really? No, I just think you're getting distracted and then defensive when I point that out. This isn't personal. Aren't you supposed to have a better practice of remaining neutral about the things a patient says? I'm not trying to hurt your feelings at all. Believe it or not, most people think of me as a pretty sweet kid."

Dr. Peters: "Well, yes, that is rather surprising, I admit."

Gila: "Ouch."

Dr. Peters: "It seems I'm not the only one who takes things personally then, yes?"

Gila: "Nice."

Dr. Peters: "I'm glad you approve. Now back to what I began to say...Where was I?"

Gila: "You were going to say something simplistic."

Dr. Peters: "Oh right, yes, *that*. Well, I guess I was thinking that perhaps you are describing difficulties talking because you haven't actually worked through your loss around your father when you were younger. I was thinking that talking about that might help you feel more comfortable talking about other things."

Gila: "No."

Dr. Peters: "No? Care to expand on that?"

Gila: "You are completely wrong. So, no. I don't need to talk about my fucking childhood. That stuff is boring. Over. Old. I need to find a way to talk about the things I'm thinking now in real-time. Like when I'm walking with Prof. Raynite and she looks at me and says, 'your turn.' I need to be able to answer that. To have the guts to self-express. I don't need more of a shitty childhood."

Dr. Peters: "Yes. But, perhaps those issues will make more sense once we understand better what you've been through? I know it may be hard to believe, but I *do* know something about trauma and grief. Some of my colleagues might even say it is my *expertise*."

Gila: "That may be. But do you know that line from Eminem, where he talks about not being understood because – you're looking confused?"

Dr. Peters: "Did you say, Eminem?"

Gila: "The rapper, yes. Do you know him? No?"

Dr. Peters: "You do?"

Gila: "I love Eminem. It's not all Chaucer and Steinbeck and Henry James for me. I started listening because for years it's all D would be blasting from his room, and I figured if I could understand what he liked that maybe I could relate to him better. Make my way of talking closer to how he understood things. And I've loved him ever since. You should give him a try."

Dr. Peters: [smiles, a little uncomfortably] "You were saying something – about what you've been through? What you DON'T want to talk about here?"

Gila: "Yeah, I don't remember. It doesn't matter. You're seeing me as some condescending smart-ass grad student trying to intellectualize, but that isn't right. I'm not saying you don't know anything. Just that you don't know me. I don't know how to insist on that distinction without offending your sense of *expertise* or whatever."

Dr. Peters: "Yes, well, perhaps you will come to trust me more eventually. You seem to have developed fondness for these other teachers in your life. Therapy is different, of course. But, you might see that I do know a thing or two. Our time is up in a moment or two, but if you'd like to come in the same time next week we can continue this. And maybe I will understand you better. Shall I put you in for this same slot next week?"

It is a classroom, rectangular with fluorescent lights. It is a few minutes into the first day of class. The new students are unfamiliar to each other and the space. They are sitting around the u-shaped seminar table waiting nervously for class to begin. Gila is at the back, directly opposite where the teacher will sit. She is twenty-four, with hair just past her ears, plastic glasses, playing with a pen, looking skeptical. Some people are chatting amongst themselves. The Professor is late.

She ambled in, one shoulder weighted down by her briefcase, marching awkwardly and reluctantly to the front of the seminar room.

"Is it me or is it dark in here?" She looks around knowing exactly what she'll find, "Are there no windows here? Holy shit, that sucks for us! Although, after all, it is a course on trauma, so what the hell! Maybe it helps! Anyone want to check if there are chimneys nearby?"

She was wearing faded black unfitted jeans that seemed like a relic from the 1980s and a dark purple blouse with a wide open neckline that seemed like someone else's idea of what dressing fancy looked like. As she walked, her feet seemed to stomp and drag behind. When she finally made it to the table's head, she seemed, all at once, beleaguered and bemused. Or, exasperated but willing to put on a show of being the brilliant professor preparing to unveil the truth.

"So, hi!" she said with cheer that was so palpably at odds with the wounding etched into her furrowed brows and worried face.

"I'm Professor Raynite. Obviously."

She dumps her pile of books and endless loose leaf papers on the table and, with difficulty disproportionate to the task, shuffles her thin, muscular, boyish fifty-year-old body into the schoolroom's plastic seat. She shoves her sleeves upward, as if they're in the way of whatever rugged task she's about to launch into and leans forward. Her legs spread out wide under the table inelegantly, her eyes wide open assessing the new batch of bodies she'll have to find a way to teach.

"I guess this is like Trauma 101 or something. It's fucking 8am, so someone should tell me if I'm in the wrong place. Huh, anyone? Which, since no one is saying anything, means either you're terribly nice – are you all such well-behaved graduate students you'll sit through a class with the wrong teacher teaching the wrong thing – or, maybe this isn't wrong and that's just my brain on little sleep you're hearing. I'm an insomniac and there are studies now that tell us we need like – what is it? Six hours? No? Am I the only one who cares about this stuff?"

The Professor scans the room, smiles, and giggles.

"Okay, well, anyway, this is what happens when you don't sleep enough, which by the way is not exactly unproblematic from an ideological standpoint. Since if you're thinking about insomnia, you're also needing to be thinking about the worker and the state and capitalist constraints that make sleep basically a bourgeois privilege. So, really who am I to kvetch about not-sleeping? And, yet it isn't like the university is somehow outside capitalist modes of exchange. What are you paying for tuition these days? Don't answer that. I don't really care. Still, no one is running out, so I guess this is the class. Or, you really are so timid it makes me want to cry. Oh well. So, hi again! We're going to be stuck together every morning here, so let's just start with what we're doing here, okay? This is a course on trauma. So, I get that no one with "happy" childhoods is cramming to get a seat in here. Not like "happy" is something we wouldn't want to deconstruct, but, anyway, maybe some of you actually had happy childhoods. What the hell do I know? But, seriously I don't care about whatever bad thing has happened to you. Okay? I know it might seem like I do because we'll be talking about painful stuff and all this Holocaust and sexual abuse stuff makes everybody sentimental, but I mean it when I say that I don't want to hear it. This is a class on theory and literature. If you need to talk about your feelings, go to therapy."

She looks around the room to survey the squirming her opening number engendered. Students caught red-handed, seeking confession and relief.

Referring to how hard she is to follow, she sometimes called her talking-style "jazz," except that what makes her shtick so untouchable and stunning is that she alone self-propellingly plays every single part. She speed-talks and then, at certain words, hard-stops abruptly. She scans the room for signs of comprehension, weakness, disarray, signs of anything at all to feed her vigilance and play.

ح

It is the campus coffee shop attached to the university bookstore. It is bustling with students buying lattes, wraps, hovering over their laptops, talking. Prof. Raynite goes to the table where a student is waving to her. The Professor looks besieged by the weight of books she is carrying and dumps them on the table before sitting down.

Professor Raynite: "Hey! Do I know you from somewhere? You waved, so I kind of assumed that was directed to me, but who knows?! People make outrageous assumptions all the time based on their own psychological needs. Duh! Ideology critique! I mean and that's what we're reading about all the time, isn't it. Anyway, that could be what just happened. For all I know you were stretching your muscles or something. Were you stretching your muscles? That would be kind of funny I think. You haven't said anything yet. Oh dear, are you really not the student I'm supposed to be meeting? You look kind of familiar though. Do I know you from somewhere? Are you in my class? Say something, you're making me nervous."

Gila: "Uh, yes, sorry. I'm sorry, yes, Gila. I'm in your trauma theory class."

Professor Raynite: "Phew! That would have been inconvenient. Although, not really, I mean we both could have learned something by encountering otherness where we expected something else. A teachable moment! Ah well, instead we'll just have to settle for some kind of normal teaching or whatever it is you think I can do for you."

Gila: [smiles uneasily]

Professor Raynite: "Is there a reason you are not talking right now?"

Gila: "Um, no, sorry. I didn't realize that I was supposed to be saying something. I'm sorry, I –"

Professor Raynite: "Holy shit, you need to chill out. Seriously. What's with all the apologizing? We're meeting to talk about papers, so what is it you need to ask me? Don't just sit there. I have things to do. And you should have a list of questions you've prepared. I'm kidding. Relax. They don't need to be in list form. Although, that would be nice, save me having to listen to you finding your question and focusing on it. Whatever. What are you writing about? It's the first paper. You're nervous. Everyone is. What is it you want to know?"

Gila: "Um, yes, of course. I'm really, I think I'm really interested in the trauma material. In the theory. I've never learned anything like that before. So, I wanted to write something about that I think."

Professor Raynite: "Yes, and?"

Gila: "And?"

Professor Raynite: "And that's not a topic. Trauma theory is the subject of the class. What is it you like? Freud? Caruth? Lacan? Be specific."

Gila: "Everything. All of –"

Professor Raynite: "Would you mind if I got lunch? I don't think I've eaten yet today. Let me think about that for a minute. Nope, don't think so. I'm going to go and get something, okay. And maybe while I'm gone you can think about an actual question to ask me as opposed to just falling over yourself about liking the class. Okay? Be right back!"

Gila: [waits for Professor Raynite to settle down with her plastic containers of chickpeas and iced tea] "Maybe memoir. I think maybe I'm interested in memoir."

Professor Raynite: "Great, now who? Or, what kind? Are you talking early American memoir, slave narratives, religious confessions, trauma memoir? You can't just say *memoir*. Be specific."

Gila: "Oh. Sorry. I didn't really know...I don't..."

Professor Raynite: "It's fine. Keep going. What memoir specifically?"

Gila: "I don't know. I was thinking maybe –"

Professor Raynite: "And, by the way, this should be obvious to you already, but, just in case it isn't, you should really know the differences among the genres the next time we meet. I mean, its fine with me for now, you're just starting out as a graduate student and whatever. But, seriously, it isn't scholarly to say just *memoir,* as if that has meaning on its own. Got it? So, you need to do your homework."

Gila: "Okay, of course, I'm sorry. I –"

Professor Raynite: "And can you stop apologizing for god's sake! Seriously, it's distracting. Are you *that* nervous? I mean, I know I'm intimidating but come on! Usually students get over it eventually. Where are you from?"

Gila: "Toronto."

Professor Raynite: "And, what's your deal? Are you interested in this course because of some major childhood trauma or something?"

Gila: "Um, no. Yes. I don't know. I don't think so. I don't –"

Professor Raynite: "Wow! You don't even know the answer to personal questions!"

Gila: "Sorry. I mean, no, I'm not sorry, not, excuse me. I just. I don't know why I'm interested. Maybe because of things that happened. I never knew there was such a thing as trauma theory. I –"

Professor Raynite: "Yeah, I get it. Fine. Don't start telling me about your childhood, please. I was just curious if you're, like, overwhelmed by the material or something or if this is how you always are. But, it's fine. Keep going. Memoir. Eggers. You were saying?"

Gila: "Yeah, yes. His memoir *Heartbreaking Work of Staggering Genius.* I was thinking maybe I could write about that?"

Professor Raynite: "Sure. Why?"

Gila: "Because it's different."

Professor Raynite: "How?"

Gila: "Because he's deliberately trying to write against the way most people talk about grief."

Professor Raynite: "Good. What are ways most people talk about grief?"

Gila: "That you get over it. And if you don't, there's something wrong with you."

Professor Raynite: "What's wrong with that?"

Gila: "I don't know."

Professor Raynite: "You can do better than that."

Gila: "I don't know."

Professor Raynite: "Try. You say he's doing something unconventional. I agree. Eggers is great. I love Eggers. You'll never get into a PhD program if you write about him, mind you, because most people don't take postmodern trauma memoirs seriously *to say the least*. But, anyway, he's awesome. Fine. Do whatever you want. Have you read his other books by the way? I'm assuming you're going to before writing about this, because when you write about an author you have to read across their oeuvre. You can't just read one text, obviously, anyway. Who knows? Maybe you don't care about your career prospects, do you? Are you interested in becoming an academic? Anyway, whatever, you should think about that at some point, but, not now, while we're talking. I'm just here to help you develop a vocabulary for sustaining critical inquiry, which means, by the way, that whatever you do with this paper is your responsibility, understand? But, for now, since you're in my class and we're meeting about paper topics, what is it you're trying to ask? Formulate a question. And why aren't you taking notes while I'm speaking?"

Gila: [startled] "Oh, sorry. I didn't –"

Professor Raynite: "Fine. I'm going to keep talking while you get out a pen. You should get into the habit of writing things down during meetings like these. Anyway, yes, tropes of survival. You were questioning the credibility of certain normative mourning teleologies, right?"

Gila: "I don't...I guess. I don't know. Is that...I was just trying to say –"

Professor Raynite: "Right. I know what you were *trying* to say but you're not using *critical* language. And, part of what the pedagogy of this course has to do with is training you to bring a refined critical apparatus to bear on questions such as these so that you're turning incoherence into something that can be productively engaged as a question, right?"

Gila: "Okay. I don't know how to do that."

Professor Raynite: "Do you have anything specific about the readings you don't understand? I'm here and this is your time, so you might as well ask if there's something you're not getting."

Gila: "No, I don't think...no. The Freud is interesting. All the readings are fascinating."

Professor Raynite: "Really?"

Gila: "Yeah, yes, absolutely. I have never read anything about grief or loss or anything like that."

Professor Raynite: "Okay, so go ahead and write about Eggers. Read the history of the confessional genre, obviously, and trauma theory and what it means in the development of poststructuralist self-representation to craft a narrator that is damaged and incoherent but that somehow is charged with the project of healing. I have to go now. I'm probably late. Do you have a phone or watch or something with the time on it? [Getting up] You don't have to get up too! God, you're so *formal*. Anyway, it's only a first paper. I wouldn't lost too much sleep over it. There'll be other assignments to improve your grade. Of course that doesn't mean that you should be lazy. I don't want to waste my time readings things that you have barely thought of. Good. Bye! See you in class! You should talk more by the way!"

❦

It is an office on Manhattan's Upper East Side. Prewar, cozy, the halls are laminated by dim lights and luxurious gold fixtures, carpeted hallways. In the waiting room, there are many antique chairs, some pillows, magazines. Dr. Watson is short, elderly and round with a bulb of dyed-blond hair, big tortoise glasses, gold necklace, bracelets, watch, a matching single-colored pantsuit. She has a southern accent. Gila is wearing jeans, a long sleeve shirt, a winter dark brown jacket. It is late November.

Dr. Watson: "Well, hello there! How do you do? My name is Katie. Katie Watson. You must be Gila? Is that a hard G or a soft one?"

Gila: "It doesn't matter. Hard G. Hello."

Dr. Watson: "I don't know too many Gilas. What kind of name is that?"

Gila: "Israeli. My father was Israeli."

Dr. Watson: "Is that so? How interesting. It is a lovely name."

Gila: "I've always hated it."

Dr. Watson: "Oh, well. I'm sorry to hear that. Maybe one day you can tell me why that is."

Gila: "Okay."

Dr. Watson: "So? Do you want to start by telling me what brings you in today?"

Gila: "I guess."

Dr. Watson: "Okay then, well, whenever you're ready."

Gila: "I'm not sure where to start."

Dr. Watson: "Well, just start anywhere you'd like. That's what I tell people. What matters is your comfort. There's no hurry here. We don't have to cover everything. It would just be helpful to start by getting to know you a little bit and finding out who you are and what you're looking for."

Gila: "Okay. Whatever. I never know where to begin. My dad died when I was small – that kind of thing?"

Dr. Watson: "Oh, sure, yes, if you want to start with that. Whatever feels most comfortable."

Gila: "*None* of this feels comfortable so whatever, but you guys typically want to know the history-biographical crap. So, I thought I might as well start there."

Dr. Watson: "I'm sorry to hear that none of this feels comfortable to you. Do you know why that is?"

Gila: "Um, I don't know. Going over the same irrelevant childhood material I guess."

Dr. Watson: "You don't think it's relevant that your father died when you were little? How old were you? I didn't catch it."

Gila: "I didn't say. 12. He was sick for a while, so it wasn't exactly a shock. And, no, of course, I don't think it's irrelevant. It's just not what I want to be talking about. And, as soon as I open with that, you all get caught up in how traumatized I must be feeling."

Dr. Watson: "And, it seems like you're saying that getting *caught up* in that would be the wrong response. Is that right?"

Gila: "Yeah. There's nothing necessary to say about my father. He was the person I was closest to. I have a mother and a brother, but I take care of them. It's not the same as it was with him. He talked to me. He listened. Stupid stuff like that."

Dr. Watson: "Why would you call that stuff silly? It sounds heartbreaking to me that you were so close to your father and then, while you were still so young, he died unexpectedly. And then to be left with, did you say a brother and your mom? It sounds like they weren't very supportive."

Gila: "Being sick for four and a half years isn't exactly *unexpected*. And, secondly, about my mom and brother, it's just more complicated. I don't like when people start assuming she was evil or anything like that. She couldn't manage anything, and he's severely incapable of functioning in a normative way but we made it work. I don't want pity. It sucked for him to die. But, I'm not some stricken victim not knowing how to cope."

Dr. Watson: "Well, sure, I suppose that's true. But, it doesn't change the fact that you were very young. And, here you are, losing the person you're closest to. That's such a sad story and I can see why maybe you'd prefer not to talk about it."

Gila: "Wait a second there. Are you implying that I don't want to talk about my dead dad because it hurts too much? You must be joking."

Dr. Watson: [surprised] "That doesn't sound right to you? Well, who knows? I could be wrong. It just seems to me that sometimes when things are hard to talk about it is easier to avoid them. That's all. Everyone does that."

Gila: "I don't."

Dr. Watson: "What is that? You don't do *what*? Can you explain things to me better, so I can understand them?"

Gila: "Well, I can try. You're obviously very nice and well-intentioned and this folksy style you have is charming. It really is. Almost disarming. But, even if I do explain, that's not a guarantee you'll understand the point I'm trying to make."

Dr. Watson: "And, what point is that?"

Gila: "That I don't need to talk about my father. Or his stupid getting sick and dying. It was gross. It was disgusting. Do I wish it never happened? Absolutely. Do I wish he didn't leave me to take care of them, especially when it was an uphill battle with a teenager who refused to listen to anything and a child who really can't function? Yes, of course. But, I survived that stuff. Which is not to say I'm not still wounded, damaged, or just plain old fucked up, if you don't mind me swearing in here. But, I know about all that already. I've *talked* about that. What I need now is different."

Dr. Watson: "Who did you talk about that with?"

Gila: "*That's* your question?"

Dr. Watson: "Yes. It made me curious to hear that you have talked about this with someone. I was wondering if you could tell me a little bit about that."

Gila: "Tobin. She was a teacher in high school, English. She is the closest person to me. When I go back to Toronto and there's nowhere to sleep in my mother's house, I have stayed at her place. She has five children, but she has kind of adopted me as one of her own. I don't know where I'd be right now without her."

Dr. Watson: "You feel she's helped you that much."

Gila: "She saved my life."

Dr. Watson: "How did she do that?"

Gila: "I don't know what you mean? She was my teacher. She saw I did so much, and didn't eat too much or sleep at all. She made sure I went away to school. To Boston. She still thinks I do too much for the two of them. But, she doesn't really get that it's my job. The point is...I don't know. She knows me. She's the only one."

Dr. Watson: "It sounds pretty special – what the two of you have."

Gila: "Um, yeah, it is. I know I'm very lucky. I have no idea why she has taken me under her wing the way that she has, but I'm grateful. I really...I can't imagine where I'd be without her."

Dr. Watson: "That's really something, isn't it? Gila, I can't help notice that you said Toobin? Was that her name? Oh yes, Tobin. That this Mrs. Tobin noticed you didn't *sleep* or *eat* too much? Is that a recurring issue of yours that you're struggling with?"

Gila: "Are you asking if I'm anorexic?"

Dr. Watson: "Well no, not exactly. I just...well, I guess I am. Maybe I am. I am trying to get more of a sense of what your concerns are. And, since you said she was the only one you talked to and you mentioned that she noticed these things..."

Gila: "Wow. No. I am not anorexic. Nor do I have any other eating disorders. Or self-harming tendencies generally. I'm quiet. Smart. Serious. I am devoted to work, writing, trying to think. Wanting to do good somehow. I don't drink or smoke or anything. I never have. I never had the time. Or even interest, I guess. No. The point I'm trying to make is different. I wish that you could listen to what I'm *actually* trying to tell you instead of worrying about all these other irrelevant things."

Dr. Watson: "Well, I'm sorry that you experience my questions as irrelevant. I'm just trying to get to know you better, that's all."

Gila: "Then, why don't you start by paying attention to what I'm *actually* saying?"

Dr. Watson: "And what is that? I apologize if you feel you're being misunderstood."

Gila: "I don't just *feel* that way. It's true! You're sitting there asking me if I barf up my food after I told you about the most important person to me! You're telling me my dead dad is important after I told you that the problem is in the *present* tense. I really don't understand what's wrong with your training. Do you *learn* to ask these misguided, inaccurate questions, or do they come naturally to you?"

Dr. Watson: "I hear that you're really disappointed with the questions I've been asking. Maybe there are reasons for that – that we can explore later on in the treatment? It sounds like it's hard for you to trust someone. And, with the loss you've had, that makes a lot of sense. It takes some time. Sometimes, it's just putting one foot in front of the other together and slogging it through?"

Gila: "What? Can I ask what in god's name you're talking about?"

Dr. Watson: "Oh, sorry if I wasn't clear. Treatment. I'm talking about treatment. I'm telling you that I understand how skeptical you might be feeling and I'm telling you that it's okay. This process takes a lot of time. But, I can be patient. I'm not going anywhere anytime soon. Alright? Gila, how does that sound?"

Gila: [silence] "Idiotic. No offense. First of all, you have no idea whether or not you're going anywhere anytime soon. Seriously. I can't believe you just said that to me. My father was healthy one minute, the next minute –"I have four months to live" – so spare me, please, these bullshit promises you are not authorized to make or keep. You seem really nice, genuinely. You really do. And so I feel bad being harsh with you. But, I don't think you're listening. Or, maybe, in spite of this great effort that I think I'm making, I'm still not being clear. I was in school last year in Chicago. I studied trauma theory. Does that make sense? I studied *trauma* theory, like how it works, like what is happening to the mind when something comes from nowhere and breaks it. I *wrote* about these things. I had a teacher whom I adored. She had some similarities to Tobin I suppose, but also different. Brutal. Brilliant. Raynite. I can't try to talk about her here and even begin to do justice to how special she is. But anyway, the point is that I wrote things: about Joan Didion's memoir of losing her husband, Eggers losing his parents. I wrote about Freud. *Mourning and Melancholia.* That work kept me awake at night for *weeks*. For *weeks* I couldn't think of anything else. It was exhilarating. For the first time I was studying things I was *actually* interested in. Given that I've been in school for years, I had four majors! And, I've always done so well and never had to break my head, not once, not ever. It was such a treat to actually *need* to think. Hard. To think hard about something and try to figure it out. Does that make sense? It was amazing. Really. Feels like what I've been intending to do my entire life. Thinking about what motivates people to do the things they do. Trying to understand them. Using philosophy to take apart the mind and make some sense of it. Writing theoretically. I learned things I didn't *know* existed. Or, maybe that's not exactly right. More like I learned there's a way to talk and write about things I have been dying to write about for as long as I can remember. Raynite taught me that. She said, "Turn things you don't know into questions and then go ask them." And, I did that. I *did* that. And then you know what happened? I got stuck. Whenever it was time to say something, I couldn't. I'd get quiet. I would mumble. Raynite said it drove her crazy. I know it did. I couldn't help it. I tried to talk. Whatever. I don't get it. I would feel so much, but, instead of *using* it, my head got quiet. Can you follow what I'm saying?"

Dr. Watson: "I'm not sure I can, not really. I would love to try to though? Do you think that that can happen over time?"

Gila: [looking around the room] "You have a lot of Freud here but no Lacan? Or, Klein? Some Winnicott, I see. That's good. Who doesn't love Winnicott? He's such a sacred cow, as thinkers go."

Dr. Watson: "Is it important to you that I have the right books?"

Gila: "There aren't any *right* books. There are only the books you have and it's always interesting to me, that's all."

Dr. Watson: "I'm a little lost. Forgive me."

Gila: "Forget it. I'm not saying anything. Just getting a sense for what you're interested in. What were we saying? Oh, yeah. Is there anything in what I said that makes some sense to you?"

Dr. Watson: [shifting her weight in the chair] "Well, let me see. I think you've said so much, and it's all important really. You've talked about your interests at school. And that seems really valuable and meaningful. You talked about this teacher of yours. I can't quite recall her name this second, but it was another teacher who helped you a great deal. And, that seems important too. So, I understood all of that, yes. It seemed very interesting. And, talking about writing about grief. I imagine that must have been very cathartic for you, isn't that right? And, I think, although we're almost out of time for today, so I won't be able to say too much more but I think you're also talking about how important your mental and intellectual life is to you. I see that, certainly. I see that loud and clear. So, I'm glad that you told me as much as you did. Does it feel like I understood things? I know we're out of time, but if there's anything you'd like to add please do feel free. We can stay an extra minute or two."

Gila: "Thank you for your time. I don't want to stay overtime. There isn't any need for that. I appreciate how hard you tried."

Dr. Watson: "Alright then, wonderful. I'm glad to hear we made some progress. I can put you in for next week? Does that sound good?"

It is a classroom. Gothic architectural exterior, inside plain beige walls, white boards, a long rectangular seminar table the graduate students are sitting around. It is Chicago. Late November. It is the early afternoon. The heat is working, but the temperature in the room is frigid. The teacher wears a purple scarf while lecturing, and the table is covered with water bottles, mugs of coffee, books all opened to the same pages.

Professor Raynite: "So. Hi. You all look cold. Wear layers. Tell me about *Nachträglichkeit*. Anyone?"

Student #1: "Deferred Action?"

Professor Raynite: "Yes. And?"

Student #2: "Um, something about trauma?"

Professor Raynite: "Okay. Not really an answer. But keep going. Can anyone here speak in full sentences?"

Student #3: "I think Freud is talking about how we process trauma, and that, like, you're always late to it or something like that. I think."

Professor Raynite: "Good, better. Yes. There is a time delay. Why is there a time delay? What kind of delay are we talking about here?"

Student #3: "Like a delay in processing or something like that. I think Freud is talking about why you can't process trauma while it's happening, or that –"

Professor Raynite: "Why?"

Student #3: "Well, I think because it's too horrible or something like that?"

Professor Raynite: "Anyone else? Think about the text we read today. That dream of the burning child. What happens in that dream? Why are you all looking at me? You should be looking at the text. [reading from the article in front of her]

"This is Freud: 'A father had been watching beside his child's sick bed for days and nights on end. After the child had died, he went into the next room to lie down but left the door open so that he could see from his bedroom into the room in which his child's body was laid out, with tall candles standing around it. An old man had been engaged to keep watch over it and say beside the body murmuring prayers. After a few hours' sleep, the father had a dream that *his child was standing beside his bed, caught him by the arm and whispered to him reproachfully: "Father, don't you see I'm burning?"* He woke up, noticed a bright glare of light from the next room, hurried into it and found that the old watchman had dropped off to sleep and that the wrappings and one of the arms of his beloved child's dead body had been burned by a lighted candle that had fallen on them.'"

[the Professor stops reading and looks around the room]

"Holy shit. This is so powerful. Every time I read it."

[the Professor shakes her head]

"What's happening here? What does this child mean, 'Father, don't you see I'm burning?' What makes this so haunting? That the child in the dream is reprimanding the father for letting him die. But, what do we do with the fact that the child is also actually burning again in real life? So, in a sense, it's as if the father is dreaming that his child is reproaching him for letting him die, but it is by *dreaming* of it that the father *actually* lets the child burn all over again. So, at first it looks like, yeah, maybe this dad is telepathic! He goes to sleep and dreams his child is burning when in fact his child's sleeve has caught fire in the other room. Great. Fine. Whatever. But, forget about the temptation to think about this purely along those lines for a moment and think about the trauma. A dad has *lost* his child. He goes to sleep because grief is so goddamn exhausting and then he has a dream in which he *fails* to see that he's *allowed* his child to die. The child says: 'Father, don't you see I'm burning?' Why would a father *dream* something like this? You should be asking yourself this question. Why would a father have this kind of dream? It seems unbearable, doesn't it? And, yet that's not it, right? Because what's happening here is that the father has a dream that he's being reproached for allowing his child to burn and, by the very fact of having this dream, I mean, *the father is sleeping and not being awake like he should be,* he is *allowing* the child to burn. Is this hitting you? Are you as blown away by this as I am? It's fucking heartbreaking."

[the Professor shakes her head]

Student #2: "Yeah, I was confused about that. Why wouldn't the father awaken when he heard his son calling him? Because, otherwise, it's like, he sleeps through what's happening. Whereas, if he got up, he could have rescued him from the candle falling."

Professor Raynite: "Right. It's like the child in the dream is telling the father what's happening in real life. Right? So, why doesn't he listen? Why doesn't the father, who we assume wants his child to live, listen to his child telling him that he's on fire?"

[silence, no one raises their hands]

"Think about this business of the *time lag, Nachträglichkeit.* There is a time delay in trauma because the event is too unbearable for the mind to assimilate at once. What does this mean? That the father keeps sleeping because in the dream, as opposed to real life, his child is still alive. The father doesn't wake up because, if he wakes up the child is gone again, he is back in a reality where his ill child is dead. The father dreams about the child still being alive because he can't yet be present to the fact of his child's *actual* burning. I'm assuming you're all following this. The father would rather *dream* that his son is burning than be awake and find out that his child has *already* died. There is a time delay. The father *can't* be awake and also be conscious of the fact that his son is no longer living. So, he *dreams* that the son is still living. And he'd rather stay sleeping and hear his son reproach him than wake up and find out the son already died. Any questions? So, what does this have to do with the *time lag* that we're talking about? What are we learning here about the way the mind works?"

[the class is silent. No one moving or rustling papers]

"It's so haunting. I know. I know. It's awful. But, let's try to understand it. Lacan teaches us about a *time lag*. What does this mean? C'mon guys. *Time lag*. No one? That when something happens that is too unbearable for the psyche to assimilate, to tolerate, or to take in, then it goes away, the mind dissociates. What does this mean exactly? That a person can't be a witness to her own unbearable event. And, as a result, the person misses it. It happens – the child dies, the house burns down, a rape takes place – but it's traumatic so the person doesn't *know* it happened. Is this making sense to you? Some of you are taking notes, but all of you should be because this is complicated and it's the basis for understanding trauma and how traumatic narratives are constructed. How subjectivity can function in a belatedness that is constitutive of its being. I'm going to continue. What *time lag* is teaching us is that we can't help but be late to those events which have affected us traumatically. It's as if we are affected but we can't really know it. So, it's as though, in spite of the fact that it happened to us, since it was too impossible to understand or take in or just plain goddamn bear, we end up circling ourselves endlessly, trying to get back to the moment when the world fell apart and we missed it. It happened to us, but we didn't get to witness it take place."

[silence]

"Questions?"

"You" [the Professor is pointing to Gila, who is sitting directly across from the Professor at the end of the seminar table]. "You're staring right at me, looking like you're thinking something. What can you say about this dream or any of this?"

Gila: [stunned] "No. I'm not...nothing. I don't...I can't. I wasn't thinking anything. I don't –"

Professor Raynite: "Really? Because you look really intense, like you know something or have something to say."

Gila: "No, really, please. I don't understand it really."

Professor Raynite: "What part?"

Gila: "Um, I don't know."

Professor Raynite: "*Méconnaissance? Nachtraglichkeit?* What is it that you don't understand? You need to give me more to work with. Other people? Let's remember that we're trying to comprehend this with tools of critical theory and practice. Let's be scholarly. What about this dream do you have questions about?"

Gila: "I don't...know. The time lag."

Professor Raynite: "What about it?"

Gila: "I don't understand it. I don't understand how it works."

Professor Raynite: "Try. I or someone else here will correct you if you don't make sense. Go for it. Stop worrying so much if you're getting it right. You people need to learn to put yourselves out there and be willing to be wrong. That's how you learn. You want to skip the step where you're fumbling around in the dark trying desperately to make sense of things. Well, let me spare you the suspense and tell you that you can't. Well, not if you want to be real intellectuals, you can't because you're going to have to accept at some point that you have your ideas in public. And, sometimes what you say is profound and sometimes you're making a fool of yourself. So what? Maybe someone else will learn from what you're not getting right. You need to share. Intellectual life is not a place to be ungenerous and withholding. Well, actually, sadly it is, but it doesn't need to be! Gila, go, you were saying? You were about to teach us what you don't understand about time lag."

Gila: "Yeah. Um. I don't know. You disappear from something that you can't confront while it's happening. But then...I don't think I get it. How do you catch up later?"

Professor Raynite: "You don't."

Gila: "But I thought...that's what I don't understand."

Professor Raynite: "That's what is so powerful about the father's dream. That's why we're talking about it. Because the father is dreaming that his child is alive and he's having this dream because he keeps desperately trying to return, in his mind, to the moment when he can see that his son has just died. But when he closes his eyes and falls asleep, what does he hear?"

Gila: "Father, can't you see I'm burning."

Professor Raynite: "Father, *don't* you see I'm burning? Right. But, as soon as the father hears his child ask him this question, it's already too late. Just as in reality the child is already on fire in the room next door. So for the father, by the time he hears his son ask him this question, he has already failed to save him."

Gila: "But I don't understand."

Professor Raynite: "The father is traumatized. Do you know what that means?"

Gila: "No."

Professor Raynite: "Anyone else know what that means? It means he keeps replaying the impossible moment when his son tells him that he's dying and the father isn't stopping it. There is a fire in the room next door. There is a fever that makes the child ill. It doesn't matter. The point is still the same for the father – he let his child die. And this is impossible to bear."

Gila: "Why?"

Professor Raynite: "Why *what*? You need to put more language around your questions. This is a graduate seminar, guys. Why what?"

Gila: "Sorry. Why is it impossible? Or, why can't he just wake up and get the child away from the burning candle?"

Professor Raynite: "Because the child is dead. That's the whole point. The father, who's traumatized, dreams that the child is alive and asking him a question, but what the dream is also about is the fact that the father isn't there when the son needs him to see that he's dying. The father is gone. The father is sleeping. So, when the child tells his father,'Can't you see I'm dying?' The answer is, 'I can't.' Because if I could see it, then I wouldn't be having this dream. I'd be awake and rescuing you from the fire. But, instead I'm sitting here dreaming. And I'm dreaming about how I was *too late.* And I'm dreaming it because I'm trying to catch up. I keep trying to get to the moment before you ask if I see that you're burning. But *I don't see it.* I *hear* it instead. And, by the time I hear it, it's too late to save you. It's always already too late."

[the Professor sighs and looks around the room]

"Are there any other questions? How about you? Gila, did this clarify what you were asking about?"

Gila: [sitting as if frozen, transfixed, staring at the Professor]

Professor Raynite: "Okay. I think you probably understand it fine. I'm not convinced you can't say more about this. But, okay. Can someone else push this question forward, so we can create some intelligibility here? It isn't good enough just to have feelings about all this. We're learning to be scholarly and critical and to use the apparatus of theory to develop vocabulary for precisely those things which make us incoherent to ourselves. Come on. I can't do all the work myself. Did I see a hand somewhere? "

❧

It is a first floor apartment on Manhattan's West End Avenue. It is a quiet, wide street lined with prewar residential buildings and no stores. There are many families going into and out of the buildings, doormen holding taxi doors open, children with their backpacks slipping off as they bolt toward home. This apartment enters through its own door on the side and inside there are several rooms, each with different doctor's names on the doors. Mrs. Barish is in her mid-fifties, thin, with short chestnut hair and rimless glasses. She speaks very softly, with a faint New York accent. She walks slowly but confidently out to greet the new patient. Gila is in jeans, sneakers and pinstriped dress shirt. She is wearing a short winter jacket, a bomber, and gloves with the fingertips cut off. It is late December. It is snowing.

Mrs. Barish: "Hello."

Gila: "Hi. Where should I sit? There are a lot of chairs."

Mrs. Barish: "Anywhere you'd like. Choose what is most comfortable."

Gila: "Then I'd sit outside."

Mrs. Barish: "Oh. I see."

Gila: "Yeah."

Mrs. Barish: "But it's so cold outside. It's snowing."

Gila: "I know. But the snow isn't going to make me feel like I'm doing something wrong."

Mrs. Barish: "And this will?"

Gila: "Probably."

Mrs. Barish: "I wonder why that is."

Gila: "Probably for a lot of reasons. Not least of which is that I don't know how to be a good patient."

Mrs. Barish: "What's a *good* patient?"

Gila: "I don't know. Someone who sits down and talks about their *feelings*. Or their *childhood*. You're looking at me like you don't know what I mean."

Mrs. Barish: "That's because I don't."

Gila: "Really? I'm not sure I buy that. But, if that's how you want to play it, it's fine."

[long pause]

Gila: "Are you going to say anything?"

Mrs. Barish: "What should I say? I think this is your time and you should feel free to talk about whatever is important to you."

Gila: "You're quiet, aren't you?

Mrs. Barish: "I'm not sure what you mean."

Gila: "I don't know. It's just...other people talk a lot more."

Mrs. Barish: "Is it a good or a bad thing? My being quiet."

Gila: "Good."

Mrs. Barish: "That's good."

Gila: "Yeah. I still don't know what to say though. I heard from someone that you specialize in trauma. So I guess maybe you know something that maybe other people don't. I don't know. I studied trauma but theoretically, not really clinically. I don't know the clinical theory on it, not really. Except that I think Freud is wrong about something. But, I haven't worked that out yet, exactly. I finished graduate school in philosophy and literature last year, and now I'm here in the city taking some course work in psychoanalysis and trying to decide if I should go on to apply for a PhD. I want to, but I'm not sure. Professor Raynite says I could, but that I shouldn't necessarily go in that direction since I'll lose some of the human dimension that I'm interested in. She says that academic work won't necessarily get me closer to what I really care about – understanding how people work.

Mrs. Barish: "Do you agree with her?"

Gila: "I think so, yeah. She teases me about that, says what I want to do isn't 'normal science.' I don't know what that means but she's probably right. Seeing something I don't really see. She's right that I wouldn't be happy just writing academic papers. I *do* want to figure out how the mind works or something like that."

Mrs. Barish: "How the mind works. You mean psychologically?"

Gila: "Yeah."

Mrs. Barish: "Is that something you've always been interested in?"

Gila: "Yeah, I think so. Ever since I was small. Wanting to understand why people act as they do. What motivates them. My mother is crazy, kind of. I don't know if that's an official diagnosis or what hers would be. But, she's difficult to deal with. I imagine that factors in somewhere in terms of what I'm interested in. Although maybe not, who knows? I have no idea really."

Mrs. Barish: "Yes, it's not uncommon for people to be interested in using their minds to process difficult emotions."

Gila: "But that's not what I said."

Mrs. Barish: "Oh? It isn't? Perhaps I misunderstood."

Gila: "No, I don't think you did. You're probably just conflating rather separate psychological endeavors. The difference here is that I'm not trying to *work through* something, I'm just trying to *understand* it better."

Mrs. Barish: "And those are two different things?"

Gila: "Yes. Of course. I'm not trying to use my mind defensively but just trying to use whatever insight I have, having *been* the kid of certain kinds of people, to make some sense of things. Produce knowledge. Put it out in the world. Be critical and try to produce intelligibility."

Mrs. Barish: "Uh-huh. I think I understand what you're saying. You want to make a difference."

Gila: "Sure. I guess that's part of it."

Mrs. Barish: "What a noble aspiration that is."

Gila: "Are you trying to flatter me? Don't try to flatter me, please. It just annoys me. Makes me wonder why you'd feel the need to do that. Makes me wonder what you're *really* thinking. That kind of thing."

Mrs. Barish: "Oh. I'm glad that you're telling me you're hearing it that way. I wasn't trying to flatter you at all. No, not at all."

Gila: "You don't have to justify yourself. It's fine. Whatever. You didn't do anything wrong. I'm just telling you what I don't like, but there's no way you could have known that. It's fine. Really."

Mrs. Barish: "You seem worried that I would feel bad. Is that true?"

Gila: "I'm not being *nice* or anything, if that's what you're implying. Trust me. I am *not* a nice patient. I'm terrible. Difficult.
You're going to hate me soon."

Mrs. Barish: "Oh dear, I can't imagine that's the case."

Gila: "Why would you say that? You have *no* idea. You don't
know me one single bit."

Mrs. Barish: "That's true, I don't know you yet. But there's
nothing wrong with you telling me what you need from me. I
consider that a strength. It helps me get to know you better."

Gila: "You're reading this wrong. I know you can't see that
right now. You're thinking I have anxiety and guilt about my
needs or something, and so you're encouraging me to express
myself. You're reassuring me. Don't reassure me. That's not
what's going on."

Mrs. Barish: [smiles] "If you say so. What *is* going on Gila?"

Gila: "Well, it's more like when you're wrong about something
you say or you say something dumb, I can't help myself. I *have*
to point it out. But, this was nothing. It was just a tendency
perhaps, on your part, to identify and join my feelings. Which
is fine as a clinical technique with a certain kind of patient.
But, it doesn't work with me that way. Not when I care more
about the fact that you *understand* me than that you think
you know what I feel."

Mrs. Barish: [smiling]

Gila: "Are you going to say anything? Why are you smiling? Was
something I just said *amusing?*"

Mrs. Barish: "Not *amusing,* no. But you really do speak quite
differently than most people do."

Gila: "I know. That's why I told you I couldn't be a good patient."

Mrs. Barish: "Well, but that's not what I said. I didn't say you *couldn't* be a good patient, just that you're not really, or, so it seems to me, a typical one. But, why should that be a problem? Who said I need you to be a typical patient?"

Gila: "I don't know. But it always seems that way."

Mrs. Barish: "Well, that might say more about the clinician than it does about you."

Gila: "I'm not so sure about that. You're feeling like you understand me so you're saying that. But wait. We're only just beginning. I haven't told you yet that you're an idiot –"

Mrs. Barish: [laughs] "When you put it that way!"

Gila: "No, I wasn't saying that. I was just saying that I *might* say that. When you say dumb or inaccurate things, I can't help myself. I'll have to correct you because I need you to understand what I'm really trying to get at."

Mrs. Barish: "And, accuracy is really important to you it seems?"

Gila: "Yeah. Of course. But, I think *precision* is the better word. So yeah, precision is important. Otherwise, how do you ever get at the truth?"

Mrs. Barish: [laughs]

Gila: "Why are you laughing?"

Mrs. Barish: "Because that was a case in point! I said one word and you refined it for another, more *precise,* one."

Gila: "Oh, I guess so. Yeah. They're different words though. And the difference matters."

Mrs. Barish: [smiling] "Indeed. I am seeing that."

Gila: "I don't understand your tone. Is something wrong with demanding precision in how one analyzes something?"

Mrs. Barish: "No, I wasn't criticizing you. I was just observing that accuracy is important to you. But that there might be other ways."

Gila: "Precision."

Mrs. Barish: [smiles] "Precision."

Gila: "What other ways are there?"

Mrs. Barish: "Oh I don't know. Say, feeling?"

Gila: "Feeling? What about feelings?"

Mrs. Barish: "Well, it's just that you're talking so much about *accuracy* and being *understood* and I am wondering what about your feelings."

Gila: [looking at the bookshelves] "It's hard to see the titles on these shelves. They're far away. I see a lot on trauma stuff but no early development? Attachment theory not your thing? There's Kohut though, that's a pleasant surprise. Maybe it's good I can't see the shelves too closely. It's always distracting."

Mrs. Barish: "Looking at bookshelves?"

Gila: "Yeah. You were saying something about feelings. Well, what *about* them? Is there a question there? I didn't hear a question."

Mrs. Barish: "Um, I'm not sure yet. More of, well, an observation."

Gila: "Of what? What are you trying to say? Can you just say it please?"

Mrs. Barish: "Well, I'm not sure yet. I think maybe it's simple. Just that you're talking so much about needing to make sure that someone understands you and I'm wondering what you're feeling about things. And whether or not it's important to you that someone can also share some of your feelings."

Gila: "What feelings are you talking about?"

Mrs. Barish: "Well, I don't know yet. I don't really know you at all. But, I found myself wondering if feelings were getting lost here somehow."

Gila: "Tell me you're not trudging out that tired old bullshit thinking and feeling divide?"

Mrs. Barish: "Maybe I am and I didn't even know it?"

Gila: "I think you are. I think next you're going to tell me that I'm *too much in my head.* That maybe I'm even in denial about my loss or something. Or better, I'm *dissociated.* That's a *popular* word with you clinicians these days."

Mrs. Barish: "You sound dismissive of that possibility."

Gila: "What another good observation that is." [silence] "Are you going to say something to that?"

Mrs. Barish: "I'm not sure yet. I believe you just insulted me. So, I'm thinking for a minute."

Gila: "I didn't insult you exactly. You shouldn't take things so personally."

Mrs. Barish: "Uh-huh."

Gila: "Are you upset with me now? This is what I warned you about. That I was going to be difficult. No, no, you said, I can handle difficult and then the first thing out of my mouth.

And, I wasn't even annoyed with you just now. Well, so much for trying to tell me you can try to understand –"

Mrs. Barish: "Now just hold it there, Gila. I didn't say that I couldn't handle anything. I just said I needed a minute to think about how to respond. There's nothing wrong with taking a minute. Not everyone thinks on their feet as quickly as you do. Did that ever occur to you?"

Gila: "Okay." [long silence] "My father died when I was twelve. I realize I didn't say that, but I know you people care about that sort of thing. He was sick for 4 and a half years, rare blood cancer, disgusting, died and then it was me and my mother and brother. They're kind of like my kids, kind of, I guess, I don't know. I take care of them, run the business – it's a bakery. It's fine. Another brother died then too, but I guess the big event is my dad and all that crap."

Mrs. Barish: "Thank you for telling me. Yes, I think that's relevant, don't you?"

Gila: "Sure."

Mrs. Barish: "You mention that you help *run* the business? What does that mean? Are they living nearby?"

Gila: "No, no, they're still in Toronto. My mother is remarried, kind of. I'm not sure. She gets married and divorced depending on her moods. It's better now, I guess. Or, maybe not. I don't know. My little one is there too. He is my baby. He has a hard time but he's managing. I talk to him a few times a day. And her too. They call frantically when something isn't going the right away, and I talk to them. It's harder to do from far away but it works out. I go back often too, every two months or something to check on the business and things like that."

Mrs. Barish: "That's a lot of responsibility, wouldn't you say? For someone so young as yourself."

Gila: "*No*. Why would you say something like that? I'm not too young at all."

Mrs. Barish: "Maybe I'm not fully understanding something. It seemed from the way you were describing it like it was a lot of responsibility for someone in their twenties to manage the affairs of their family."

Gila: "I don't know what you're talking about."

Mrs. Barish: "Oh?"

Gila: "The bakery is *my* business. D is my littlest one, and she – well, it would be nice if she were more independent but she's not there yet. But, I hope she will be. One day. I don't know. I don't get what you're telling me."

Mrs. Barish: "Gila, it just seemed like a lot of responsibility. That's all. Even if you feel very close to your brother."

Gila: "That isn't making sense to me. It is my *job*. And, we're not close in a typical way. You're misunderstanding it. We don't talk or anything like that. He isn't very verbal or his sentences don't work like yours and mine do. It's...almost kinetic. He's like a raw wire or something, and I help by formulating his reactions into language. Or, something like that. It's always been that way."

Mrs. Barish: "Do you think it's possible that maybe you have other feelings about that?"

Gila: "What?"

Mrs. Barish: "Do you think it's possible that a part of you, maybe not the logical, reasonable part, has other feelings about everything you are doing for your family?"

Gila: "Can you just say what you're trying to say, please? More directly."

Mrs. Barish: "I didn't think I wasn't being direct."

Gila: "Well, you're not. Please get to where you're going more swiftly. That sounded harsh. I'm sorry. I'm just not getting what you're trying to say and I want you to stop hedging incessantly."

Mrs. Barish: "I can try. I mean, don't you think there is a part of you that could have feelings of resentment with everything you have to do? Other people your age aren't dealing with these kinds of things. You can acknowledge that. Maybe you are angry with it. Or, at least there's a part of you that is."

Gila: "But, I'm *not* angry. Or frustrated. Exasperated sometimes, absolutely. She can drive me crazy. And him, I can't ever be more than two minutes away from my phone. I don't know what he'll do if I'm not there in time to talk him down a cliff or intervene or...But, what you're saying, about some secret part of me being secretly angry makes no sense to me. Besides, *who* would I be angry with? Them? They can't help it. I'm only relieved he isn't dead or in jail and she hasn't lost everything yet."

Mrs. Barish: "Maybe you are angry with your father?"

Gila: "For what? It's not his fault."

Mrs. Barish: "Well, in a certain sense, his dying is what led you to have to deal with this stuff."

Gila: "It's not like that. Not that simple. I mean, yes. It did technically. But...but, it's also that...I promised."

Mrs. Barish: "You promised what?"

Gila: "That I'd take care of them. I *said* I would. Who else would –"

Mrs. Barish: "But, that's a very heavy burden, Gila."

Gila: "No. It is the *job*. There isn't any other way...Or...even if it sucks sometimes, it's...I don't know how to say it...what I *do*. It's how the system works. We can't be dead or in a ditch or homeless. The way you say it...it's...I don't know. It's as if I chose it, or I have a choice. As if I'm doing something I secretly resent. But you can't resent the thing that keeps you, all three of us, alive. That would make no sense. There isn't any other way. I'm not saying there aren't *moments* when I wish that I could have a day *off* from ten phone calls a day, *really* off, or do my readings for class without being interrupted by one of them frantically telling me to fly to Toronto and bail this or that one out of court or...But, until they're independent and can manage on their own, there's nothing I can do. I told you. It's just reality. It's the *job,* even if it isn't normal or ideal. "

Mrs. Barish: "It certainly seems like you're doing a very good job at that."

Gila: "That's *not* what I'm saying at all. I think I suck at what I'm doing. Maybe because I'm here instead of there? Even though it wasn't any better when I was physically there all the time. I don't know. The boy is barely keeping a job. I speak to him a bunch of times a day, but it never feels like enough. I speak to him every morning to get him out of bed and off to work. Then, when he's done. Then, when he's angry. Then, when he almost smashes another car with his own because he's furious the coffee is hot or the light is still red. Then, at night when he says he won't go to work ever again because his boss insulted him and he can't calm down when he's running through scenarios of how people he doesn't know are out to get him. She is married, divorced, almost broke. – I can't keep track. Always telling me the business is going to be taken away because it's making no money. I look at the books and money coming in, so I don't exactly get it. But fine. I make business plans but...I don't know what she does with them. I don't know. The man she lives with is kind of a tyrant. I have no *idea* what you mean when you say I'm doing a *good* job. I'm failing. I'm trying but failing. You're just flattering me again. And I can't stand bullshit. Please, don't lie to me to prove you understand something you clearly don't, in the least bit, understand."

Mrs. Barish: "Oh-kay."

Gila: "Are you offended again? I thought I told you not to take things personally."

Mrs. Barish: "I'm just processing what you're saying to me. I'm not always as fast to speak as you are, remember?"

Gila: "Yeah. Fine."

Mrs. Barish: "Did it occur to you that maybe I'm not smart enough to be your therapist?"

Gila: "Oh god, you're really going to get discouraged that easily? I can't believe that."

Mrs. Barish: "I wasn't getting discouraged."

Gila: "Yes, you are. Why else would you say that? You're trying to get rid of me by saying you can't possibly change the way you relate to me, so it must be that I need someone different."

Mrs. Barish: "Well?"

Gila: "Well, what?"

Mrs. Barish: "I really don't see that as trying to get rid of you. I'm just –"

Gila: "Well, it is."

Mrs. Barish: "I don't think so. I really am just trying to help you and I want you to get the best person to help you. You seem to be getting impatient with me so that got me thinking that maybe with someone else who was maybe quicker on their feet –"

Gila: "No. That isn't true. I know it's hard to believe but I like you. I like how quiet you are. And, you're unflappable. You're quiet and you seem almost fragile but you're tough in your own way. Although, it's hard to tell at first. This session's going well. It may not seem that way to you but trust me. I've said more here than probably to anyone, anywhere else in this context."

Mrs. Barish: "Oh! Well! That's helpful to know."

Gila: "Yeah, so, just try not to take things too personally. Okay? Can you just remember that or something?"

Mrs. Barish: "I can try."

Gila: "Okay." [silence] "We're almost out of time."

Mrs. Barish: "Yes. We still have a few minutes though."

Gila: "Do you think you can help me?"

Mrs. Barish: "What do *you* think?"

Gila: "No. No, answering-a-question-with-a-question bullshit. I want to know what you think."

Mrs. Barish: "Is it okay if I need more than one session to come to a decision about that?"

Gila: "Well, then, is there anything you *can* say? Can you at least tell me what you think the problem is or what I need help with? What your *observations* are?"

Mrs. Barish: "Hmm. Let me think about how I want to word this." [silence] "I think that you clearly have a lot of feelings and maybe you need an opportunity to talk about them. You're very comfortable using your mind to work things out for yourself, but maybe what you need is a space where we can talk about your feelings."

Gila: "But I don't *know* them."

Mrs. Barish: "Well, maybe that's something we can figure out together. Over time. Slowly. Some things take time, you know?"

Gila: "And, let me guess. You're *good* at going slowly."

Mrs. Barish: [smiling] "I think so, yes. It comes in handy sometimes." [she tilts her body slightly forward] How does that sound?"

Gila: "Whatever."

Mrs. Barish: "Whatever?"

Gila: "Yeah. Whatever. Fine. We'll try it your way. *Slowly.* Whatever that means. Even though I have *real* questions. *Actual* things I need to understand and I don't see...how going slowly is going to get us anywhere...whatever. Slowly."

Mrs. Barish: "I'll see you next week."

It is a hallway in a university building, long and winding with a wooden bench against the wall. They are sitting on it. The Professor is wearing a black leather jacket and black jeans with a loose fitting blue patterned t-shirt underneath. She has big black plastic glasses on and short curly hair that is messy but clear of her face. Gila is wearing jeans and a purple V-neck sweater. Her messenger bag is draped over her shoulders and chest. It is snowing outside. It is March.

Gila: "Thank you, Professor Raynite, for meeting with me. I really appreciate it."

Professor Raynite: "Yeah, yeah, sure, I know. Shoot. What did you want to meet with me about?"

Gila: "Thank you, yes, I –"

Professor Raynite: "Vivian."

Gila: "Sorry?"

Professor Raynite: "Vivian. Can you call me by my first name? Or, would that be too traumatic for you? Seriously. You're so freakin' formal! Are you always like this? What's that about anyway?"

Gila: "Um, well, I don't know. Maybe, not, I don't know. It depends."

Professor Raynite: "On what?"

Gila: "Excuse me?"

Professor Raynite: "You said it depends, so I'm asking *what* it depends on."

Gila: "Oh. Sorry. I don't know. I think my father was kind of formal. I'm not blaming some childhood shit for my own shortcomings or anything, it's just –"

Professor Raynite: [laughing] "Okay, okay, see – that's what I mean! You're funny! I can tell by your writing that you see a lot more than you're ever willing to say out loud. Why is that? It's not nice to be withholding."

Gila: "No. I know. I don't know."

Professor Raynite: "I don't know, kiddo, if I'm buying this whole scared-to-death-of-me routine. Because, from what I can tell, you have a very sophisticated sense of what you think about things. I mean, sure you don't say much in class, but your paper last month was great. I don't say that lightly, but really. Holy shit. Where did that come from? Who knew? You never raise your hand or say anything, so I was taken aback to find you had it in you to write the critique you did of Didion's memoir. I was surprised, frankly, which I love. I love being surprised. Are you ever surprised? It's good. It means you're open to being teachable and transformative moments and that's what's necessary to effect social-political change, isn't it? So, teachable is good, as long as it's not the traumatizing kind, which of course it always could be. I mean *you never know.* That is the whole point Lacan is always making, isn't it? About the indeterminacy of the signifier and how context could determine the impact of a given event?"

Gila: [staring at the ground]

Professor Raynite: "What's up? Why are you so shy? I know you're thinking something. *That* much is clear. What did you want to ask me about? I don't have all day."

Gila: "Sorry. I was wondering if you would be my advisor for the thesis, if you would –"

Professor Raynite: "I don't really have the time. You can work with someone else. You're smart enough. Find someone. You shouldn't have waited this long into the term. People were asking me months ago."

Gila: "I know. I'm sorry. It's just that – I don't know. I couldn't yet."

Professor Raynite: "It's like, how far into the second term? I can't take on more students. Have you asked Professor Samuelson?"

Gila: "It has to be you."

Professor Raynite: "Excuse me?"

Gila: "I'm sorry. It has to be…I have to work with you. You *know* this stuff."

Professor Raynite: "Wow. That's like the first time you've looked at me directly, instead of at the ground. Okay, well, of course I know this stuff. So what? I write about it and all the rest. But, so do others. Take Katie –"

Gila: "It's not the same. I've taken courses. Other people's. I've been in school my entire adult life. It's not the same. I will do anything, I –"

Professor Raynite: "Relax, okay? Stop prostrating yourself, it makes me uncomfortable." [laughs] "You're just idealizing me, projecting the wish for someone who knows something onto me. So, I can bear it, because you can't. I get it. You probably can't help it. But you have to chill out a little, can you? Seriously. Okay? If this is so important, why didn't you ask me sooner when everyone else was coming to me a few months ago? You're so shy! I never hear from you in class."

Gila: "I don't know. I'm sorry. I never know what to add."

Professor Raynite: "Really? 'Cause you look like you're thinking a lot."

Gila: "I'm sorry, I just never knew this stuff existed. I thought trauma was all about how victimized you were or something and that kind of sentimental angle which I couldn't stomach –"

Professor Raynite: "Why not?"

Gila: "Um, I don't know. Because it sounds too simple, maybe? I don't know. I couldn't relate. Maybe something about the stories people tell, I couldn't ever talk like that...or, maybe, just that something terrible happens and then you survive. I wasn't in a war or had a leg blown off. I more or less had food that I could easily enough obtain. I went to school. I didn't think anything that horrible ever happened to me, but I know that things were...complicated. And, yet even when there was some un-fun stuff once upon a time, it wasn't ever like *that*."

Professor Raynite: [smiling] "So, you *do* have a lot to say!"

Gila: "I don't."

Professor Raynite: "But you just articulated the poststructuralist critique of subjectivity's normative tropes!"

Gila: "I did? No, I was just saying –"

Professor Raynite: "Right. I know what you were saying but it's what we're trying to get at in this class with Derrida and Lacan. And, Foucault of course. The fantasy of an intelligible subject who always *knows what* event has compromised his precious self-coherence. But how it wouldn't be *trauma* if the subject *knows*!"

Gila: "Because what trauma does is compromise your ability to know yourself?"

Professor Raynite: "And remember Freud's burning child, right? Trauma is the very thing you couldn't bear to know, observe, and be a part of. When it happened, you were gone."

Gila: "So, then how could you say, *x is the bad thing that happened to me.*"

Professor Raynite: "Exactly."

Gila: "That part about not knowing *what* the trauma is."

Professor Raynite: "*Nachträglichkeit.*"

Gila: "Yeah. That."

Professor Raynite: "What about it?"

Gila: "That seems so true somehow. I don't know. I hate how everyone is always presuming they know *automatically* what the worst part of something is or where the damaging thing occurred, or something. But, really, how do you know because...yeah...you can't. You might just be too busy or...it's just..."

Professor Raynite: "Or, too tired. People underestimate how hard it is to *know* yourself when you're just scrambling or hustling, scraping by, just trying to survive. All this *knowing* is so damn heroic all the time."

Gila: "And especially – never mind."

Professor Raynite: "What?"

Gila: "Nothing."

Professor Raynite: "Oh, come on. What were you gonna say?"

Gila: "Just that, well, *how* do you know? That's what I never understand."

Professor Raynite: "What do you mean?"

Gila: "I don't know. Just...what if you couldn't go to therapy? What if it didn't work for you? And you didn't really talk about things personally with people. I don't know what I'm asking. I just –"

Professor Raynite: "That's what reading's for!" [laughing]

Gila: [smiling] "I guess so...I'm sorry I didn't ask you sooner if you could be my advisor. I didn't think...I waited because I needed to see first if I could do the work."

Professor Raynite: "I don't know about any of that, but that Didion paper was awesome. Seriously. I couldn't believe you wrote it because you're always so quiet. Great work. You should take the compliment! I don't give them often."

Gila: "Okay."

Professor Raynite: "You're not really listening, are you? That's fine. That's your business. Being gracious is a skill though, by the way. It does no good to discredit what you're good at. There's enough out there you can't do right. For example, you should have been more critical of the theory. You didn't develop an argument that expressly challenges the theory, which is what I thought you wanted to do."

Gila: "I did want to, yeah. How do you –"

Professor Raynite: "Well, that's *your* job to figure out, isn't it? But, start by really figuring out how to use the book to critique the theory. Basically, don't assume the theory is necessarily right about what's it saying, get what I mean?"

Gila: "Yeah. I don't think it is."

Professor Raynite: "Continue."

Gila: "Oh, just that something doesn't add up in what we're reading about trauma. Or grief. The idea that you mourn and then you're over it. Eventually."

Professor Raynite: "You don't agree with that?"

Gila: "I don't know if it's that I don't *agree*. I probably don't understand it well enough. The material is hard, but –"

Professor Raynite: "I think you understand it. What else are you trying to say? Spit it out. Stop mumbling."

Gila: "Sorry, I...I don't know. I don't understand the model of *mourning* that is acceptable versus the kind that Freud is calling *too much*. He's trying to say that certain kinds of grief make sense and others don't, and I don't know. I guess that's true, but something...I don't know yet. Something isn't adding up."

Professor Raynite: "Keep going."

Gila: "I don't know. I love Eggers because he has the guts to say to the reader: You know what? Fuck this conventional traumatized trope. Don't pity me. My parents died. Bad shit happens. I'm making it work."

Professor Raynite: "And, what about that do you love?"

Gila: "Everything. I don't know."

Professor Raynite: "Try. I do too, by the way. But, you need to articulate it."

Gila: "That he tells it like it really is. No easy answers like my *mother died and therefore I am x.* I hate that crap. It makes no sense. It feels good, maybe, but it makes no actual sense."

Professor Raynite: [smiling] "See? This is what I mean! Look how opinionated you are! You have so much to say about these things. And, you're funny. Stop hiding behind some *aw-shucks sorry I don't know anything* routine. I don't buy it for a minute. Seriously, you need to get over whatever hang-up you have about talking out loud and *do* it, in class, in person, whatever."

Gila: "But, it's not an act."

Professor Raynite: "Well, whatever it is, you should get over it."

Gila: "But, I'm not *doing* anything. This is –"

Professor Raynite: "Oh, please. I've seen you sometimes before class, chatting with people, being friendly. I even saw you laughing! Don't deny it. It's true. And, yet, whenever we talk, you're silent, deferential, whatever."

Gila: "But it's different talking to you."

Professor Raynite: "Why? Don't let it be. I'm not that scary. Besides, what are you afraid of anyway? I don't get the sense you're trying to impress me, which is unusual but it doesn't feel like you're just an anxious or ambitious student, even though you're anxious about *something,* so –"

Gila: "It's nothing like that."

Professor Raynite: "Yeah, I didn't think so."

Gila: "It's just talking to you is different than to anyone else. Sure, I can talk and be funny and even charming. People tend to like me. I don't know why. I listen. I'm well-behaved. I say smart things. I had a teacher in high school that I talked to. That's the only other time I felt something like this. With everyone else, I don't know. It's not the same...they...you *see* everything."

Professor Raynite: "So, you have a thing for teachers."

Gila: "No. I don't think…"

Professor Raynite: "Relax. I'm teasing you. Kind of. What were you saying?"

Gila: "That you see so much. It's…I feel you understand."

Professor Raynite: "So do you, I bet."

Gila: "No, no, I don't –"

Professor Raynite: "I think you do. I think you see a hell of a lot more than you ever let on. I see the way you are in class. Taking everything in. I don't know you anywhere else, so what the hell do I know? Maybe nothing. I could be totally wrong. But, my guess is, you'd have a lot more to say if you actually said what you're thinking."

Gila: "I don't –"

Professor Raynite: "Remind me. Where are you from again?"

Gila: "Toronto."

Professor Raynite: "Canada! I love Toronto."

Gila: "Yeah, everyone does."

Professor Raynite: "Not you though?"

Gila: "No. I don't know. It's fine. I don't really know it, to be fair. I grew up in a bakery business."

Professor Raynite: "No way! How cool is that? So your parents are bakers or something, is that it?"

Gila: "Yeah, something like that. My father started it when I was born. Gave up whatever he was doing before and told my mom let's start making cakes! So yeah, they did that and we were just always around it. You know how it is with small businesses...Anyway, and then when he died I kind of took over or something like that."

Professor Raynite: "Huh. That's interesting. Does your family still have the bakery?"

Gila: "Yeah, my mom is there in Toronto. She makes the cakes. I have a little brother too, but he's not really involved. He likes cars and things like that. I go back often and help out, or I try my best to manage things from here."

Professor Raynite: "Cool!"

Gila: "Yeah."

Professor Raynite: "Eggers writes about taking care of his brother after both parents die. Is that what you like about the book?"

Gila: "Maybe? I don't know."

Professor Raynite: "Don't look at *me*. *I* have no idea. It's just most people find him kind of obnoxious as a narrator, so it's interesting that you like him."

Gila: "He has the guts to say that there's no such as thing as *normal mourning.* Or, that what counts as *normal mourning* is actually just a delusion and the real process is messier and doesn't end when you think that it will or the way that it will. That you can be fucked up a long time."

Professor Raynite: "And, what's your deal? Are you like one of those kids who always wanted to be an English professor or something? You don't strike me exactly that way, but who knows? I have no idea."

Gila: "I don't know. No. I don't think I want to be an academic."

Professor Raynite: "But, you want to write. Clearly."

Gila: "I guess. I don't know."

Professor Raynite: "Oh, please. Don't be disingenuous. It's clear you have a mind for thinking theoretically. If you could talk more it would help. But maybe you have to figure that out on your own time or something. Not my business. Have you always been interested in psychoanalysis?"

Gila: "I haven't read it, until your class, until now."

Professor Raynite: "No way! I don't believe you."

Gila: "Yes."

Professor Raynite: "Wow. Really? Did you do your college degree in a cave or something? Then you're even better at this then I thought. Fine. Did you not study this in school or something? What college did you go to?"

Gila: "Brandeis in Boston. I got a full scholarship. I'm only saying that because I don't know if I would have chosen it, but I wouldn't have been able to afford to come to the States otherwise."

Professor Raynite: [laughing] "Relax, you don't need to worry. I *won't* think you're arrogant. Promise. What did you study there? Molecular physics or something? How come you didn't come across psychoanalysis?"

Gila: "No, not science. I had a few majors. But I never learned theory."

Professor Raynite: "Can you look at me while you're talking? I bet you can be even a *little* bit more comfortable than this. It makes me feel like I'm a scary person, which I kind of am, but not *this* scary."

Gila: "Sorry. I can try."

Professor Raynite: "And, stop saying sorry."

Gila: "Sorry."

Professor Raynite: [laughing and rolling her eyes] "So, you were telling me you never learned theory? That's hard to believe. You just avoided it or something? Didn't it come up in your gender studies coursework?"

Gila: "I didn't take any gender studies classes."

Professor Raynite: "What?"

Gila: "Yeah."

Professor Raynite: "But you're so –"

Gila: "The type that would be interested?"

Professor Raynite: "I don't know. I guess. I wonder what I'm trying to imply. Hm. That's interesting. I have to think about that some more."

Gila: "It's embarrassing how little I know about any of that stuff. I want to take a course. You're teaching gender studies in the spring? I just never got around to it, I guess. Got married young and then just focused on more traditional subjects. Probably I'm just putting off some bigger question, or –"

Professor Raynite: "Wait a second. Did you just say you're married?"

Gila: "Yeah, I know. It's –"

Professor Raynite: "Holy shit, seriously?! But you're so –"

Gila: "Young?"

Professor Raynite: "Yeah, for one thing. How old are you? Twenty-five? I thought so."

Gila: [laughing] "I know. We got married young."

Professor Raynite: "That's seriously young. Were you fleeing something? That's not just *young*. You're like a child bride or something."

Gila: "He's in law school. I'm here in this program. I don't really think of it as *married* in that conventional sense."

Professor Raynite: "Wait a second. To a man? You're straight? I don't believe you!"

Gila: "I know."

Professor Raynite: "Wow. [playfully punching Gila's arm] Well, kiddo, married is married. Even if you are *ambivalent*. Which you clearly are. I never noticed you wearing a wedding band?"

Gila: "I don't wear one. I can't. Makes me feel trapped or something. I told you. It isn't a typical marriage. We're doing things together. It is a partnership, but not, well, domestic or...I can't explain."

Professor Raynite: [laughing] "Yeah. *Ambi-valent* means two directions at once. Just saying. But, wait, you must talk to your husband more comfortably? Doesn't that mean –"

Gila: "No. It's different. Talking to J isn't anything like this. We do things together, we're committed to getting certain things we want. But, I don't...I don't talk about this stuff."

Professor Raynite: "Gender? Trauma? *Ambivalence*?"

Gila: "Yes."

Professor Raynite: "Hm. But, you don't talk with *me* either. You just listen and let me do all the talking."

Gila: "I know, but I don't mean to. I just don't know enough to say anything yet, but I want to –"

Professor Raynite: "Sure you do."

Gila: "But not like I *want* to."

Professor Raynite: "You mean you can't talk in a way that's commensurate with your understanding."

Gila: "Yes. How did you know that?"

Professor Raynite: "So learn."

Gila: "I know. Can I ask you something? How did you learn to talk about these things? You know this stuff, what it *feels* like but also how to *think* about it. You don't get overwhelmed."

Professor Raynite: "I am a teacher, of course I know so much. And, who says I don't get overwhelmed? Don't assume you know what my defenses are. You know this stuff by reading it, rereading it, practicing producing intelligibility despite your incomprehension."

Gila: "But not just know so much about the theory. It's like you *know* so much. About the pain. Or, loss or something. Sorry. I don't know."

Professor Raynite: "So do you though."

Gila: "Know something?"

Professor Raynite: "You're unusual, you know that? Do people tell you that a lot?"

Gila: "Yes. People tease me that it's because I didn't have a child-hood or something. I don't mean this to mean that I'm a victim. It's just a fact. No Sesame Street or playing with toys. You're six. Here's Dostoevsky kind of thing."

Professor Raynite: "It's because you were busy baking cakes!"

Gila: "Well, no, not at the age of four I wasn't. I don't think. But, then who knows? My father wasn't always sensitive to the difference between adults and children. Anyway, maybe that was it. Combined with his European formality or something –"

Professor Raynite: [laughing] "That's funny."

Gila: "No."

Professor Raynite: "What? Did that make you uncomfortable or something? Girl, you need to chill out! It would be so much more fun if you could just be more *comfortable*. Really. Trust me. Or don't trust me, whatever."

Gila: "I know. I'm just not used to talking. Like this."

Professor Raynite: "Like what?"

Gila: "Like this. Like with you. Where I can say what I'm actually thinking."

Professor Raynite: "Are you busy being *good* all the time? That kind of thing? Is *that* what your problem is? I was like that a little too when I was younger."

Gila: "Something like that, yeah. Being quiet. Saying what people want me to say or expect me to say. Having no preferences. I have no preferences ever. It's actually a skill! Comes in quite handy when you're running a business and raising some kids. Anyway, yeah, what I think doesn't matter. It can't."

Professor Raynite: "That sucks. But you're gonna need to get over that somehow if you want to think and write for a living, you know that right?"

Gila: "I know. I don't know how though."

Professor Raynite: "You seem to be doing alright. More or less. When you're not falling over yourself and apologizing every two seconds and staring at the ground, you're actually kind of fun to talk to. Who knew?!"

Gila: "Were *you* always like this?"

Professor Raynite: "You're going to have to be specific. Always like *what*?"

Gila: "I don't know. Always able to talk in this way. I don't know. I'm not sure what I'm asking."

Professor Raynite: "I'm not sure either. But, the short answer is *kind of,* yes and no. I had phases of self-destructiveness – things I did to try to stop the world from spinning out of control, stupid, desperate shit, which, of course, didn't really help. *As you know,* so yeah, it wasn't always like this if, by this, you mean that I seem stable and organized and that kind of thing?"

Gila: "I just don't know how you get there."

Professor Raynite: "Where?"

Gila: "I'm not sure. To where you can talk about this in some way. Or, understand how it works."

Professor Raynite: "Who said I understood how it works?"

Gila: "I mean, it's just that you can *talk* about trauma and not just feel it. Or, it doesn't stop you from speaking. I think maybe I get so overwhelmed or something. I don't know what happens. It's as if I can read this stuff and feel so much and have so much that I want to say but then I can't talk about it. Or, maybe it's more like I can't really *think* about in any productive way. I just get so quiet. Inside. Maybe it's because I'm overwhelmed and it's stopping me from being able to use my head the way I'm used to? I don't get it. I don't know. I've never had a problem *thinking*."

Professor Raynite: "You'll learn. You're overwhelmed. This stuff can be *intense*. Really. You're only just starting. Be patient. Besides, you just told me that you're not good at saying what you actually think. Don't be so hard on yourself."

Gila: "How did you learn not to get overwhelmed?"

Professor Raynite: "You mean, how do I manage the affective impact of this material in such a way that enables me to transform feelings into intelligible thoughts?"

Gila: "Exactly. Even that sentence –"

Professor Raynite: "I compartmentalize! [laughing] No, seriously. I don't know. That's what inhabiting a critical vocabulary is for. That's what I keep trying to teach you guys. Listen. As kids we used to joke that compared to our mother, at least *Hitler* liked his *dog*. Which was more than you could say about our mother. You get the picture? So yeah, sure. I'm interested in trauma for a *reason,* as they say. But, I'm teaching you that there is a *language* out there, tools for learning how to *think* about the problem critically, in theoretical, historical, structural terms."

Gila: "And, that will help?"

Professor Raynite: "Of course *I* tend to think that organizing emotional experience in theoretical terms is helpful. That making incoherence intelligible is a good and worthy critical enterprise and all that stuff. But then, on the other hand, my shrink thinks it's a defense, so what the hell do I know?" [both start laughing]

Gila: "I just want you to know how much this means to me."

Professor Raynite: "I get it. It's fine."

Gila: "But, I mean, *really*. Like, I didn't even know trauma was a field of study. And now I'm trying to understand it. And use this theoretical language."

Professor Raynite: "That's a good thing!"

Gila: "Yeah, I know. I want to thank you. Because –"

Professor Raynite: "Oh please, spare me this scene of your prostrating yourself. Seriously. It makes me anxious. I don't know what all that's about but, seriously, you need to chill. I'm just a teacher who knows this stuff better than you do, so far. This is my job to teach this material."

Gila: "It's more than that. You're different. You understand this stuff. Most people don't."

Professor Raynite: "What did you say your question about Didion was? Sure, I'll be your advisor. Just to be clear –"

Gila: "I will take up no space or next to no space. I promise. Thank you. Oh my god, thank you."

Professor Raynite: "Fine. It's fine. I know you don't need me to hold your hand and that's a good thing because I don't have time for that."

Gila: "I won't. I promise. I'll work by myself. I'm good at that."

Professor Raynite: "I'm sure. Do me a favor though? Before the next time we meet, work on your anxiety or something. So you're not just sitting here falling over yourself. But, actually talking, like a graduate student about the material. Stop thanking me and apologizing. It's making me anxious, okay? You need to practice getting it under control. Do that and we're good. Yes? Go. Start reading. I don't need to tell you to read around Freud if you're going to begin to deconstruct his argument about mourning? You have your work cut out for you! I am exhausted. I still have papers to write and read this evening. It's exhausting when you never sleep. Or, don't sleep well. Or, dream. Anyway. Do you still bake?"

Gila: "I'm allergic."

Professor Raynite: "To what?"

Gila: "Flour, dairy, sugar. The business basically."

Professor Raynite: "Get out. [teasingly punching Gila's shoulder] Are you for real?"

Gila: [looking bashful, smiling] "Yes. It is ridiculous, I know."

Professor Raynite: "That's *hilarious*. You are a walking symptom! Do you know that about yourself? [shaking her head] It's –"

Gila: "So obvious, I know. It's kind of embarrassing. I mean, *really*? The daughter of a baker allergic to sweets. That seems to be as transgressive as my unconscious gets."

Professor Raynite: [laughing] "Sometimes I'm afraid my dreams are boring too. I mean, I'm supposed to be wanting revenge for old abuses, shit like that. My shrink says there is rage somewhere but sometimes there are just these kittens there who want me to pet them you know? Or, feed them or teach them, ha! Something domestic and sentimental like that. And, I wonder: am I being a bad patient or is this really the scarier wish?"

Gila: [laughing]

Professor Raynite: "Oh, like *you* should talk! Miss I'll make these cakes but I won't *eat* them, *ever*."

Gila: [laughing] "I wasn't being rejecting!"

Professor Raynite: "*Of course* you are, in your own way. That's how symptoms work! Have you read Phillips on "the symptom"? You would love it. He describes how we're all more or less desperately attached to some idea of ourselves as having a personality that is somehow beyond these knots of fixations and compulsions but, of course, that *is* our personality! So, anyway, take my kittens. Maybe I'm afraid of tenderness, who knows? Were you always allergic? We can walk together out the building. What time is it? Shit. I have a meeting I am very late to. Oh, well. We were talking about the genealogy of psychosomatic truth-effects in us. Continue."

ॐ

It is a sunny afternoon, mid-winter, in Mrs. Barish's office. The sunlight is shining through the windows in the garden floor office apartment. Mrs. Barish is wearing dress pants, a thin purple turtleneck and a dark navy blazer. Gila has arrived to the waiting room early. She is wearing sneakers, jeans, and a short wool peacoat. There is still snow in the ringlets of her curly hair when Mrs. Barish, in hushed tones escorting her last patient out, comes over to say it's time for their session.

Gila: "I don't know what to say."

Mrs. Barish: "That's okay."

Gila: "Is there somewhere we can start or something?"

Mrs. Barish: "You can start anywhere you'd like."

Gila: "There *isn't* anywhere. I don't know how to do this."

Mrs. Barish: "You can just talk about whatever is on your mind."

Gila: "It doesn't work that way. I can't just sit down and...it's not even that. I have no idea what I would talk about."

Mrs. Barish: "Anything."

Gila: "I need more guidance than that, seriously."

Mrs. Barish: "Let me see. How about right now? Do you know how you're feeling right now?"

Gila: "Nothing. Cold."

Mrs. Barish: "Yes. I noticed you are keeping your jacket on."

Gila: [begins to take it off] "Sorry. Yes. It's cold outside. I should be used to it, being from Toronto, but I never am. Why do people always say, 'you're from Canada you should be used to cold weather!' How do you get used to cold weather? That's like getting used to being hungry."

Mrs. Barish: "You don't like the cold."

Gila: "I don't know. I don't *mind* the cold. I just hate winter clothes."

Mrs. Barish: "Oh, yes, you're not wearing boots!"

Gila: "Nope. I hate them. And winter jackets, as if we're skiing all the time. And gloves and hats and scarves. I know, I know. It's no wonder then, I'm freezing. Ms. Tobin scolds me all the time about this. I mentioned her to you, I think? The teacher from high school who saved my life? Fed me, told me I should go to school, that sort of thing? You aren't nodding. I didn't then? Anyway, that was her. She is the person closest to me. When she sees me in Toronto, when I go back, she yells at me, in a parental way, about needing to suck it up and put on some clothes but still I can't do it."

Mrs. Barish: "It sounds like she's giving you good advice."

Gila: "Yeah, she always does. She has five kids. She told me once she doesn't mind a sixth. But, she wants to kill me when she sees me like this in the cold." [smiling]

Mrs. Barish: "She cares about you."

Gila: "Yes. I don't know why. We talk about books. I know this might be hard for *you* to imagine, but I can be pretty good company."

Mrs. Barish: "That isn't hard for me to imagine."

Gila: "Yeah, so. I see her when I am in Toronto or when she comes here. She has a farmhouse in Vermont and I've joined her there a few times too. It's peaceful when I'm with her."

Mrs. Barish: "So, what do you think it is about the winter weather that you don't like?"

Gila: "I didn't say I didn't like the winter weather. I said I didn't want to wear the winter GEAR, as if I'm skiing when I'm walking, that kind of thing."

Mrs. Barish: "So, what is it that you don't like? Is it the style or the effort it takes? Something like that?"

Gila: "Not being able to feel things as closely. I don't know how to explain it, but with gloves on, you can't know exactly what you're touching. Does that sound strange? It probably does. But it's like, with boots, you don't feel the ground. All that fake material blocking what the environment feels like. It scares me. Everything being so far away in that way. There but *not* there. Like you're in some artificial self-created bubble and everything you touch is something you can't actually *feel*. Ew. I hate it."

Mrs. Barish: "Hm. I never thought about winter clothes in that way. That's interesting."

Gila: "I'm not sure that it's so *interesting*. It's just an idiosyncrasy of mine, I guess."

Mrs. Barish: "Well, but it *is* interesting to hear you talk about what you don't like."

Gila: "Why?"

Mrs. Barish: "Because you're describing how important it is for you to *know* what you're doing and where you're experiencing all the time. Knowledge is very important to you. And, if you can't have that, then you feel unstable."

Gila: "Is *that* what you heard in what I said?"

Mrs. Barish: "Yes. It is."

Gila: "Because that sounds dead wrong. You're interpreting my attachment to knowledge. You're saying that I *need* to *know* things all the time. And, that's plain wrong. I *like* to know things. I *strive* to know things. But, if you were listening to what I was *actually* saying, you'd hear that I emphasized how the sensation I am most disturbed by is being blocked from *feeling* my surroundings."

Mrs. Barish: "And, what does that mean to you?"

Gila: "That I'm not this cerebral, defensive, basically intellectualizing machine that you're imagining me to be."

Mrs. Barish: "Who said I'm imagining you that way?"

Gila: "Oh, please. *Of course* that's what you're saying. But, I said something else that's so much more important. I can't believe that's what you heard."

Mrs. Barish: "Hm. Well. Maybe we can have two different ideas about that?"

Gila: "*What?* That's even worse than the wrong thing you said."

Mrs. Barish: "Really? Oh dear. Only *your* idea is right and my idea is wrong? Now that doesn't sound fair, does it?" [smiling]

Gila: "Are you trying to be condescending? That's how it sounds. Or, patronizing? Or, whatever. I don't appreciate it. I'm not saying 'I'm always right because I am me.' That is ridiculous. Do you think I'd ever say that? What is this, second grade? I wouldn't have said that when I was *in* the second grade. I am offended. Seriously? No. I'm saying that contradictory interpretations often reflect incompatible hermeneutic strategies. Not to mention that different ideological structures undergird the different things we privilege when we're reading, or, in this case, listening. I'm saying that –"

Mrs. Barish: "And, what is your interpretation that is different than mine?"

Gila: "Why are you cutting me off?"

Mrs. Barish: "I didn't mean to."

Gila: "Yes, you did. But it's fine. You're signaling that you won't take up the argument."

Mrs. Barish: "Was I doing that? I thought I was just asking you to share what your idea was, since it seemed that mine was so wrong."

Gila: "You're being condescending."

Mrs. Barish: "I'm sorry you're hearing things that way."

Gila: "That's how you're *saying* them!"

Mrs. Barish: "I don't think so. Maybe this is a miscommunication. Because –"

Gila: "A *miscommunication*? Seriously? Did you really just say that?"

Mrs. Barish: "I did. What's wrong with that? Is there something wrong with that word?"

Gila: "There's nothing wrong with the *word* in and of itself, of course. But, isn't this *psychoanalysis*? In which case, don't we kind of dismiss the idea that the things we say are *irrelevant* or *accidental* or *meaningless,* even if they *seem* that way at first? In fact, isn't that the whole edifice upon which this therapeutic enterprise is constructed? The belief that we should take even the littlest things we're feeling, thinking, doing, *seriously*?

Mrs. Barish: [silence]

Gila: "Why aren't you saying anything?"

Mrs. Barish: "I'm thinking about what you're saying, that's all."

Gila: "Can you think more quickly?"

Mrs. Barish: "I don't think as quickly on my feet as you do, remember?"

Gila: "Yes. You like to do things slowly. Which is fine, I guess. Even though I don't like being kept in suspense."

Mrs. Barish: "I am wondering why it seems so important to you that you know what I'm thinking."

Gila: "Because we're in this room together talking? Because I need a mind that I can trust?"

Mrs. Barish: "You seem annoyed."

Gila: "It's an annoying question."

Mrs. Barish: "Why?"

Gila: "Because you're implying *again* that all I care about is obtaining knowledge, certainty, whatever. You're not hearing a single thing that I'm saying."

Mrs. Barish: "Oh? I didn't see it that way."

Gila: "Well, of course you didn't. You *wouldn't*. You prefer to proceed as if your questions are innocent and psychologically mindful. When in reality you're asking me why I need to spend so much time arguing with another person's mind."

Mrs. Barish: "Well, why do you?"

Gila: "See! That is your question."

Mrs. Barish: [smiling] "You know I really fail to see the problem with what I'm asking you. You're telling me that everything I'm saying is wrong and then, when I'm quiet you ask me what I'm thinking. But, if you don't like what I'm thinking then you ask me *why* I am thinking it, and then you want to talk about *that*."

Gila: "You're saying that I'm defensive."

Mrs. Barish: "I didn't say that."

Gila: "You didn't need to. It's the only answer that every road leads to. You're describing me as difficult and demanding and severe. You're saying that all I care about are *ideas* and differences and distinguishing between what is right and wrong. As if this is a classroom. Which I know in moments it can feel that way...That's true. But that isn't what I'm after. I'm trying to connect to you but I need your mind to meet me there. What's wrong with that? I need to know how your mind works, how you move through thoughts and problem-solving."

Mrs. Barish: [smiling]

Gila: "You're smiling again. Why are you smiling? Was something I just said amusing?"

Mrs. Barish: "It's just not typically what *therapy* is about."

Gila: "I don't understand."

Mrs. Barish: "Well. Typically. And, I understand that you're not typical. But, *typically,* therapy is about working through what the patient *feels* about things. What they feel about their conflicts or their needs or their loved ones. Or, in this case about who they've lost. It isn't supposed to be about how *my* mind works. It's supposed to be about what *you* are *feeling*."

Gila: "But...I don't get it. What if my mind and feelings are connected? Like, what if I don't know how I feel about things unless I can have a frame for thinking about them too?"

Mrs. Barish: "Yes. That's what I was trying to get at earlier when you took offense."

Gila: "When? And, I didn't take offense. Or, maybe I did. What part?"

Mrs. Barish: "When I tried to say that you're more interested in *knowing* things then *feeling* them. I was trying to point out that you have a very well-developed intellectual apparatus. And, clearly a powerful mind that serves you well in your endeavors. But, that part of you is not letting another part of you express how you feel."

Gila: "I don't understand."

Mrs. Barish: "It isn't that hard to understand. It is what happens when people, especially when they're young and have powerful minds like you do, go through a traumatic event. Their feelings become scary for them, so they approach the world through their *thoughts* instead. It's not unusual."

Gila: "I don't see how that's what I'm doing. Because I use my mind to feel secure?"

Mrs. Barish: "Sure, that's part of it. But it's more general than that."

Gila: "How? You're not making sense."

Mrs. Barish: "Let's say there are two Gilas. There is the intellectual one who knows so many things and is powerful and secure and can reason her way through any situation. And, then there is also this more emotional Gila who is scared and maybe sad, grieving still. She has a lot of feelings about things that have happened to her. But she doesn't talk about them.

She has learned that it's safer to just be smarter than everyone else."

Gila: [silence]

Mrs. Barish: "You seem to have gotten quiet."

Gila: "Yeah."

Mrs. Barish: "That's okay."

Gila: "I guess."

Mrs. Barish: "We can just sit here quietly for now."

Gila: "I don't know."

Mrs. Barish: "It's okay not to know."

Gila: "Is it time to leave yet? Is the session almost over?"

Mrs. Barish: "No, we still have some time. You don't need to worry about that right now."

Gila: "Whatever."

Mrs. Barish: "You seem nervous. Do you want to just sit back in your chair for a moment? You look very worried. We still have some time. And, we can always pick up where we left off the next time."

Gila: "You talk very quietly."

Mrs. Barish: [nodding]

Gila: "I like how quiet you are."

Mrs. Barish: "That's good."

Gila: "I feel tired all of a sudden. I don't know."

Mrs. Barish: "Maybe it's a lot to take in."

Gila: "No."
　　[silence]
　　"I think you're right about feelings. There's something to do with feelings here that's important."

Mrs. Barish: "Yes. I think so."

Gila: "Well I already know *you* think so. I'm saying what I think. I'm not sure about the two-Gilas thing. I'm not sure that's right. You make it sound like...I don't know. Like I'm defensive. Like my mind is primarily or essentially a defensive machine. Cerebral, intellectualizing. Like my primary mode of operating is to intellectualize the things I'm feeling so that I don't have to feel them. But, that's so...I don't know. So conventional. Which doesn't mean I'm special. That's not my point, just that I *know* about that already. I've gone down that road and wondered if that's what I'm doing and...it presumes that I'm holding things back."

Mrs. Barish: "Sure. Not consciously. But, that it feels safer to think about things than to feel them."

Gila: "Yeah, I get it. Non-consciously, of course. That whole repression business. But, I don't know. It feels like something else is going on."

Mrs. Barish: "Like what?"

Gila: "Well, I don't know yet."

Mrs. Barish: "Maybe you think I'm saying that something is wrong with you but I'm not. There's nothing wrong with intellectualizing or with splitting the self off into different components. Sometimes, it's what you need to do in order to survive."

Gila: "I know. I've read the literature. That isn't it. It isn't that I'm feeling blamed or something. Or, maybe I am also. I don't know. That's just distracting. No…it's something else…"

Mrs. Barish: "I just want to let you know that we're almost out of time for today."

Gila: "Okay."

Mrs. Barish: "We still have a few minutes. I just wanted to warn you. Please, finish your sentence."

Gila: "Thank you, yeah. I don't know though. It's like the intellectualizing thing presumes I'm holding something back. I'm trying not to feel too much. That thinking is a way of making me feel *less*. But, it doesn't work that way for me. *Thinking* helps me sharpen *what* the *feelings* are. I think this is related to what happened at Chicago. I know there isn't time now…but, the point is that…I don't know. That something is holding me back, but it isn't *me* that's doing it. I don't know how to say this. But, it's more like I don't know. Like, I can *tell* there is a feeling there inside me somewhere, but there's nothing I can do to get it. I try and nothing…That's what I'm looking for. That's why I'm here. That's…yeah. We're out of time, aren't we?"

Mrs. Barish: "We'll have to continue this next week."

Gila: "Did what I said make any sense?"

Mrs. Barish: [shuffling her feet, getting ready to stand] "Yes. I think sometimes it can be a very long process to trust one's feelings. And, to work with defenses that are very strong indeed and very powerful to get them out of the way and allow the feelings to come out."

Gila: "Okay."

Mrs. Barish: "I'll see you at the same time next week?"

Gila: "Actually, do you have anything at the end of the day? I like to have the day at least before it. Since I can't really do anything after the sessions."

Mrs. Barish: "Let me look." [finding her calendar on the side table and checking it] "Five o'clock?"

Gila: "Thank you, yes. That's good."

Mrs. Barish: "Five o'clock then. I'll see you next week."

❧

It is a café under the El train stop, a station in Hyde Park, the South Side of Chicago. The walls are painted white and bright orange. Several tables are occupied with people from the university campus, which is nearby. It is early summer; the school year has almost ended. It is early in the afternoon, humid, and people are in t-shirts, tank tops, shorts. At a small table near the window, the Professor is in a black long sleeve shirt and black jeans. Gila is in jeans and a buttoned-down navy plaid shirt. There are cups on the table, a glass of iced tea, which the Professor has nearly finished drinking, and a mug of coffee that Gila ordered but hasn't touched and is getting cold.

Gila: "Thank you for meeting me. To talk about the paper. I appreciate it."

Professor Raynite: "Yeah, no problem. I'm happy to discuss your work. I love this place. Is it okay to meet here instead of on campus? It's right near my house."

Gila: "Yes, please, anything is fine, of course."

Professor Raynite: "So, what's on your mind? You seem upset."

Gila: "I don't know. What did you think of it?"

Professor Raynite: "I gave you an A+! Are you seriously wondering what I think of it? It was fantastic! Did you want another +? You realize that stuff begins to look ridiculous in graduate school? I mean a PhD program isn't going to care how many pluses are after the A's. Or, about A's for that matter generally. Is that what's making you doubtful?"

Gila: "No. It's not that."

Professor Raynite: "Then what? I never give that grade. And, I mean *never*. But your paper was fantastic. I mean, I can't believe you're the same student who couldn't pronounce Lacan when you first started here in September."

Gila: "Thank you. Yes."

Professor Raynite: "Well then, why do you seem so upset about it? Other students in your place would be ecstatic. Your paper was chosen as among the best in the program! What's *wrong* with you?"

Gila: "I don't know. I don't care about the grade."

Professor Raynite: "Well then, what is it? [leaning forward] I've never seen you this upset before."

Gila: "I know. I'm sorry. I just – I tried my best and –"

Professor Raynite: "Gila, listen to me. It is better than most graduate papers I read, okay? Seriously. I wouldn't be saying this normally but you look like you really need some perspective. You did a close reading of Eggers through trauma theory that you routed through gender theory and sexuality. Two months ago when we were talking, you had never read a gender theory book! The ground you've covered since then, but also since I've met you, is incredible. Listen to me – I've been teaching twenty plus years and I have never seen someone absorb as much as you did and put it all together, as if they were a pro. Okay? You should feel really *good* about the work."

Gila: "Thank you. But something's missing."

Professor Raynite: "What do you mean? What kind of –"

Gila: "I take the paper as far as I can take it, but at the end, when it's my turn to say what I *think* about how trauma works, I can't do it."

Professor Raynite: [staring at Gila]

Gila: "It's true, isn't it? I critique the preexisting theory. I say there is a problem with the narratives we use of trauma. They all adhere to the familiar tropes. I'm grieving, now I'm healed.

I was broken, now I cohere. I was blind but now I see, fine. I saw the link to sexuality. How non-normative sexual practices give us a way to challenge the frameworks we use for thinking about how the experience unfolds, what it means, that maybe not everything ends with children and a fence and being *properly* mourned. I did that well enough. I know. Who cares. But –"

Professor Raynite: "But Gila, six months ago you could never have articulated that series of thoughts. Give yourself a little credit."

Gila: "I can't. Because I set out to say *more* than that. Or, to say something different. Bigger. That...I don't know what. About –"

Professor Raynite: "But, Gila it takes time. You're how old? Twenty-five?"

Gila: "That's not the point, you know it. You don't need to make me feel better. I know the paper didn't make the point I meant it to. It failed, didn't it?"

Professor Raynite: [staring at Gila] "It started to say that grief can be unconventional but, no, it didn't say how or what you mean by that."

Gila: "I said the stories that we tell of grief are all straightforward, easy. Even when they take a longer time or someone does it Holden Caulfield style, there's always a catharsis and relief. There's always, somehow, a heroic moment of seeing you're beyond your losses. Even Eggers, playing frisbee on the beach. But I don't get it. I don't see how you can lose the things that keep you whole and then regain them, ever. Everything I read keeps saying there's a moment that's *beyond* what happened. You grieve and then, at some point, there's the other side and magically you got there. But there's something I don't understand. What if you've given up the voice, the ghosts, and still you aren't free? The nights are yours, okay. You aren't the same kid who talks to those who left a while ago, but you aren't back to normal either."

Professor Raynite: "Loss is complicated. You don't need to understand it all in a single graduate paper."

Gila: "I'm not just trying to understand it, there was something I was trying to *say*. I used the words we learned in class. I used the readings. I learned everything, and –"

Professor Raynite: "And *then* some."

Gila: "Fine. I read *a lot*. Reading is easy. You always told me not to hide behind the reading but to say what I actually *thought*, what I actually *saw*. But I didn't do that, did I? Couldn't. Grieving doesn't look like letting go. But then *what is it?* It isn't simply stuckness. It's more complex. It's neither letting go nor holding on."

Professor Raynite: "It sounds like you're onto something with that thought."

Gila: "Then why can't I *finish* it? If it's neither of those things, what is it?"

Professor Raynite: "What do you think?"

Gila: "But *that's* just what's wrong, I *can't*."
    [the Professor looks at Gila, tilting her head concerned. Gila looks at the ground]
    "And this time, I'm not being shy. Or, holding back. I have the language that *you* taught me. I can say, 'there's something incoherent about the teleology of losing' but when it's then my turn to say just what I mean, it's quiet in my head, it's blank. Do you know why this is happening to me? I don't get it. I don't get what I did wrong? I thought...I thought if only I had *language* I could channel what I *feel* but don't know how to say. But then I get there, when it's time to formulate what I know of grief, and I can't say *any*thing. It's quiet still.

And, I'm not overwhelmed this time. I don't get where I went wrong in all of this. This is the first paper I ever worked so hard to write."

Professor Raynite: "You wrote a fantastic paper, Gila."

Gila: "I took my thought as far as I could take it and then...it's like the film reel ended."

Professor Raynite: "Do you want to be an academic? You could get in anywhere you wanted to go. I'm not saying that's what you should do necessarily, but you can spend years working on questions like these, if that's something you're interested in."

Gila: "I thought so, maybe. But not if this is all I'm capable of."

Professor Raynite: "Come on, Gila, don't you think you're being a little harsh with yourself? I mean, don't get me wrong, I'm game for all kinds of self-hating habits, but really? Maybe you just need more time to think this through?"

Gila: "*Time* is if my mind was tripping up but that's not happening. It's not my *brain* that's getting stuck. It's not something I'm having trouble *thinking*. I know this doesn't really make sense, Professor Raynite, does this not make sense? It's like I'm having trouble *seeing* what I think. Does that sound weird? What's wrong with me? I feel like something must be wrong with me. I gave up everything that held me back. I left. I let him go. I said I have to do my own thing now. I served as I had promised but...I'll watch them still, of course, but now I'm David. I am David now, running where I feel like it, doing my own thing...I'm free. I'm free. Why can't I *see* the place my thinking takes me? I am a former prince who ran a kingdom once, until Ms. Tobin said, "I bet you *behind every prince there is a young man yearning to be free,* be free." And, I went once and went again and then came here and here you taught me how to talk about the things I know and now...What's wrong with me? Can you please tell me? Help me see? I'm sorry, I said more than you care to know, I'm sorry, I just –"

Professor Raynite: "It's fine. I don't know what to tell you though."

☙

It is mid-winter, in Mrs. Barish's garden floor office on the Upper West Side. The streets outside are quiet in that late hour after school, before dinner. Mrs. Barish is wearing a dark blue turtleneck and slacks, her suit jacket hanging over her chair. Gila is in jeans and a pin-stripe pink buttoned-down shirt, loafers, her messenger bag. Mrs. Barish is sitting, slightly reclined, in her analyst chair across Gila who is upright, at the farthest edge of the office sofa.

Gila: "I don't know what to say."

Mrs. Barish: "That's okay. We can take our time."

Gila: "Is there anything you can ask me? To help me start?"

Mrs. Barish: "Maybe you can talk about whatever is on your mind?"

Gila: "What if I can't?"

Mrs. Barish: "Maybe you can just let yourself see what it feels like to try."

[long silence]

Gila: "I don't know."

Mrs. Barish: "What don't you know?"

Gila: "What to say."

Mrs. Barish: "Well, what are you feeling? Why don't we start with you telling me about that?"

Gila: "Oh."

Mrs. Barish: "Oh what?"

Gila: "That isn't any easier."

Mrs. Barish: [smiling] "Feelings are hard to talk about, aren't they?"

Gila: "I don't know. I guess."

Mrs. Barish: "Sometimes the defenses we use in one instance in our lives are no longer good for us at other moments in our life."

Gila: "Oh yeah, you were saying something along those lines the last time."

Mrs. Barish: "Yes."

Gila: "If I'm understanding you correctly, you're basically suggesting that I use my intellect as a defense against my feelings?"

Mrs. Barish: "What do you think?"

Gila: "What do I think? I think you're dead wrong."

Mrs. Barish: "Oh?"

Gila: "What I don't understand about that interpretation is that it doesn't account for what I was trying to tell you last time, and also the first time I came in here. About what happened in Chicago. How I tried to write about grief and then I couldn't. How I got stuck."

Mrs. Barish: "Yes, I remember you talked about that."

Gila: "You don't seem to be registering what a big deal that was."

Mrs. Barish: "What is it you feel I'm not understanding? Maybe you could explain it a little better for me."

Gila: "I'm not sure I necessarily can because it seems so obvious how relevant that story is but if you don't think so then I think maybe it wasn't...I get discouraged easily. But I really think it's kind of essential to understanding what I'm trying to describe."

Mrs. Barish: "Go on. Please."

Gila: "Do you think you could try to do a better job of paying attention, please?"

Mrs. Barish: [smiling] "I'll try."

Gila: "So, I told you that I was writing a paper on grief and that I was deconstructing Freud's argument on the difference between 'mourning' and 'melancholia,' wherein he basically designates the difference between healthy and pathological mourning as a difference in scale and length of duration. The right kind of mourning is linear, straightforward, more or less abides by normative tropes of progress and self-development, that whole thing. And, on the other hand, there's melancholia, where the mourner does not let go, holds on tightly to the lost object well past the point when he should be doing so and has a kind of haunted semi-life as a result. I talk about Eggers and gender and sexuality and all manner of things that aren't relevant here, to you, but the part that is has to do with the fact that I wanted to say something *isn't* working about this model of the psyche."

Mrs. Barish: "That paper by Freud is a very interesting one."

Gila: "Right, but I was trying to deconstruct it. By which I mean *critique* it. I thought it didn't get things right."

Mrs. Barish: "Uh-huh. But you know, Freud isn't saying that all melancholia is necessarily a bad thing. He understands that there's a range of ways of mourning."

Gila: "Okay, sure, but that isn't really my point."

Mrs. Barish: "Oh?"

Gila: "No, I'm not having an issue with Freud, per se. And, I'm not saying this theory is being dogmatic or formulaic or whatever. I get bored with those kinds of arguments. I'm saying something else, about how mourning doesn't work that way."

Mrs. Barish: "It's more complicated than that."

Gila: "Yeah. Exactly."

Mrs. Barish: "Of course. I don't think any clinician actually believes that mourning has to fit into either one of those categories."

Gila: "Okay. Right. But, that isn't really what I'm saying either. I'm not trying to say some version of this theory is outdated. Or, simplistic. I'm saying there's a flaw in the underlying logic by which Freud imagines that loss can adhere to a certain kind of developmental template."

Mrs. Barish: [smiling] "Do you want to say more about that?"

Gila: "Well, just that I think Freud is trying to superimpose a familiar way of thinking about growth onto the way trauma works and I don't think they work the same way. Growing up may follow a certain pattern but losing someone doesn't, necessarily."

Mrs. Barish: "And, what does it mean to you, this argument about Freud?"

Gila: "What do you mean, what does it mean to me? Aren't you understanding what I'm saying?"

Mrs. Barish: "I think I am, but I'm trying to focus on how this is relevant to what's going on here."

Gila: "I'm *telling* you how this is relevant. I'm telling you that I think grief works differently than we tend to think it does. And, I can work through his argument, pointing out the inconsistencies. But then, when I have to say how I think it *does* work, something happens, and I can't. I want to say something about how mourning isn't a straight line, or even just a messier one, but something else. That it's not like: you were there and now you're here and healed, and we get it, you've *been* through shit, you're broken but...that it's something else."

Mrs. Barish: "You're talking about how painful it is."

Gila: "No. I'm not. I'm talking about how it isn't *good enough* to say, you've been through stuff and now you're damaged, ravaged, riven, torn."

Mrs. Barish: "Why not?"

Gila: "Because it's more than that. Because you're fucked up, in some deep way that you don't get over, even after years or months or talking or whatever they say helps you move on."

Mrs. Barish: "Do you think your ideas about this are influenced by your experience?"

Gila: "Are you serious? What else would they be influenced by?"

Mrs. Barish: "Yes. So, what's the problem then?"

Gila: "The *problem* is that I can't say what I actually think is going on. How grieving *actually* works. Okay, it isn't conventional or the conventions need to be changed. But then, what's going on? The thought is right there, in my mind, but I can't touch it. I can't say it, clearly. Can't *say* it at all."

Mrs. Barish: "Hm. But aren't you saying it to me, right now?"

Gila: "No, not really. I'm just saying something about x doesn't work, but I'm not saying what *I* think instead. What is happening when we lost something we needed? What happens in the mind? I am circling the answer but every time it is the time to say it, I can't see it. It goes blank inside my head. Or, quiet. Something...I don't know. There's something I'm not seeing but it isn't that my brain's not working. It isn't –"

Mrs. Barish: "Maybe it has to do with feelings."

Gila: "Say more, please."

Mrs. Barish: "Well, I was just finding myself wondering what you're *feeling* about grieving and if that is relevant here."

Gila: "Continue."

Mrs. Barish: "Well, just that maybe what you need isn't really to *think* about it more, but to *feel* something about it."

Gila: "Well, you're right, it has to do with feelings. That's where I got to, also. After Chicago. That's why I'm here. It seemed to me that I know my mind well enough to tell that the problem isn't technical, so to speak. I read everything. I read so much. I understand it. That part is easy. But something is getting stuck."

Mrs. Barish: "I think you have good instincts Gila."

Gila: "I don't know. I don't see what else it could be."

Mrs. Barish: "I think you're right that your feelings are what need attention."

Gila: "So, what do I do?"

Mrs. Barish: "What you're doing. You start to talk about your feelings. Like you're doing."

Gila: "But, this isn't getting anywhere. Or, not getting where the feelings are."

Mrs. Barish: "Yes, but we're just starting. I think that over time it will."

Gila: "No, I don't agree. These aren't feelings that I'm expressing now. These are ideas. Let's not get distracted with classifying different states of being. I only mean, that I'm not feeling something now. I'm just talking about what I think."

Mrs. Barish: "Hm. Well, can you try to talk about your feelings?"

Gila: "I don't have any!"

Mrs. Barish: "Maybe you're just letting your mind do all the work so you don't have a chance to know what you're feeling. Maybe we can pause this conversation for a moment and try to see what you might be feeling?"

Gila: "I'm *not* feeling anything."

Mrs. Barish: [smiling] "Perhaps this is what we were talking about the other day, that you have two different parts of yourself. An intellectual and an emotional self, and the mental side is just so much more powerful than –"

Gila: "You aren't listening. I'm not being defensive."

Mrs. Barish: "Of course you're more comfortable talking about mourning in the abstract, but that's what makes therapy different from writing a paper."

Gila: "I'm going to ignore the implicit hierarchization of self-reflective activities because that would take too long to deconstruct. Although, it *is* annoying, by the way, how you can't acknowledge the power of thinking and writing to organize and push feelings forward. Anyway, yes, I was saying that writing about mourning isn't abstract! I have more feelings reading papers and talking about them than I *ever* do in here when you ask me, when we're talking about things that I'm *supposed* to have deep feelings about! Reading Eggers, Henry

James, AIDS memoirs, Joan Didion, John Donne, *that* stuff brings me to tears. This stuff...I can't relate to what you're asking me."

Mrs. Barish: "Maybe that's because it's harder to have your own feelings."

Gila: "But, I do have my own feelings! Just not when I'm sitting here talking to *you*."

Mrs. Barish: "Well, maybe that's because I'm asking you to talk about things that are uncomfortable for you."

Gila: "Like what?"

Mrs. Barish: "Like your feelings about your loss, for one thing. Or, about your past more generally. You don't say anything about your mother even though I'm sure you have a tremendous amount of feeling about her. It sounds like she was very difficult? You never mention your husband, so I don't know anything about him. There is a whole lot that most people talk about in here that you are refusing to approach and I think we need to start there if we want to get to know you better."

Gila: "But, this *is* getting to know me. Why would I need to talk about that stuff? It's so goddamn boring. I wouldn't survive the process of telling it to you. There is this scene in Eggers where he says, *there, I've told you all the gruesome details of my parents' deaths, you even know many times a day I masturbate, now what do you know? I have given you nothing. This is like a snake shedding its skin!* I love that moment; it's how I feel in here. I wish that you could understand –"

Mrs. Barish: "But, Gila, you haven't told me those details, about the losses you've endured. You refuse to talk about them at all."

Gila: "Because they're *not* relevant. To my question. To this. They are relevant to my life, of course. To how I ended up here, to why I talk in this way, and whatever, but they are not the reason I can't see what I'm trying to say, or that something is blocking me. You're looking for some terrible thing I've repressed, but I haven't. Can't you understand that?"

Mrs. Barish: "I didn't say you were *repressing* anything."

Gila: "No, maybe not but that's the logic you're using. And also, why do you keep saying I'm *refusing* to talk. I'm not refusing in some obnoxious way. When I say I'm a good kid everywhere else, it's because I would do whatever you wanted me to if I could. I don't *want* to be difficult anywhere, ever, with anyone, but this isn't about my personal preferences. I thought we were trying to figure something out? So, if I'm not going certain places, it's because they aren't in the right direction. You reading it that way. though, suggests to me that you're interpreting my behavior based on your own sense of being injured by the way I'm asking to be heard."

Mrs. Barish: [smiling] "Gila, does it occur to you that maybe you don't always know the right direction to go in?"

Gila: "You're smiling like you think it's obvious that this whole diatribe of mine is really a defense."

Mrs. Barish: "Well? Do you think it's possible that maybe *I* know something about where you need to go?"

Gila: "No. No offense. But no."

Mrs. Barish: "Maybe that's a problem. That you don't trust me."

Gila: "You're getting distracted."

Mrs. Barish: "Excuse me?"

Gila: "You're getting distracted by stupid things like do I trust you? *Of course* I don't trust you. Why would I? But, that doesn't matter. I need you to set aside your own shrink-ego for a moment, please."

Mrs. Barish: "What matters then?"

Gila: "I don't know. At least that's finally a better question though."

Mrs. Barish: "You say the past is irrelevant. That you don't need to talk about it in order to understand what's happening now. But, what about your feelings about your family? Do you think any of that is relevant to what you're going through now?"

Gila: "I don't know. Like what?"

Mrs. Barish: "Like losing your father. You must have been angry? Or, your grief at being left with your mother. That must have been difficult. I'm sure it wasn't easy to be fighting with your mom right after your father died."

Gila: "But, I *didn't* fight with her. I have never fought with her."

Mrs. Barish: "But, you mentioned that she was difficult and –"

Gila: "She was. She made everything ten times more difficult than it ever needed to be. But, I couldn't *fight* with her. She couldn't help it."

Mrs. Barish: "You feel protective of her?"

Gila: "You're not getting it. It's not that kind of thing where I have secret feelings about her that I've *repressed* and now you're going to get me to *express* them. It was my *job* to raise them both, that's all. That's what I tried to do. Do you get mad at a teenager for being a teenager? Maybe sometimes, but you *understand* it. That's how it was with her."

Mrs. Barish: "I'm not trying to say there are certain feelings that you should have felt, I just think there must be a lot of feelings there."

Gila: "Maybe, but not the way you're looking for them."

Mrs. Barish: "How can you be so sure?"

Gila: "I'm *telling* you how! Because, I don't have that *feeling self* that you keep looking for. You keep saying, what about *this* feeling? Let's go back and be defenseless and talk about *that* feeling. If only I would stop my mind from getting in the way, all would be revealed etcetera, but you don't seem to understand that I don't *feel* things in the way that you're describing. Never have."

Mrs. Barish: "Yes. But, I think that's because your intellectual self is more powerful and you need help letting your emotional self out."

Gila: "Again with that dichotomy! What if I don't have the kind of emotional self you're talking about?"

Mrs. Barish: "Of course you do. It's just that you're resistant because that is the part of you that doesn't know everything all the time. That's vulnerable and you don't want to be in that place, which I can't blame you for. But, that's where we would need to go if you want this work to help you."

Gila: "But…I don't get it. It doesn't add up."

Mrs. Barish: "Sure it does. Everyone has resistances, Gila."

Gila: "Fine. Yes, maybe. But, what I *don't* get is why you're talking about this, about me as though my cerebral self is somehow like a gate that we need to slip past to get to my feelings."

Mrs. Barish: "I couldn't have said it better myself."

Gila: "But, *I'm* not saying that. That makes no sense."

Mrs. Barish: "Of course it does. You just said yourself that your feelings are blocked."

Gila: "But not by my thoughts!"

Mrs. Barish: "This is semantics, Gila."

Gila: "Are you kidding me? This is language. And, we communicate in *language,* for better or worse."

Mrs. Barish: "I just think you're doing here exactly what you're describing. You're trying to bring an emotional moment under the control of your rational mind."

Gila: "I can't believe you're *actually* saying this, actually *believing* that I have a feeling 'self' hiding behind an intellectual one. It is so simplistic that it's embarrassing. It is so...you obviously didn't hear the part where I explained that I am trying to talk with you. That I am *not* holding my feelings back."

Mrs. Barish: "Well, sure I did, I heard you say that, but then I can also see that you're *not* sharing your feelings with me."

Gila: "I know but not because I am *resisting,* or whatever. I'm *trying* to talk to you."

Mrs. Barish: [throwing up her hands, exaggeratedly] "Well, then what's going on?"

Gila: "I don't know! *That's* the problem I'm trying to solve! Why can I only have deep feelings when I'm reading or talking to teachers? That's what *I* don't understand. Because it's more than just small differences, or that I don't trust you, or that you ask distracting, often inane questions. That all seems beside the point. I can't even *relate* to the person you're describing, who's been through shit and feels some things about it. It's like you're describing someone else. When I listen to Professor Raynite or when Ms. Tobin talks to me, I know that there are things I feel. But otherwise, I don't know, it isn't there."

Mrs. Barish: "I think by now this kind of verbal acrobatics is probably second nature to you."

Gila: "Meaning?"

Mrs. Barish: "That your intellect is a very precocious machine, protecting you from unwanted feelings. So that even when you try to feel something, you can't."

Gila: "I can't believe this! It doesn't seem to matter what I say. In your mind, my feelings are there but I don't want to talk about them because...I am resistant? Because I'd rather be a shithead, going from therapist to therapist, each one calling me a different version of an asshole? You're right, my feelings *are* in prison and I'm the guard holding the keys. I'm just too *fucking* comfortable or resistant or chicken shit to let them out. My mind is precious armor, lucky me! That must be why the *only* time I've gotten *close* to any feelings that felt deep, it was with people who could *think* with me. Why I have the most intensity of emotion when my *mind* is helping me to sharpen what I see."

Mrs. Barish: "I'm not saying your mind is the bad guy."

Gila: "Yes you goddamn are! I can't believe it."

Mrs. Barish: "I think you're misunderstanding me. Your mind is very important to you, and no one is taking it away from you. I'm only saying that it has a defensive function as well."

Gila: "But, you're absolutely *wrong*. Not that a mind can't be defensive. Not that I can't intellectualize. Not that I can't enlist my mind in the service of some heavy-duty resistance to the cure. But, that's *not* what I'm describing here. I want to know the things I feel. I am desperate to find out what I know. For god's sake, I write and have always written. I break my head. I talk to teachers. I always want to know what's true. I am begging you to help me see the things I can't see, but you're just getting distracted by some reductionist distinction that misses the point and, therefore, the problem and...whatever, it doesn't matter."

Mrs. Barish: "But, Gila, I *am* trying to help you."

Gila: "Then, tell me what I need to do. I know something isn't working."

Mrs. Barish: "I *am* telling you what I think you need."

Gila: "To talk?"

Mrs. Barish: "That's right."

Gila: "About my feelings."

Mrs. Barish: "Yes."

Gila: "Even though I say I can't."

Mrs. Barish: "I think you can."

Gila: "I should just check my thinking at the door and surrender to what's buried deep inside."

Mrs. Barish: "Well, hey, you don't have to check your mind anywhere. You have a wonderful mind. Maybe we can trust that it will still be there, when you need it."

Gila: "What if I don't think the two parts are separate?"

Mrs. Barish: "I can't force you to talk, if you don't want to. You know that."

Gila: "But, I didn't say I didn't *want* to."

Mrs. Barish: "Well, then I think you can."

Gila: "Whatever."

Mrs. Barish: "I'm not sure what that's supposed to mean."

Gila: "It isn't. Nothing."

Mrs. Barish: "Well we're out of time for today. But, maybe next time you can tell me what it means?"

Gila: "It means you aren't listening. I'm sorry. I like you but –"

Mrs. Barish: "I like you too."

Gila: "I wish I could be different, so that maybe I could work with you. I'm sorry. I am. It's probably my fault. But I'm not built that way. I can't."

It is the end of January. Bitter cold temperatures, hard ice, and snow. On this Saturday morning, in Midtown Manhattan, the auditorium is being warmed by the crowds of eager students and clinicians filling its seats. The famous Dr. Caroline Jaspers is lecturing on the future of feminist thought within psychoanalysis. Gila is sitting in a row at the back, alongside other students and friends taking courses on psychoanalysis that term.

Before the lecture begins, Gila has been saying to the person next to her that she has never read any of Jaspers's work but thinks it's a little more historical-political than what she's usually interested in. They are chatting and laughing before the lecture begins. As soon as the lecture is over, Gila, restless to get up, says to her seatmate that she has to run down the auditorium steps, to the edge of the stage. When noticing Gila's nervousness, the girl asks her if everything is okay. Gila says that she can't breathe, she needs to talk to Dr. Jaspers, needs to find a way to introduce herself before she leaves.

Caroline Jaspers is in her late sixties, a small, angular frame, rugged open face and bright blue eyes. She has short and shaggy white hair that she runs her fingers through periodically. She is wearing faded black jeans and a black half-zip sweater, looking mannish, confident, and athletic. She looks simultaneously sprightly and immersed intensively in thought. She has an accent but it's not traceable to any particular language, so much as the culmination of multiple fluencies: German, French, English, the American Midwest. After a train of people have come on stage to congratulate her on her lecture and shake her hand, and some familiar friends have spent excited moments catching up, Dr. Caroline Jaspers glances over at Gila, who is looking up at her on stage, waiting. Dr. Caroline Jaspers notices that Gila is still there. Ten, then twenty minutes later and when there is a break in the parade of people vying for her attention, she takes a few steps to the edge of the stage and bends her knees, leans forward, asks, "Are you waiting for me?"

Gila: "Yes."

Dr. Caroline Jaspers: "What can I do for you?"

Gila: "My name is Gila. Ashtor. You need to be my analyst."

Dr. Caroline Jaspers: [smiles broadly and looks surprised] "Is that so?"

Gila: "Yes, please. I am begging you. I know that you don't know me but I've been looking and...it's you. You need to please say yes. I am a student, I finished a degree and now I'm planning a PhD. I study philosophy and literature, I –"

Dr. Caroline Jaspers: "Whoa, okay, hold it there. What did you say your name was?"

Gila: "Gila."

Dr. Caroline Jaspers: "Now, Gila, I am very flattered that you think maybe I can help you. But, this is a little unusual."

Gila: "I know, I'm sorry. It's just that I've been looking. Everywhere. And just now, the way you talked. I know that I can talk to you. Please. I will do anything. I will –"

Dr. Caroline Jaspers: "Now, now, let's not get so far ahead of ourselves, okay? How about I give you my card? I am sure I have a card somewhere."

[she begins rummaging through the pockets of her jeans. Then, not finding one, calls to an assistant nearby to pass her a card, which she does]

Dr. Caroline Jaspers: "Good. Here it is. This is my card. What do you say you call me and we can make arrangements to talk about this more in person? What did you say your name was? Ah, yes, Gila. I'll remember. Call me and leave me a message and we'll make a plan to meet, okay?"

࿓

It is a frigid and bright January winter day on New York City's Lower East Side. The streets, normally bustling with skaters, dealers, high school kids and local area inhabitants, is deserted and quiet in the morning. Like most buildings in the area, this one is decrepit: the paint is peeling off the doors, the buzzer isn't working, and there is faded graffiti across the residents' directory. Gila checks the business card again and again, walks back and forth to see the addresses on other buildings, to make sure this is the right one. She is wearing jeans, a buttoned-down navy sweater and loafers. After waiting for someone from the building to leave so the door can open again, Caroline Jaspers appears in the same faded black jeans and black half-zip sweater.

Dr. Caroline Jaspers: "Oh, come in, come in! It is so cold outside! This buzzer isn't working, eh? Ach! Come and get warmed up."

   [Dr. Jaspers winds them through to a dimly lit corner basement apartment, at the back of the building. There is a single bookshelf of dusty hardcovers, a desk with piles of papers covering its surface, two leather armchairs with end tables propping up lamps and a small dark chestnut velvet couch]

Dr. Caroline Jaspers: "Come in, come in. Would you like some tea?"

Gila: [startled] "No, thank you. It's okay."

Dr. Caroline Jaspers: "I have a kettle here, it's very easy? Will you let me know if you change your mind? I drink so many cups of tea sitting here all day."

Gila: "Thank you, very much. Thank you for agreeing to meet me."

Dr. Caroline Jaspers: "Yes, well. It's not everyday someone comes up to you at a conference as you did and says what you said, eh? Pretty unusual? And I've been doing this a very long time. But we'll get to that a little later. You can call me Caroline, if you'd like. I tell my patients and my students to do whatever feels comfortable to them."

Gila: "Thank you, Dr. Jaspers."

Dr. Caroline Jaspers: "Yes, I didn't think you would elect to use my first name. There's something very formal about you, isn't there? So unusual for your age. That's okay, whatever helps you feel at ease. Get comfortable, please. You look so nervous."

Gila: [shifts in her seat, tries to lean back but then sits upright again] "Thank you, yes, I can get very nervous sometimes. I'm sorry."

Dr. Caroline Jaspers: "We all do, don't we? And, it's just so cold out there. I apologize you had to wait out there. These aren't very fancy digs for a scholar of psychoanalysis, yes? Ach, it'll have to do, won't it."

Gila: "It's very warm."

Dr. Caroline Jaspers: "You like it? Good, I'm glad to hear that. It is my corner. I can't complain. Of course, it would be nice to have more space and slightly better, more, how shall we say, presentable surroundings. I know so many of my colleagues are uptown on the West or East Side. But, I have always been here. I'm rather comfortable with it, I have to say. It's a little rough. But, it is warm, isn't it?"

Gila: "Yes."

Dr. Caroline Jaspers: "So. Would you like to tell me a little bit about yourself? You mentioned that you are a student, is that right? I don't think I caught the nature of your studies, do you mind telling me again?"

Gila: "I studied literature and philosophy at Chicago. Now I am taking some courses in psychoanalysis. I want to continue on to a PhD, I think. I love psychoanalysis, but I miss the rigor of academe and...I don't know. I came here, to the city, trying to figure something out about myself, but I don't know how to be in therapy. That's why I came up to you the way I did. I know it is unusual. I'm sorry. But...the way you lectured. It's like, I already trust you. I know that sounds very strange but I've felt this way before with certain people. So, I know that I'm not wrong. Even though it sounds like I'm basing it on almost nothing."

Dr. Caroline Jaspers: "I'm not too concerned with how unusual it sounds. I believe you can see something in someone pretty quickly. That doesn't sound so hard to comprehend. Now I'm not exactly sure what you saw in *me,* per se, but that's a different matter. I understand the general feeling you're trying to describe, I think."

Gila: "Thank you, so much, thank you. I was worried you would dismiss me out of hand. I brought things that I've written in school, so you can see that my interests are related to things you're interested in. In case that will help you decide to take me on as a patient."

Dr. Caroline Jaspers: "Oh? If you brought me papers that you'd like me to read, I'm happy to do so. Sure. Of course. It would be a good way to get to know you better."

Gila: "Thank you. Oh, thank you so much. I am so grateful; I don't know what to say."

Dr. Caroline Jaspers: "Well, but let's hold it there a moment, because it's not that simple. You see, I'm leaving psychoanalysis. Well, not leaving the field, of course, but I'm moving to a different country, where I will focus more on writing. I have been appointed the general editor of Winnicott's papers, which is a lovely honor of course, but also a tremendous time commitment. I am winding down my practice here, you see? I can't take on new patients."

Gila: "But –"

Dr. Caroline Jaspers: "I know, this must be terribly disappointing for you and I'm deeply sorry about that. You seem like you're really and very determinedly searching for something. I am sorry because I can see that you thought that I could give it to you. But there's just no way around it. It isn't personal, you can see that, I hope?"

Gila: "But you would be perfect. I can't go back, out there, to looking. I can't. You don't understand. I have...I met so many people. I tried. Please. You have to hear me out. This isn't typical. I –"

Dr. Caroline Jaspers: "I know. I'm sorry. I can see this is terrible news for you. I am very sorry. Now, would it help, do you think, to tell me a little bit about what you're looking for? Or, what it is you think I understand that other people don't? Maybe it would help me get to know you a little better to hear some of that. Shall we try that?"

Gila: [shaking her head, looking at the ground] "I don't know. I've tried to be in therapy. I keep trying. Different therapists. So many different kinds. More Freudian, less Freudian. People who specialize in trauma, in Kohut, in working with grief, whatever. But all I hear, from everyone, is that I'm defensive. Or, resistant. That I don't know how to be in therapy. That I don't know how to talk. Which is true. I don't know how to talk. Except to certain people that *aren't* therapists. Everyone has told me that I'm either playing games, protecting my defensive self, or refusing to surrender. They all say different versions of 'you aren't willing to do the work of really being a patient,' even though I don't think I'm *doing* anything at all. I just can't talk the way they want me to. I don't know why."

Dr. Caroline Jaspers: "Hm. Why do you think they're saying that?"

Gila: "Because it's difficult for me to talk. And, when they try to ask me questions, I get distracted by their underlying assumptions, which I can hear in their questions. But, when I try to point that out, it just devolves. And then they say I'm intellectualizing or displacing my emotions or distracting them on purpose so I don't have to be the vulnerable one. I can see how it would look that way. I can be very rude, I guess. But, I'm not doing what they *think* I'm doing, I'm really not. I'm *trying* to talk, but I can't do it. Not like that."

Dr. Caroline Jaspers: "Well, I can see, I think, how that might happen. People don't take too kindly to having their prejudices pointed out to them, now do they?"

Gila: "No. But it's my fault, really. I know it is. I am impatient. And I don't talk about what I'm supposed to talk about."

Dr. Caroline Jaspers: "And, what is it that you're supposed to talk about?"

Gila: "I don't know. My childhood. My father died when I was 12. He got sick when I was eight. He had a rare blood cancer. My mother is difficult and I took care of her and my baby brother. She is volatile and destructive. But we got along, made it work. And, the bakery business. I ran that when I was there and now I take care of things from afar. Which is different but we're all very close. I had an older brother too – who died."

Dr. Caroline Jaspers: [sighing and rustling her hair] "I'm sorry to hear that. It's awful to have so much loss when you're still very young. You said you were how old?"

Gila: "Eight when he got sick, twelve when he died."

Dr. Caroline Jaspers: "Such a pivotal age."

Gila: "I don't know."

Dr. Caroline Jaspers: "Well, sure you do. You have read something of child development, I presume? So, you know that 12 is an age when you are going from being a child to becoming an adolescent. It is puberty. It is such a difficult time where so much change is happening. And, for you to lose your father then [shakes her head]. It's such a difficult time for that kind of loss. You were close to your father, I take it? From the brief way you described it, I gathered that was the case."

Gila: "Yes. Very. We talked. We could connect that way. I couldn't ever do that with anyone else."

Dr. Caroline Jaspers: "You mean with your mother and brother?"

Gila: "Yeah. They are both very different. I get along with them fine, it's nothing like that. I just...I never talked to them. I only could do that with my dad."

Dr. Caroline Jaspers: "That's a tremendous loss then, isn't it, of course?"

Gila: [her voice is beginning to crack] "I don't understand why I can feel the effect of that here but not when I'm talking to others, other therapists."

Dr. Caroline Jaspers: "Hm. I wonder. What do you think?"

Gila: "I don't know. With you, when I say these things, they have meaning, somehow. Like you *understand* it. But, I don't feel that when I try to talk to others. I end up thinking it all means nothing, I have no feeling, or something like that. I'm so confused."

Dr. Caroline Jaspers: "Hm, yes, that is interesting. I wonder what you're trying to tell me."

Gila: "It's like you know me, somehow. Already. The way you listen. I don't know."

Dr. Caroline Jaspers: "I'm surprised because I don't think I'm really listening in a particularly special way. I'm just hearing what you're saying."

Gila: "But then, why do I feel comfortable? Why do I trust you?"

Dr. Caroline Jaspers: "Well, I don't know, why do you? Do you think it's something I said in my lecture? Did something seem meaningful to you then?"

Gila: "No, I don't think so. The truth is, I don't even know what you said in your lecture. I couldn't really concentrate. As soon as you started talking, it was your voice. All I could pay attention to was the *way* you sounded."

Dr. Caroline Jaspers: "And what way was that?"

Gila: "I don't know. Rigorous. Warm. Tender and severe. Precise. I felt that I could tell you anything and you would understand it."

Dr. Caroline Jaspers: "Hm. Interesting." [she runs her fingers through her hair, then folds one leg across the other and leans an elbow on her knees] "So, perhaps it's something then about my being an academic. A professor. Perhaps, it has something to do with that?"

Gila: "Yes, maybe. It's like I know your mind is solid. I can trust it with my thinking and I guess the feelings follow afterward?"

Dr. Caroline Jaspers: "Ah-ha. Yes. That makes some sense."

Gila: "It does?"

Dr. Caroline Jaspers: "Sure. Yes. You need to know there is something solid, as you say, underneath you. And, without that, you feel unsafe."

Gila: "But then, why is everyone saying my thinking is defensive?"

Dr. Caroline Jaspers: "Well, I don't know. Of course thinking can be defensive. But, as I'm sure you know from what you've read, *anything* can be defensive."

Gila: "But, does that mean I can only talk to someone who is also a professor? Please, that can't be true. I have been looking for so long and everything always ends up the same way. Is there any way you can talk to me long-distance? Anything? Please. It is impossible for me to talk to anyone."

Dr. Caroline Jaspers: [leans her head back and then brings it forward again] "Gila, don't I wish I could. I see how much you long for some kind of understanding. It is palpable, your yearning for relief."

Gila: [starts to cry a little] "Please. I will do anything. I am a good student. I can take a course? I can visit wherever you'll be once in a while?"

Dr. Caroline Jaspers: "Oh, Gila, it isn't *like* that. Believe me, if I could take you on I would. I would do it in a heartbeat. But –"

Gila: "Then, please. You have to help me. I am so lost out there and I just keep thinking I don't know how to change enough to work with some of the people I've met."

Dr. Caroline Jaspers: "I know. And, believe me when I say that if there was any way I could do it, I would. I really would. Which doesn't mean it wouldn't be a battle between us, you and I, for sure. But, I could take it on, or at least I think I could."

Gila: "But, maybe it doesn't have to be a battle? I will be very good."

Dr. Caroline Jaspers: "Oh no, I don't *want* you to be very good! It would be a challenge, there's no doubt. But, I would do it, I would, if I were continuing to stay in private practice. And, in the country. But, I'm leaving, you see. When you get to my stage in life, it's about time to redirect things and I simply don't have the time to write the way I'd like to when I'm working with so many patients. This was a very tough decision, trust me. Precisely for reasons such as these. I feel drawn to try to help you, but what can I do? I am leaving in a few weeks."

Gila: "But. What...I don't know what to do. I really don't."

Dr. Caroline Jaspers: "Yes, that is the question isn't it?" [leans forward, runs her fingers through her hair, exhales, and leans back again]

Gila: "I wish I knew how to be like this with other people, but I don't. I can't. I never know what to talk about. Or, *how to* talk."

Dr. Caroline Jaspers: "And, you can't start talking as you have done here, with me. Because you don't yet trust their minds and so you don't feel that they'll understand. Yes? I see. But then the process of trying to know their minds, so you can feel comfortable, ends up making you seem like you're defensive and intellectualizing, yes? When really I think you're trying to steer them in a different direction?"

Gila: "Yeah, *toward* my feelings. I don't *want* to get caught up arguing about what I think about x or y."

Dr. Caroline Jaspers: "But, that happens anyway?"

Gila: "Because they think that I'm resistant instead of actually struggling. That I'm *withholding* feelings or something. But, I'm not! That's what I don't know how to make them see."

Dr. Caroline Jaspers: "Ah yes, I think I'm starting to understand. They assume that if you can be so eloquent about what you're thinking that you must be able to talk about what you're feeling as well."

Gila: "And, that if I'm not, I'm being difficult. But, I'm not *being* difficult. I don't think? I don't know anymore. Maybe I am without realizing it, I don't know. I keep trying to tell them that I don't have the feelings I'm supposed to have. I don't know why this is."

Dr. Caroline Jaspers: "No one is seeing that you're scared. You're not withholding. No, that isn't right, no. I see that clearly. You want the *truth*. That is clear. Some patients *don't,* and you have to understand that too. It is something you see in this work all the time. You have to respect that and move slowly... Remember Freud said that patients come in and say, doctor I am sick, fix my symptom, yes? You remember that? Of course. Well, so you can see that not everyone wants to really know what's going on in their own minds, but I see that you *do*. You are hungry to understand what's going on with you. It's very admirable, Gila, very brave."

Gila: [shakes her head and stares at the ground, trying not to cry] "How did you understand all that? It is exactly right, exactly what happens. It doesn't matter what I say, it ends up seeming like resistance of some kind. I don't know how to say what you just said. But also, I don't know how to talk to them if they can't understand that, right away. Why can't other people see it, like you do? You know me even less than most of them. I don't understand."

Dr. Caroline Jaspers: "This is difficult work. And, actually, I think the truth is that you don't really need someone who *understands* things better, per se. I think you understand quite a bit already. I think you're probably far more brilliant than you're even willing to let anyone see. But in time, that will take time. You're very nervous. Very restricted. You haven't leaned back in your chair a single time. You know that? You're very scared, but of *what* I'm not exactly sure."

Gila: [staring at the ground] "I don't know either."

Dr. Caroline Jaspers: "My hunch would be, based on the little I know, that you don't really need someone who can *explain* things to you. You need someone who can listen. Who you can trust and who can listen. My analyst was a man who said very little and every now and then he would cough just to remind me he was there! He teased me about it, of course, that I was doing the work for both of us. But, he was on to something as well. I didn't need someone to interpret things for me, and I suspect neither do you."

Gila: "No."

Dr. Caroline Jaspers: [leaning forward and resting her elbows on her knees] "But you *do* need something. Because when I sit here looking at you I see a very frightened girl. How old do you think you are right now? Maybe twelve years old, even a little younger. Yes? And, she needs to talk, and someone needs to listen."

Gila: [her head is bent towards the ground; tears are falling on her sweater]

Dr. Caroline Jaspers: "I really wish that I could give you what you want. And what you need. It would be a pleasure, really, I want you to be able to hear that, okay? What can I do instead? I can't think right now of someone I could recommend. Hmm. There are people, smart people of course. Where will you do your PhD? I can find colleagues in any city, that won't be a problem of course...but ah, you know? I also am not sure it's what you need right now. What do you think? Especially after this, after our meeting, it will be hard to suggest someone new, I think. You will want to feel *this* right away, but that's not very easy, as I'm sure you know."

Gila: "Yes. I do."

Dr. Caroline Jaspers: "Hm. [leaning back in her chair, stroking her chin] "I'm not sure what to suggest. There are smart people out there, of course, many smart people who have written smart books. People I think you will like, but there is also something you feel *I* specifically can teach you, yes? And, if that's the case, I don't know what good it would do to send you to try again with someone else. Tell me, since you know about yourself better than I do, what do you think you need right now, given these less than ideal conditions?"

Gila: "I don't know. I'm tired. Of meeting new people and trying to say something and seeming like a jerk all the time. I...I feel that I must be either crazy or very difficult. I will go to someone if you think...I don't know. That they can help me. But I don't know –"

Dr. Caroline Jaspers: "Yes, of course. It must be very draining."

Gila: "Discouraging."

Dr. Caroline Jaspers: "And that too, of course."

Gila: "Is it my fault that this only seems to work for me when the other person knows so much about me without my having to explain it? Does that mean that the problem is with my having to explain myself? Is that where I trip up? Maybe I should learn to do that better?"

Dr. Caroline Jaspers: "Oh, Gila, I don't know that it's so simple. And that question sounds to me a little like you think that it's your fault?"

Gila: "But, it *must* be! If it keeps happening. *I* am the only common denominator."

Dr. Caroline Jaspers: "*And* therapy, don't forget."

Gila: "What do you mean?"

Dr. Caroline Jaspers: "I mean this is a process, a very particular one. And, like any complicated system, it has its strengths and weaknesses. It has blind spots. Like you and I have blind spots. That is to be expected. *You* read Freud. In his better moments, even he understood that, sometimes better than anyone else. It's not for everyone. It sometimes takes a lot of work. "

Gila: "But, I was trying, I really was, I –"

Dr. Caroline Jaspers: "Yes, I'm sure you were. I'm sure you were. You don't strike me as the type to give up easily, on anything. Very persistent, yes?" [smiles warmly] "Just like you're sitting here now because you felt that I could maybe help you."

Gila: "I *know* you can."

Dr. Caroline Jaspers: "Indeed. So you say. You may be right. I know I would certainly try to. I am not perfect either, eh? You know that."

Gila: "It's not about the person being perfect. It's...in graduate school, Raynite would always tell me that I shouldn't idealize her, she didn't have all the answers, etc., and I kept saying that isn't the point. I don't think you're a god. It isn't like that at all."

Dr. Caroline Jaspers: "No?"

Gila: "No. It's about how you know something about me that I don't really know yet. Something like that. And, with everyone else, I'm just trying desperately always to explain myself but never manage. Then with you, it's like, you listen to me differently. You hear it differently for some reason."

Dr. Caroline Jaspers: "I have been doing this a long time."

Gila: [shaking her head] "It isn't anything like that. It's you, who you are. I am sorry if that sounds silly. It always made Professor Raynite uncomfortable. But, I don't know how else to say it. I hear it in your voice. When you lectured. When I heard you talk, I knew a few sentences in that – I knew."

Dr. Caroline Jaspers: "You mean it is something about my *voice* that you feel drawn to?"

Gila: "That sounds ridiculous, doesn't it? I'm sorry, I know it does. But as soon as I heard you speak. You sound familiar. Your accent, intonation, everything. And when you lectured, there was...I don't know...so much sharpness in your arguments. The way you made them. Maybe it is the precision? Makes me feel safe. Like I could trust you. Like you would understand. You could *think* about things with me and...I don't know...I'm not sure why that's important...maybe then I wouldn't be so alone, I don't know...I don't..." [looks down at her hands and tries to hold back tears]

Dr. Caroline Jaspers: "Ach Gila, I am sorry you have had such a hard time finding someone you could talk to." [she leans forward and bends down, resting her elbows on her knees] "It sounds from the way you describe this feeling, that you've felt this way before, perhaps in other instances. Is that so?"

Gila: "Yes. Two other teachers. They are brilliant too. In different ways. Tobin knows exactly what she wants, she sees everything. Raynite is magnificent. I think she sees more than she can bear. They saved my life, both of them. I can't even imagine where I'd be without them. They...I felt this same way then too, immediately. I knew."

Dr. Caroline Jaspers: "Ah-ha. We are your three guardian angels then, yes?"

Gila: [smiles and looks up] "Yes."

Dr. Caroline Jaspers: "You mentioned that you were considering going on to do a PhD, is that right? Do you *want* to do that?"

Gila: "I think so. I don't know."

Dr. Caroline Jaspers: "You remember Freud's paper 'On Negation'? What did he say there, eh? That there is no *no* in the unconscious. *I don't know* means I don't *want* to know!

Gila: [blushing] "But, I really don't –"

Dr. Caroline Jaspers: "*Try* to know."

Gila: "Yes. I have applied, but I'm not sure. My professor, who I worked with, says I would be missing things in academe and maybe wouldn't like it. But, I've always wanted to think and write. There's so much I want to learn and do. I just don't..."

Dr. Caroline Jaspers: "Yes? Well, academe isn't perfect, of course. But, you must do it. The PhD. It will be good for you. There will be plenty of things you don't like, no doubt, but you need it too. To refine your inborn skills."

Gila: "Thank you. I haven't been sure. I was worried that..."

Dr. Caroline Jaspers: "No, no, [brushing her hair away from her face] nothing to worry about. It will be good for you. I'm sure about it. And then, we can talk more about philosophy, yes? Who are you interested in? Maybe you'll visit me, if you're ever in Montreal and we can grab lunch or something. How does that sound?"

Gila: "Oh, yes, of course. Thank you. I appreciate –"

Dr. Caroline Jaspers: "Well, it isn't what we hoped for, is it? No, but it will have to do for now. You can write to me. Would you like that?"

Gila: "But, what if my notes are too long? I wouldn't know what is appropriate."

Dr. Caroline Jaspers: "Ah, so much fear, Gila. So much restriction! Eh? You need some help with that, yes? Always feeling so nervous. Always checking yourself. Stopping yourself. You must feel so constrained. That's okay. It will take time. Yes, perhaps a lot of time. And help. I think you could find someone eventually. But, it will be good for you to start a PhD, begin to do your scholarship. I don't believe I exactly know what you're interested in? Maybe we can talk about that a little bit, if you'd like. It will be good to have a little rest from this search for a therapist, I think. You never know, maybe in a different moment, depending on what you're working on or thinking about, things will shift and move around a little and something that was hard before may feel a little different. From a different angle, that kind of thing. What do you say? Does that sound like a reasonable plan? You are so constricted, I can barely tell if you're nodding, you poor thing! Perhaps a PhD will help you with that too. It will be good to gain some grounding and the mind is a wonderful way to do that. Don't let anyone tell you otherwise. Of course it shouldn't come at the expense of a vivid emotional world, but I suspect that's not quite a risk for you. You seem to feel things very deeply, very intensely from what I can tell. I believe it could be different at a later point. And, who knows? Perhaps our paths shall cross in the academic world? For now, what about we say you'll write to me and I will be sure to always write back."

Gila: "But –"

Dr. Caroline Jaspers: "No, no. No hesitation. Shall we say that then? You'll write to me, whatever length you feel like, and I'll write back. Now, of course, my letters may be briefer than yours because I have commitments that I have to be accountable for, you understand that, of course? And, you won't take it too personally, I hope?"

Gila: "Yes, I can try that. Thank you."

Dr. Caroline Jaspers: "I know it isn't what you were hoping for. I understand that. We can meet a few more times before I leave, if you'd like? Try to get to know you a little bit better?"

Gila: "I wouldn't know what to say, I..."

Dr. Caroline Jaspers: [sitting upright] "Then let's do that, yes? I think my next patient may already be here and that means I'm going to have to go to the door. We don't want her standing outside now, do we? [standing up] We can walk to the door together; would that be okay? I'll see if she's already here. I haven't cured her of her tardiness just yet, alas! Shall we? Why don't you tell me what philosophers you'd like to research?"

❦

It is one year later. Early summer. Sunday. Sunny. Near a public bench in a small leafy park in the East Village, New York City. The streets are bustling with people riding bikes, walking, talking, skateboards cutting across concrete. There are sounds of music and honking and brunches at restaurant patios filling the air. Gila has just bought a scoop of mint-chip from a boutique dairy-free shop, a treat for finishing the first year of her PhD coursework. The cell phone in the pocket of her jeans is vibrating. It is a call from D, she lets it go to voicemail. The day is beautiful and maybe it can wait. A few seconds later, when he calls again, she plants the spoon into the scoop and answers.

D: "Yo."

Gila: "Hi there. What's going on today?"

D: "Don't know. Nothing much. Whatever."

Gila: "Are you okay?"

D: "Why?"

Gila: "Because you don't sound okay. What's going on?"

D: "Nothing. Don't know, I – Whatever."

Gila: "You need to say a little more than that, please. What's going on? Fill me in. We talked last night and you seemed fine?"

D: "Yeah whatever, I – It's – Fuck it, I don't know. Don't fucking know."

Gila: "Hm. That doesn't sound too good. What's going on, D? Fill me in, okay? I can't read your mind. Can you help me out? Let's help me out. Please. I'm listening."

D: "It's nothing, just – I'm – Fuck it, G, I'm done."

Gila: "You're done? What are you *done* with?"

D: "Everything."

Gila: "You can't be done with everything. What happened? Did someone do something confusing or offensive? Did you get into another fight with Mum? Tell me, so I can figure it out. Okay? Come, I'm listening. Please try to talk."

D: "I'm just done, yo, fucking done. I've had it. Everything – It's fucking everything, okay, it's – everything. I'm – gonna go, okay?"

Gila: "*No,* it's not okay. Where exactly do you think you're going?"

D: "It doesn't matter. Forget it."

Gila: "Um, I don't think so, buddy. Where exactly do you think you're going?"

D: "I'm just done, okay? So fuck it, really. Don't try to talk me out of it. You can't, you – can't do anything. I did this and there's nothing you can..."

Gila: "D, tell me right now. What did you do?"

D: "I got in trouble – bad. Fuck yeah, this girl – She's bad news, she's – has something. I don't know. Can't say what. Doesn't fucking matter, but – if I go with her, like live with her, some shit like that, she says it'll all work out – Okay, I'm going. I decided."

Gila: "You are going *nowhere,* understand? Is this girl the girl you have been dating for the past few weeks? You told me she was dangerous, that's why you broke up?"

D: [laughs] "Fuck yeah. Didn't think – Hoped you wouldn't. I should have fucking known that you'd remember – fucking – anyway so what? She seemed that way before, but now – it doesn't matter 'cuz I'm heading out."

Gila: "I don't understand. Why? Who will you talk to? How will you deal with stressful things by yourself, if you're saying the person you are going to be with is crazy?"

D: "Yeah, she's some crazy ass – anyway, I know you don't like when I talk that way but – seriously G, I'm finished here."

Gila: "I know you say that when you get discouraged about something, but let's figure out what's getting to you and we'll go from there. Okay?"

D: "I'm fucking done okay – Okay? What kind of life is this? I can't do anything. A fucking waste of life I am. At least she likes me..."

Gila: "You are not a waste of life, don't say such things, you're brilliant. You have a job that you're managing very well in. Think about it: just last year you were almost in jail, okay? Look at that improvement. Because you work so hard. There are days that are discouraging, so what? I have them too. But, then you have to just stick with it, talk and think it through."

D: "No more. I can't no – can't do it anymore. I'm not like you, okay?"

Gila: "I know that, okay? I never asked you to be anything like me. Do I? I'm just saying you can't run away somewhere with someone dangerous when things get hard."

D: "They're always hard."

Gila: "Well yes, but..."

D: "I'm fucking *done*. G, you have – You are the best. You are – have – done as much as possible but maybe I'm too – fucking lazy."

Gila: "That *doesn't* mean you just give up, and hurl yourself off a mountain cliff, okay? It means you take a step back and breathe and talk and –"

D: "I can't."

Gila: "You can."

D: "I can't."

Gila: "I know you can. You are despairing. That makes sense. I'll come to Toronto tomorrow, and we'll find a therapist. A good one. I already have someone in mind. A colleague of someone I know in Boston. I think he's good. I would have suggested him before...maybe I should have. I didn't think you would be ready, but maybe this is the right time. Also, we can look to find another job, okay? We can..."

D: "I can't. I have no money. Can't just do shit like you make it sound – so easy. It isn't like that isn't –"

Gila: "I will take care of that, for now. Okay? I've always worked. I have savings I can use. And, you'll see that maybe this will be a moment you can deal with things. Confront things you've been unable to address before. How does that sound? I'll fly in tomorrow, and we'll have some lunch, at the business, or maybe somewhere else. And then, we'll get to work, and find things to make things better."

D: "It's so much work."

Gila: "I know. It is. But I am right here with you. I have always been. And this is just the next step, okay? This makes a lot of sense. You're getting older. You want a more fulfilling life. That takes some time, for you to get better at some things, but it can happen."

D: "Not for me."

Gila: "Yes, it can. Stop saying no. Stop being so despondent. You are not alone with this. I'm right here. We are going to make things better. Find you a better job? Working with your hands? I've always thought that would be a better fit."

D: "Is that shit more school?"

Gila: "No, I don't think so. We'll find one that isn't. How about that? Okay? I promise you, we'll find something. We always do. As long as you just stick with this, it is a process..."

D: "Feels fucking stupid."

Gila: "Well, yes, I know sometimes it *feels* that way. Sometimes the world is hard for me too. But you put one foot in front of the other and..."

D: "Fuck it. I'm not like you, G. Just give it up, okay? Just fucking forget you ever knew me. Forget. Stop with this shit about how things will be one day. I'm tired, fucking tired, do you – understand?"

Gila: "I do. But..."

D: "What's the worst shit – Okay, name the worst thing."

Gila: "That can happen? If you run away with someone who you've described as volatile and violent and whatever else?"

D: "Yeah that shit. So what? What's gonna happen?"

Gila: "I don't know what's *going* to happen, only that that kind of instability isn't safe for you. It takes a lot of work to make sure you don't get set off, aren't reeling all the time, but here you're throwing yourself right into it. Into something that will set you off in ways you can't manage on your own."

D: "And then what? So what? What's after that?"

Gila: "I don't know."

D: "I fucking kill myself?"

Gila: "I don't know. I can't think –"

D: "So what? Who fucking cares? Not everyone is you, G. You are good to me but – fuck everyone else – I really mean it – fuck 'em. I don't care and – they don't care. No one cares, but you. You have your own life anyways. You – I did my best, okay?"

Gila: "Now you listen, buddy, I don't like how this is going. You're despairing? We can talk about it. You have hard feelings; we can change some things. We did not make it *this* far, past so much motherfucking shit I can't even *tell* you, to have your smart ass throw your hands up one day and say, sorry yo, I'm checking out. You got it? That's not happening. You're going to put on some music, go to that new burger place you like, get something to eat, then call me when you're back home and we'll talk more. And tomorrow, I will be there and we'll figure this stuff out."

D: "Too late, G. Too fucking late."

Gila: [raising her voice] "Too late for *what*? Answer me. Too late for what?"

D: "Don't know. I'm tired, 'kay. I'm fucking done. Don't worry –"

Gila: "Don't worry? You have some fucking nerve. I goddamn raised you, little shit. You understand? I have pulled your stupid ass out of every single well you've fallen into, every hole you thought was interesting, every corner of trouble you thought you would check into. I have pulled you out, by the hands or by the hair. I don't care how or what, but I am not about to give up now. So you are going to have to..."

D: "You don't get it. You're so smart and all but – you just – don't see it. How the game – it's fucking rigged, G, fucking rigged yo. It's fucking *rigged*."

Gila: "What are you talking about? What game? I don't understand what you're trying to say."

D: "This – This whole shit we're in. It's fucking – Fuck it – Doesn't matter what I do. I won't be normal. You keep trying, saving me from shit. Stop doing that, can't you? You don't see – it doesn't matter. I just get into more shit the next day, or after that, okay?"

Gila: "That is simplistic."

D: "Whatever yo. You're lying to yourself. Thinking I am better than I am – Some shit like that or – whatever."

Gila: "I don't think I have illusions about what you are, okay? But it's my *job* to make sure you're okay. Do you understand that? D? You listening? My fucking job."

D: "You did your best, 'kay? I know that. I don't mean to be – I just can't keep doing this. It's not personal, okay. Not personal. It's just – I can't keep trying. Let me go. If I fuck up from now on, that shit's on me. Goodbye."

Gila: "Oh, don't you dare hang up on me you. Can't. This is the. Fucking job. It's not about my feelings it's. The kingdom is on fire and I hear you. Can't you see I'm burning. D. I hear you loud and clear. But listen. This is not a game. You there? It's fucking life. If you don't. If. I don't find you this whole house can burn and. Everything. He built will burn. And it's my *job*. You understand?

I am what stands between you and the blazing burning all around.
Land mines.

All the shit she pulls to trigger your outrage and loathing.
Feelings.

You can't understand or manage.

Thinking you can't reach. My words are bandage

don't do this or that or that or this. We're here together

little shit. You're going nowhere. Out this field like it's a
game?

There is no exit

only forward. Nothing left. What are you doing

saying sorry, tried my best, we're not the same? you fucking joking?

If I'm not like you, who fucking am I.

If I'm not with you, where am I. And

if we're not in this together. You're my baby

don't go acting like I'm doing favors. Like you didn't know

I did all this. This all was meant to save us

now you're leaving like-

you're *tired*?

every day and year we talk I find another.

Other better way to reach you. Teach you. I'm not stopping.

I'm not dropping out. Not giving up/

there was a vicious God coming for the last-borns first.

I said not happening.

I said not all non-talking baby boys are cursed. To be
destroyed

from inside 'cause they can't fight back. Get overwhelmed

because they have no one to teach them. I have arms.

I made a basket. Baby Moses. I didn't choose it but I.

Won't leave you alone. I made a basket baby.

Put my basket in the reeds. You can't jump ship!

I'll go down with you. Cleaving to your sneakers if I have
to

weaving myself into your jacket if I have to

running after you over the cliff and gliding faster

putting a soft net down before you land to stop disaster

this is my fucking *job*. No matter if it kills me

no matter. As a matter of fact

you think it didn't?

It is me
who watches over you. The shit you pull.
You fall apart it's
me who stands between you and exploding
hears the burning cry in every call. And answers. I live in
constant dread. Foreboding
what will the kid do next.
How will I get him out.
It's me
who fucking raised you up. And me-
how dare you call this shit a game
that you can just walk out off.

Leave. Because you're tired? Don't you think a thousand
times I dreamed of saying fuck it! No
I couldn't leave you in a house on fire
I built a tent within the battlefield. To tend to you. A
medic. This is a war. We're in it together. Here is the home I
made, it isn't much but
we are playing house.
Don't be afraid.

See here's a helmet made from meals I cook you. Armor.
You can't keep it on? It itches? I'll stand in front of you. You
get hurt anyway? I'll put in stitches.
My mind. It's working overtime. My brain
is tough enough to hold your frantic chronic melting down
to stop the train your wordless fury jumps up on.
I'm always on the other end
don't worry what the people say. I'm going nowhere till
you are safe and sound
I'm going no
where are you going?
You can't walk out. Like it's some childhood game
this is my *job* I thought
and in this game you are the boychild and I am the –
I am the –
Who the hell you calling Gila?
I am not some *sister* you can disappoint.
I have been appointed
Been anointed

Dip my head in oil my cup overflows
I am not your mother. Father. Friend
I'm not your bro. I am not your keeper
Listen boy, I'm not in charge. The king is. Dead. Is
dad said. Watch them. Dad's dead
Wait.
I'm just the helper I am
Just the.
We are waiting for the king
to come. And I'm the –
one who built a tent within a desert where the land is
burning. Father
cannot see he's gone but I can hear you. Screaming. I'm
the –
one who tells our father who art in heaven. Hallowed be
thy name.
   What's going on? The
   one who said I do, who said. I'll keep it going when you're
gone.
   Who said –
   our kindly kingly dad is dead but we are not. Yet
   who said
   this is my *job*
I have no other jobs but this. Who said
we won't survive this?
yes, we will. I promised
even if I have to be the one. Who
is the king?
Now that the boy is gone there's nothing left to lose.
Fuck it. Fuck it Gila. Fucking shit what do we do.
In the name of the father and his only son. What
have I done?
He said I'm outta here. Said G we're through. Said fuck it I
say fuck it too.
Now there's nothing left to do.
Who am I?

I don't know.
You go the game is over.

※

It is late October, windy, grey in Cambridge, Massachusetts. The office is colorful, a group practice shared by youthful middle-aged women with clinical PhD's. It is located atop a bagel shop and the waiting room smells like rye and pumpernickel, even in the afternoon. Gila is wearing jeans, a grey hoodie, and sneakers. No jacket. Dr. Teresa Betson is in her early fifties, short salt and pepper hair, angular face and olive skin, athletic shoulders, moving quickly on her feet as if she's on a tennis court. She's wearing a patterned blouse, black slacks, and clogs. She smiles readily to welcome but not to overcompensate. She found Gila in the waiting room, her head bent down staring at the ground and said, in what sounded like a lowered tone, "I'm Terri, you must be Gila?"

T. Betson: "Hi there."

Gila: "Hi."

T. Betson: "I'm Terri. You can just call me Terri."

Gila: [head hanging down, facing the ground] "Ok."

T. Betson: "And, Gila, is that with a hard G or soft one?"

Gila: "Hard."

T. Betson: "That's what I thought. Is it –"

Gila: "Hebrew."

T. Betson: "Are you Israeli?"

Gila: "No. Father was."

T. Betson: "Uh-huh. Yes, I thought it was Israeli."

Gila: [silence, staring at the ground]

T. Betson: "I noticed you haven't looked up once yet. Is it difficult to be here now?"

Gila: "I don't know."

T. Betson: "Okay. That's okay. Therapy can be overwhelming."

Gila: "I don't know."

T. Betson: "We can start with simple basic things? Like, how you found me? On the phone yesterday when we scheduled this appointment, you said you're doing your PhD around here?"

Gila: "Yes."

T. Betson: "In what?"

Gila: "Literature and Philosophy."

T. Betson: [smiling, leaning slightly forward] "That sounds really interesting. Do you have a historical period that you work in, or is that not how it works in English? Forgive me if I'm not too knowledgeable about how specialization works in your field."

Gila: "Theory. I do mostly theory. Psychoanalysis. Trauma. I like every historical period. Or, I don't really notice them. Not sure which."

T. Betson: [laughs] "I think I understand. And, was it someone on campus that gave you my name or...did you find us some other way?"

Gila: "Online. Insurance. Your name was on the list of approved providers. I promised J, my other half, I'd see someone. He's worried and I finally just said ok. Three people. You're the last person."

T. Betson: [leans back a little] "Really? An insurance list? How did you choose then? It's so random that way, isn't it?"

Gila: "I guess. I don't know. Therapy doesn't work for me anyway. I've tried, a lot. I've seen experts, people whose books I read and liked. It doesn't make a difference. I can't be a patient. So. Whatever."

Dr. Betson: "That's surprising. To hear you say how challenging therapy has been for you. You seem easy enough to talk with?"

Gila: "Yeah."

Dr. Betson: "No? Am I missing something?"

Gila: "Whatever. That was never the problem. My being able to *talk*. I can talk to anyone."

Dr. Betson: "Then what was the problem?"

Gila: "I don't know. Actually, I don't care."

[silence]

Dr. Betson: "I'd like to hear if you –"

Gila: "I *don't*."

Dr. Betson: "You knew what I was going to say?"

Gila: "Something about talking more. I don't want to. Once upon a time I could have analyzed this all with you. I can't now."

[silence]

Dr. Betson: "Can I ask then: how did you choose *me*? I mean, if it was an insurance list you had no way of knowing anything about me, right?"

Gila: "I liked your name."

T. Betson: "My name?"

Gila: [head hanging down, facing the ground] "Yeah."

T. Betson: "Hm. Well that's certainly a first. That's funny. Then you won't have a hard time calling me Terri. Or, wait, was it Teresa that you liked?"

Gila: "Yeah."

T. Betson: "Terri?"

Gila: "No."

T. Betson: "Teresa?"

Gila: "I don't know. I just did."

T. Betson: "*Really*? I've never had anyone say that to me before. Hm. Interesting. Well nobody calls me Teresa, so it's just Terri to everyone. Or Dr. Betson, but I'm not usually that formal."

Gila: "Okay."

T. Betson: "Okay?"

Gila: "I'll say, Dr. Betson."

T. Betson: "Did you just say something? You almost whispered, I'm not sure I caught it."

Gila: "Nothing. I am formal."

T. Betson: "Oh. Okay. That's okay, of course."
    [silence]
    "Do I know you from somewhere? You look kind of familiar."

Gila: [lifts her head slightly to catch her eyes, pauses for a moment, then looks back to the ground] "I don't think so."

T. Betson: "Yeah, just thought I'd ask. You're not from Boston are you? You just look a little familiar."

Gila: "Yeah, so do you."

T. Betson: "I can see you're very quiet. And that's okay, of course. Can I ask what brings you in today?"

Gila: "I promised J."

T. Betson: "J?"

Gila: "My other half. He's worried."

T. Betson: "Is he right to be worried about you?"

Gila: "I don't know. A few months ago, the summer, my brother. Left. He ran away. He got into trouble. I guess, I just, I was responsible for him and failed. And, ever since I just...I guess. Things are difficult."

T. Betson: "I am sorry to hear that. How old is he?"

Gila: "Two years younger, but don't tell me he'll be fine, please. In fact, don't say anything about him. There's no way you can understand. The other two I met just tried to talk me out of it. Don't do that, please. It's hard to understand."

T. Betson: "Okay. I think I can try to do that. What I can see is that you seem to be in a lot of pain."

Gila: [looks up for the first time] "What?"

T. Betson: "You look like you're in anguish."

Gila: "I don't know. My head hurts."

T. Betson: "Oh. I'm sorry about that. Did it just start?"

Gila: "No. Yes. I don't know. I have these headaches."

T. Betson: "Can I ask you about them?"

Gila: "Sure. Whatever."

T. Betson: "Do you get them often? Or, just at certain times of the day?"

Gila: "Always. The whole day, pretty much. Sometimes, when I'm reading, I feel it less. Doesn't matter. Just hurts like hell, whatever."

T. Betson: "And, what do you do? Does anything help?"

Gila: "Curl up on the cold floor."

T. Betson: "Oh, Gila, that sounds really awful! Have you always had headaches like this?"

Gila: "No."

T. Betson: "So, do you think – "

Gila: "Yes. I do. Related to D leaving. Everything that's going on. Yes. Doesn't make them better though, knowing that. Nothing helps."

T. Betson: "Hmm. So, they're like migraine-type headaches? I'm no expert or anything, I'm just trying to think about this for a moment because it obviously seems really important if you're in so much pain all the time."

Gila: "Whatever."

T. Betson: "You don't want to see a doctor, a specialist or something? At least for meds of some kind?"

Gila: "I did. Two neurologists. They're stumped, said something about how it doesn't fit into how migraines normally work. Shouldn't be happening this many times in a single day. But, whatever. One of them said something about a chronic condition you can get...after a really stressful event. Doesn't matter. I told them it probably is just my way of falling apart."

T. Betson: "And, what did they say to that?"

Gila: "Nothing. I don't think. They are neurologists. There are more meds I could try but I don't want to. I've already taken a bunch of different things. Nothing works."

T. Betson: "Gila, do you feel in some way that you deserve this pain that you're in?"

Gila: "I wouldn't use the word *deserve*. But, it makes sense to me I guess."

T. Betson: [leans forward and crosses her legs] "I think I can try to see that, see it your way. Maybe, I don't know but I could *try* for sure, I will, but I still don't know that you need to be in so much *physical* pain all the time. It must be excruciating?"

Gila: "Just forget it."

T. Betson: "Forget what?"

Gila: "Just forget it. The headache. Leave it alone."

T. Betson: [leans back in her chair] [silence]
        "I don't want to push you to talk about something –"

Gila: "Then don't. Just forget it, please."

T. Betson: "Okay. It's kind of hard when I see you squinting and holding your head with your hand. You look very weak. I feel responsible –"

Gila: [looks up and directly at her] "You said you weren't –"

T. Betson: "Okay, I know. I'm sorry. It might take me a little while to teach myself not to be distracted by that."

Gila: [silence]

T. Betson: "Would it help to tell me a little bit more about your brother? About him leaving?"

Gila: "I guess. I don't know what to say. I had another older brother who killed himself."

T. Betson: "Oh."

Gila: [looking down at the ground]

T. Betson: "I didn't know. I mean, of course I didn't. But, hm, that's a lot. And, you're young. Shit. Gila, is that what you're worried about? That he will do something to hurt himself?"

Gila: "He did. He *left*. I...can't explain. He's not okay. He just gave up. Finally, gave up."

T. Betson: "And, how about you? Are you thinking of hurting yourself?"

Gila: "No."

T. Betson: "Did you just say no? You're speaking very quietly and I want to be sure I'm hearing everything."

Gila: "Yeah. I said no. You're getting distracted though."

T. Betson: "I'm getting what? I missed that last part."

Gila: "Nothing. Doesn't matter."

T. Betson: "Because it would make sense to, if you're suffering so much. People have all kinds of thoughts when they're in pain. It would be important for me to know about anything like that, so that we can find a way to support you."

Gila: "There's nothing to worry about. I want to be dead. That part is true. I wish that I could do something because I can't be here, like this, without him and everything...he was my life. Raising him. Taking care of everything. There's nothing left. But I can't hurt myself. It's not my style."

T. Betson: "Oh-kay. I want to believe that you're not going to do anything to endanger yourself but let's keep talking about it, okay?"

Gila: "Not now."

T. Betson: "You don't want to keep talking about it now?"

Gila: "No."

T. Betson: "Okay, I can understand that. We can return to it later. Is that okay?"

Gila: "Whatever."

T. Betson: "Is there anything else you can tell me about what you're going through? How is your eating and your sleeping? How are you managing at school?"

Gila: "Fine. I don't know."

T. Betson: "Let's break it down then into different questions, if that makes it easier."

Gila: "School is easy. I don't know how I get there or stay in class but I don't notice it. It's fine."

T. Betson: "You can write papers like this? While you're in this state, I mean? Even with the headaches?"

Gila: "I guess. It's not that big a deal. They're papers. It's school. Anyway. Maybe being able to dissociate can come in handy."

T. Betson: "That's kind of incredible. Really. I've been doing this for, well, long enough and, frankly, it's hard to imagine someone in the state you're in being able to write papers for graduate school."

Gila: "Whatever."

T. Betson: "You don't think so?"

Gila: "I don't care."

T. Betson: "I'm sorry?"

Gila: "Who cares? I've been doing shit I have to do forever. It's adrenaline, auto-pilot, whatever. I don't notice. No one else does either."

T. Betson: "Yeah." [she exhales deeply and leans back in her chair] "Yeah. That must be very true."

Gila: "People write about this. I'm not saying anything new. There was something recent that came out...never mind, it doesn't matter. People have been saying this, how after illness or combat experience you can get used to things. Doing things, a certain way. It's no achievement, just the way things are."

T. Betson: [silence]

Gila: [pauses and continues staring at ground] "I don't have any more to say or anything, just saying. I'm explaining I guess, that it's nothing special. Nabokov said he could write with bullets flying over his head. So, yeah.

T. Betson: "Gila? where'd you go?"

Gila: "What? What do you mean?"

T. Betson: "Just now. You were telling me something about coping and how you manage and then, I don't know, your *feeling* went away."

Gila: [startled, looks up from the ground and straight ahead and directly at Betson for the first time]. "How did you notice –"

T. Betson: "I can hear it. In your voice. What happened?"

Gila: "I don't know. No one's ever noticed that before." [she shakes her head faintly]

T. Betson: "You're shaking your head."

Gila: "Yeah. I'm surprised I guess. I just...I'm not used to anyone noticing anything. Like that."

T. Betson: "It probably happens a lot, doesn't it? Feeling something and then shifting into your head and back and forth."

Gila: "I don't know. I don't...no one's ever asked what I'm feeling, in that way. Like you just did."

T. Betson: "Okay. It's subtle, but I'm trying to stay close to what you're feeling. That's what I'm interested in."

Gila: "But I don't *know*...what I'm feeling. I don't –"

T. Betson: "It's okay. We can try to find out."

Gila: "But, what if I can't?"

T. Betson: "Why wouldn't you be able to know what you're feeling?"

Gila: "I don't know. I just...I don't think I know."

T. Betson: [leans forward again, sitting upright] "I want to ask you about sleeping. How about sleeping? Are you sleeping?"

Gila: "No. Two hours, sometimes three."

T. Betson: "You can't fall asleep?"

Gila: "Don't want to."

T. Betson: "Did you say you don't *want* to? Why is that?"

Gila: "Because, then I have to wake up."

T. Betson: [exhales and leans forward, almost resting her elbows on her knees] "It's heartbreaking to hear you say that."

Gila: [silence]

T. Betson: "Tell me about waking up. Please? What's so terrible about doing that?"

Gila: "I don't know."

T. Betson: "I really want to understand so it's okay if you don't know. We can figure it out together. Do you think you're having bad dreams?"

Gila: "Sometimes. More like visions. My father is walking, with tubes coming out of his arms and wires from machines he was linked up to everywhere. He's saying something. He's a ghost but also right there, in my living room. I'm on the couch. I won't lie in my bed. My bed can fuck itself. And then, I don't know. It's more that when I wake up I know again that D is gone and he isn't coming back. Every time I sleep I have to find that out again. I can't." [she is choking up and holding back tears]

T. Betson: [makes a cooing sound that expresses painfulness] "I'm so sorry, Gila, that you have to go through this every time you wake up. It sounds traumatic."

Gila: "I don't know what trauma is. I don't know anything. I was fine, that's what I don't understand. I was *fine,* for years. And now...I don't know. He's gone and it's like they're all dying again, but for the first time."

T. Betson: "Keep going."

Gila: "I don't *know.* I don't."

T. Betson: "That's okay. Just keep saying what you're feeling."

Gila: "But I don't *know.* Okay? I *don't*...I've never had these feelings."

T. Betson: "What feelings, Gila?"

Gila: "These. This kind of...I just *can't.* I can't *do* this all without him."

T. Betson: "Your brother."

Gila: "Him, my father, everything. All of it. I can't" [starts to cry] "I am so tired. I am so fucking tired. You don't understand. There was...I raised him. I took care of him because...it doesn't matter now...I needed to but if he's gone, there is no other way to be alive. I have no other *reason.* I just don't. It's over. This time I'm really done."

T. Betson: "It's almost as if he was like your skin, or something. Protecting you from feeling so many things?"

Gila: "Yeah. And taking care of him. It was my job. *I* don't have another purpose. I don't have anything."

T: Betson: "I want to ask you too...I realize I don't have a sense of who you're living with? Are you living alone? You mentioned a partner, a husband I think? But, on the phone, I think you said he's in another city?"

Gila: [looks up, startled] "Hey. Now it's your turn."

T. Betson: "Excuse me?"

Gila: "Where'd *you* go? Just now."

T. Betson: "Where did I go? What do you mean exactly?"

Gila: "Just now. You shifted gears. We were talking about my job and taking care of things and then you asked me about my living situation. Did something happen to make you turn away from what I was describing?"

T. Betson: "Wow" [laughs a little and runs her fingers through her hair] "I thought I was good, but I may have met my match here, may I?"

Gila: "Was it something I said?"

T. Betson: "No, no. Well...maybe. Yes. I think I just got anxious that's all, for a minute. Realizing you're describing very frightening feelings and realizing that I don't know too much about you and I felt responsible to get some facts there for a moment. Sorry about that. I can't believe you noticed that, I didn't, actually. I'm going to have to be on my toes with you, aren't I?"

Gila: "Sorry that you're anxious. I do live alone, yes. I'm not going to *do* anything, I don't think. Please, you don't have to worry about that, okay. Don't get scared. I'm not...it's not something I care about."

T: Betson: "Okay. Thank you. I think that's reassuring. I think. Now, where were we? Oh, yes, we were talking about it being your job to take care of him, your brother and without that you don't know what to do."

Gila: "No. Without that there *isn't* anything. There's no secret *me* crouching behind that task. I *was* that *job*. That's it. And, when it's over, so am I."

T. Betson: "Say more. I think I'm beginning to understand."

Gila: "And, please don't say it *feels* that way. I'm not talking about some sentimental shit like that, okay? This is the truth. This is a fact."

T. Betson: "I believe you. And, I believe you are trying to get me to see something that's incredibly crucial and painful. I am trying to follow you. I want to understand, I really do. Tell me more about what you mean when you say there's no one there. What do you mean by that, exactly?"

Gila: "People always talked to me as if my taking care of him was some *defense* mechanism. Like by taking care of him I didn't need to deal with my own feelings or whatever. I knew that wasn't right but I didn't know how to describe it. But, now I see it. I get it. That I just don't exist except as the person who tried to do all that stuff. There just isn't...there's just no one else there."

T. Betson: "Gila, what are you feeling right now, when you say these things?"

Gila: "I don't know."

T. Betson: "Grief or anger? Or loss?"

Gila: "I don't know. I don't...that's the *point*. I don't know *anything*. I don't. I *did*. But that was when the world was organized a certain way."

T. Betson: "With you taking care of him. It's almost as if he was the pin in the bomb and now someone has taken it out."

Gila: "And, everything's exploded everywhere."

T. Betson: "That's horrible. It sounds like you've been working so hard and –"

Gila: "It was my *job*. I just don't have another one is all. I was a soldier. Now, the war is over. He just got up and said he's leaving, going somewhere else. And, maybe he'll be fine, eventually. I have no idea. But, I don't have...I can't" [starts to cry faintly again] "I'm sorry. I don't cry in front of people."

T. Betson: "It's okay, Gila. Really."

Gila: "No."

T. Betson: "This is a tremendous loss. And, a huge shock too. And, after everything you've already been through."

Gila: [shaking her head] "No. I'm not used to crying. And now, that's all I'm doing. All the time. I don't know what's going on with me. This isn't *me*. I've never...shit's happened before but I was fine. I felt things but I was *okay*; I was always okay."

T. Betson: "But, Gila, you're telling me that you didn't really feel things in the same way before."

Gila: "But, why not? I don't get it. I don't understand."

T. Betson: "Maybe because you were focused on helping him. And, it sounds like maybe your mother as well? You haven't mentioned her but...I'm just guessing."

Gila: "Yeah. But...where was all this feeling? I wasn't a robot. I felt a lot of things...I don't get it. I don't understand what's happening to me." [cradles her head in her hands]

T. Betson: "What's going on right now?"

Gila: [silence]

T. Betson: [leans forward and speaks very quietly] "Gila? Is your head hurting?"

Gila: [faintly] "Yeah. I can't."

T. Betson: "Keep going. What do you mean?"

Gila: "I'm crying, all the time. Like *now*. This never happens. I don't *talk* like this. I just can't...manage. Or, I don't want to. I don't know. I don't recognize the way I'm acting. I'm not *like* this. You don't understand. I'm not like *this*."

T. Betson: "I can hear that you're surprised and maybe confused as well."

Gila: "I just don't understand. I wasn't hiding from these feelings. Never. Sure I compartmentalized or whatever but this is like...whatever."

T. Betson: "What were you going to say?"

Gila: "Nothing."

T. Betson: "I want to know. Can you please try to continue?"

Gila: "Nothing. It's stupid. What I'm saying is stupid."

T. Betson: "Somehow I doubt that it's either of those things."

Gila: "You don't know that. It's so stupid. Stop asking me okay."

T. Betson: "Hm. I don't want to do that just yet, okay? I think this is really important. I want you to continue. Please. You weren't compartmentalizing before. You weren't running away. But something was happening. Let's try to figure that out."

Gila: "No."

T. Betson: "What are you so scared of?"

Gila: "Are you fucking kidding? *Everything.* I don't know anything right now. Okay? *Anything.* I thought I was okay. I thought I made it. More or less. Survived some shit. I gave up all those stupid ghosts, my father and his voice and shit. It's all I hear, and now I wake up sweating and see his body in the hospital, my older brother and his head shot through with a bullet on my birthday. All of it. It's all just there – where the fuck was all of it, until now, huh? I don't understand. [shaking her head and starting to cry] I don't *fucking* understand."

T. Betson: [leans forward and looks directly at Gila, whose head is still facing the ground] "Gila."

Gila: "What? Why are you saying my name like that? Do you understand this? Can you please explain it to me? I don't get it. I don't understand."

T. Betson: "I wish I could. I really do. I would. I don't know yet. We need more time."

Gila: "I can't."

T. Betson: "You can't what?"

Gila: "Nothing."

T. Betson: "You can't *what*?"

Gila: "Nothing. Forget it."

T. Betson: "Manage? You need to tell me what you mean. Please. I'm listening."

Gila: "Sure. Maybe. I don't know."

T. Betson: "You need to say more."

Gila: "I *can't*."

T. Betson: "Why not?"

Gila: "Because I don't know *anything*. I don't understand the words coming out of my mouth. This isn't *me*. Do you understand? I am smart and sharp and...in control of what I'm feeling and now...I can't stop hearing him tell me that it's over. It's all over. I can't stop...I can't do anything. This isn't me. My head is breaking. It isn't...I don't understand."

T. Betson: "It sounds scary, what you're telling me."

Gila: [starting to cry] "I just can't do this. Okay? I can't start again from scratch. I fucking *mourned* him. I did my time in grieving. I can't go through it all again. I *can't* keep *losing*. I can't keep...I can't *do* it. And, I don't even get it. Why am I like this? I make it through whatever's happened and then I fall apart with this? It makes no sense. I don't..."

T. Betson: "Maybe you were holding things together for him. In order to take care of him."

Gila: "But...still...why would I rather die right now then feel this? I am not a weakling when it comes to painful...anything. I...I don't understand."

T. Betson: "But, maybe this is different?"

Gila: "How? I don't understand. Why?"

T. Betson: "Maybe because then, when you were taking care of your brother, there was a limit to what you could let yourself feel. You knew you were responsible for taking care of him and you needed to be strong in a certain way."

Gila: "But...I don't understand. This is different...I can't function now. I don't know how."

T. Betson: "Say more."

Gila: "I don't know."

T. Betson: "Try. Please. I'm listening."

Gila: "I can't. I don't understand. I don't get any of this. I was fine, I thought. I made it out. I had...teachers. School. I was okay."

T. Betson: "Gila, what can't you do? When you say *function,* can you explain a little more about what you mean?"

Gila: "I don't know."

T. Betson: "Try."

Gila: "I can't *do* anything now. I can't read, not really. Enough for school but not more than that. Or, talk to people. School is different; I could be half-dead and get through that. But Tobin, who is...I always talk to her. I can't now. I can't write an email. I can't say anything. I'm...don't know."

T. Betson: "You're in a lot of pain."

Gila: "But, I've been in pain before. This is different."

T. Betson: "You're feeling everything more acutely. Do you think that's part of it?"

Gila: "I guess. I don't know."

T. Betson: "Try."

Gila: "I don't *know.*"

T. Betson: "Okay. It's okay. Let me ask you a different question, okay? Can I? You said that you experienced mourning before. You have gone through grief. Do you mean that you experienced your loss and sadness?"

Gila: "I don't know what you mean."

T. Betson: "You said you had a lot of those feelings before. I'm just trying to get a picture of you, before this, that's all."

Gila: "I felt things, but…it was different. I felt scared about what would happen. I didn't want to lose my father, I felt that. But…I don't know. It makes no sense."

T. Betson: "How about on your own behalf?"

Gila: "I don't understand."

T. Betson; "For yourself. Did you feel the impact of things for *you*? Did you get comfort out of talking about it in a certain way."

Gila: "But, I *didn't* talk about it."

T. Betson: "But, you just said there was a woman, I can't remember her name, Toobin or something? Someone that you did feel comfortable with? A teacher?"

Gila: "But, I didn't *talk* to her. I listened. She told me what I might be thinking and I just…I didn't say anything."

T. Betson: "Hmm."

Gila: "What?"

T. Betson: "I'm just wondering if you ever talked to anyone about what things have been like for *you,* Gila, specifically *you.*"

Gila: "I don't get it."

T. Betson: "What don't you get?"

Gila: "You say *me* as if there's someone but...I'm just the one who keeps things going. I didn't *have* anything to say. I just...I didn't *need* to talk. I needed us to be okay."

T. Betson: "But, Gila, isn't that part of the point? Maybe?"

Gila: "I don't get it. It was my job. I needed to do my job. Or, we'd lose everything."

T. Betson: "I understand. And, you did that."

Gila: "No. I fucked up. He is gone. I tried to. I tried and fucking failed."

T. Betson: "But I want to focus on one thing for just a moment, okay? You were entirely devoted to doing that, *job,* as you call it. And, maybe –"

Gila: "It doesn't matter. It's over now. Okay? I fucked up and it's over."

T. Betson: "But, Gila, maybe that's why you don't feel like your-self. Because you're not used to thinking about your own feelings."

Gila: [silence]

T. Betson: "Gila? You're not saying anything. Where did you go?"

Gila: "I don't know what to say."

T. Betson: "Can you try?"

Gila: [silence]

T. Betson: "Gila, where do you go when all of a sudden you get so quiet?"

Gila: "I don't know."

T. Betson: "Is it feeling difficult to talk?"

Gila: "I don't know."

T. Betson: "Hm. You seem like you might be overwhelmed."

Gila: "I don't know. How would I know?"

T. Betson: "What you're feeling? How would you know what you're feeling?"

Gila: "I guess. Maybe. I don't know. I don't know anything."

T. Betson: "Well, that's not true, that you don't know anything. You know *a lot* of things, actually. More than most, in some ways. But then, it's true, there are these moments when you get so quiet. It's almost as if you go away. I wonder what's happening then."

Gila: [silence]

T. Betson: "Gila?"

Gila: [silence]

T. Betson: "Gila? Where have you gone again? Try to tell me okay?"

Gila: "I don't know."

T. Betson: "Maybe something we're talking about is scaring you?"

Gila: "I think...I don't...have what to say. No language there."

T. Betson: "Where?"

Gila: "I don't know. When you talk to me. About what I'm feeling."

T. Betson: "When I talk to you about your *feelings,* you go quiet? Do you know why?"

Gila: [shakes her head]

T. Betson: "Oh, Gila, you seem so very young right now. Like a little girl almost."

Gila: [silence]

T. Betson: "It's almost as if this little girl has all these feelings that she doesn't know how to talk about."

Gila: [starts to cry]

T. Betson: "What are you thinking, Gila? Tell me, please."

Gila: "I'm not, I can't be a *girl,* I'm not supposed to be a little... I'm in *charge* of everything. This can't be happening. I don't understand."

T. Betson: "Can you keep going?"

Gila: "I don't know. Please stop, *please.* I don't know what's happening to me."

T. Betson: "I think maybe you're feeling things, that's all."

Gila: "I can't."

T. Betson: "Why not?"

Gila: "Because I have a *job* to do. Because...I don't understand."

T. Betson: "If you have these feelings, you won't be able to do what you need to do?"

Gila: [nods]

T. Betson: "Why is that?"

Gila: "I don't know. Because...being in charge of things means I *tell* us what to do. I do what my dad did, try to anticipate and plan for things. Protect us. If I'm doing that, there *can't* be anything else. There just can't. [shakes her head] I was just doing what he asked me...what I promised to."

T. Betson: "You were helping –"

Gila: "But, I didn't *realize* that meant that *I* was gone, that entire time."

T. Betson: "What do you mean, can you explain what you're seeing when you say that?"

Gila: [holds her head in both hands] "I *can't,* I can't believe this can't..."

T. Betson: "Please try, okay? I'm listening. I really am. I want to know."

Gila: "I kept believing I was helping. But...I got it all wrong. I got it fucking wrong didn't I? He's dead. He has been dead for 15 years. I wasn't *helping,* I was *him*. I thought...I knew I was a soldier but I didn't know. I couldn't have been a soldier if there was no one giving orders. Oh my god, my fucking...I can't, I was so stupid!"

T. Betson: "But, wait there, a minute, okay, Gila, you needed to be in charge of things, it sounds like. That's what you did. How can you blame yourself for that?"

Gila: "I would die if I was left alone with her. You don't understand. If she sees something *existing* in some way, I don't know, she...has to kill it or cause it pain. I can't explain. He was the only person there, even when he was gone. To talk to or relate to. At least I had a way of *being* something. I can't explain, I don't know how..."

T. Betson: "Try."

Gila: "I gave instructions to D and her, myself. I was doing that, all this time. Trying to keep things stable or normal or something. I knew that but...I thought it was *his* voice but it was actually mine, or my voice became the voice of reason, rules, commands, whatever. A kingly voice. What I mean...I *became* my dad, his job. That meant there wasn't anything else I was thinking or feeling. I was just him, just only that...I only had ideas about things commensurate with my post. About the business, D, mortgages, how to get this or that for him or her, I didn't think about...anything else. What other people kept asking me, what I felt or wanted, was I hungry, what I needed, did I want to travel, what city did I like, what clothes to wear, what food to eat. It didn't...none of it was...every now and then it seemed strange how malleable I was, how unassuming. Raynite used to say I was complacent. Said, what do you really think about this idea or that? I tried. My brain could make an argument but when I needed to access what my *own* sense of something or what I felt about it, I would go blank. It bothered her. And me. But, I didn't understand. How could I have *been* so stupid? How could I have been so *blind*?"

T. Betson: "You became what he needed you to be. And –"

Gila: "But, I didn't know...I thought I was just helping."

T. Betson: "And, you were."

Gila: "No. *I* was the one in charge. Who was I helping? There was no one there to help. He was dead. Can't you see? I thought I was helping him, and like an idiot I kept talking to him and checking things with him and whatever but that was all just a way of not realizing that *I* was in charge now, he was gone. I was alone with them and I couldn't stay there the way things were, the way – I hope I die after I say all this, I hope I fucking die, I can't believe I've been so blind, I –"

T. Betson: "Let's not get ahead of ourselves just yet, okay? No dying or talk of dying. When you say that thing about not being able to be the same or the way you were? What do you mean by that?"

Gila: "I don't know. It doesn't matter."

T. Betson: "I think it does. Please tell me."

Gila: "She doesn't...she...doesn't *talk,* like normal people do. She doesn't...I don't know how to say this. I was a threat to her, always. Just this thing that tormented her and she wanted to destroy. We all were but she would at least treat D like a vulnerable pet sometimes who would enchant her. Me, she hated, she still...doesn't know what I'm doing or where I live. If I say I'm coughing because I have a cold, she cuts me off, mid-sentence says – I bought a purse today! – or, if I say it snowed in Boston, she says, annoyed – you're in Boston? Did I tell you what a customer said? – I don't exist with her, I can't. He talked to me. Had a way of seeing me. It was a wasteland otherwise, a desert, or...I don't know. I *can't.* I *really* can't."

T. Betson: "She wasn't a parent, at all. And, it sounds like she was dangerous too."

Gila: "I just kept the conversation going. I just...I didn't know how else to..."

T. Betson: "But, of course you did. You stayed connected to your father, that makes sense Gila, it really does."

Gila: "No. Because all this time...I didn't know how it was working. I thought I was still *me* connecting to *him*. I even thought I was *rebelling* when I went to school. Or talked to Tobin, Raynite...what a *fool* I've been! I was terrified I would forget his voice. *Terrified.* When all along...I'm such an idiot... All along *I* was his voice, it was my own that disappeared."

T. Betson: [leans back] "And, now when we're trying to talk to the little girl inside, she has no language. She's not used to talking."

Gila: "I didn't even know it was there! I didn't know...I..."

T. Betson: "Of course you couldn't have known. You were doing what you needed to do, in order to survive. Gila, is your head hurting you now? You're wincing, as if you're in excruciating pain?"

Gila: "I just can't I can't believe...I believed there was an off-duty soldier somewhere. The one that talked to teachers, wrote smart essays. But, that was still just a soldier, writing from his tent during a lull on the battlefield. That's *why* I couldn't find a way to say something about trauma when I wanted to. Or, loss. That's what happened at Chicago. I tried but it didn't matter. I was still *in* it."

T. Betson: "You clearly have a very powerful mind. And that's good because it means that we can think through things together, we can –"

Gila: "It doesn't *matter*. You don't get it. My mind has always worked, but still – that's why everyone thinks I'm fine or just being difficult when I can't answer but – it's so easy to deconstruct an argument. I can see that, clearly. I don't need to feel anything to do that kind of thing. But, people only notice that or think it means I'm aware of everything but...I don't know how to say something about...I don't even know, I..."

T. Betson: "Yourself?"

Gila: "Personal. Anything personal. I don't *have* things I'm secretly wanting or needing."

T. Betson: "And having a mind like yours probably makes it even harder to see. Because you always have something you can say or figure out. And because you sound so self-assured when you're talking. Actually, I found myself wondering that too, when you first started talking when you walked in here, like, what does this girl need from me, she seems to know everything already, but –"

Gila: "But, I don't!"

T. Betson: "No, I know. I see that now. I do. But it's hard because –"

Gila: "But, I didn't *know* how to tell people that something wasn't working. I tried but...I couldn't."

T. Betson: "It's almost as if you're missing an internal apparatus or something, an emotional system that tells you when you're feeling certain things. Like an immune system. Or, whatever the right physiological metaphor is, do you know what I mean?"

Gila: "Yeah. That's why I don't *know* what I'm feeling when people ask me."

T. Betson: "The absence of that personal voice is subtle. In a way, it is obvious when I listen to you, but it's also subtle."
[silence]
"You're holding your head like it's hurting." [leans forward] "You look like you're in a lot of pain."

Gila: "I don't care. I don't, I *don't* understand. It didn't come up before because I just did what I knew I needed to do. Only now, when he's gone, when it's over..."

T. Betson: "It's the first time anyone's asking you?"

Gila: "It's the first time I don't have the answer. Because I'm not the king. I'm not in charge, nothing to be *in charge of.* I'm used to being him, I don't *have* another way, I don't. I really *don't.*"

[silence]

"I thought because I let him go...I thought when I stopped *listening* to him that meant he was gone. That's what people said...grieving is letting go. I *did* that. I tried to. But, what a fool I've been, an idiot! Because all this time, I wasn't *really* letting go of him. I just wasn't *aware* of holding on. Better yet, I *wasn't* holding on. It was my own voice now; *I* knew the ropes of what he would have said or done. I knew his voice by heart, I...All that *forgive me father*...what an idiot! I *was* him. I wasn't *me,* there *was* no me. That's what it meant to promise him...I can't...believe...I can't..."

T. Betson: "Gila, this is a lot to have to recognize. Okay? I want us to slow down a bit. Not let you get so overwhelmed."

Gila: "Am I getting overwhelmed? How do I *know* that? I don't know that. How can I tell?"

T. Betson: [leans forward] "I know you don't know that. But, I'm getting worried because this is a lot of material and... you're fragile now."

Gila: "Fragile? Who is fragile now? I'm not fragile. What are you talking about?"

T. Betson: "You are. Remember that little girl we talked about? Inside you. I think she's screaming for attention. I think she needs...we need to listen."

Gila: "Screaming. The little girl. The headache...But I *can't* do that. It's too late. The boy was right, D, when he said it's too late for certain things. It's too late. I'm twenty-six. I've...my entire life has been this way. I *can't.*"

T. Betson: "I know it feels that way."

Gila: "It *is* that way. I don't have anything. It's all over. I had him, a way of being, a mind I could use, not totally freely, it's probably connected. Now...I don't know how to sleep or what to eat. I can't live without a voice that tells me what to do."

T. Betson: "I know you can't. But that can change."

Gila: [silence]

T. Betson: "Gila? Are you listening? Can you nod so I know that you're here with me? You look like you're in so much physical pain. Your poor head, you just keep holding it, like it's breaking."

Gila: [silence]

T. Betson: "I think that we can do this together, okay? I want you to think about that. I really believe you have so much –"

Gila: "Stop. Please. Don't comfort me. I don't need that. Please."

T. Betson: "What do you need then?"

Gila: "I don't know. But, it's the truth. The things I'm saying. Finally, you have to bear it or don't listen, and I won't talk. I don't care. No more illusions. I won't be comforted by anything."

T. Betson: "Okay. I hear that. I do."

Gila: [crying softly]

T. Betson: "It's a lot to bear."

Gila: [silence]

T. Betson: "Gila, unfortunately, we're going to need to end soon. And, I need to know you'll be okay. Can we try to talk here for a minute about how you'll be, when you leave? This was a difficult session. We covered a lot. And, I don't know you at all, so...maybe you can give me a sense of where you'll go from here?"

Gila: [silence]

T. Betson: "Gila? You're going away again. Let's bring you back. Okay? Let's talk about how you're going to manage."

Gila: "I don't know."

T. Betson: "Well, can we talk about some things that might help? Some things you can do? Does exercise help? Would talking to someone, you mentioned a teacher? Can you call her and talk to her a little bit? Does talking to your partner help?"

Gila: [silence]

T. Betson: "You said reading isn't working right now. Maybe because you're not sleeping. Should we talk about sleep medication? I can give you the name –"

Gila: "Sorry."

T. Betson: "For what, Gila? What are you apologizing for?"

Gila: "Talking. I'm sorry. I didn't...I don't know what's happening to me."

T. Betson: [leans forward and shuffles almost out of her chair to be closer to Gila, who is looking at the ground] "You're not doing *anything* wrong. I want you to hear that, if you can. You're supposed to talk. There's nothing wrong with that, okay?"

Gila: "I'm taking time. I'm sorry for taking time. Is the session over? Did I go over? I didn't notice. I'm so sorry I didn't..."

T. Betson: "It's okay, please, it's okay. You don't need to say sorry for anything. We went over a bit but I don't have anyone right after, so it's fine. This is important. Can we please talk for a moment about how you're going to be okay? We can meet again next week, if this time slot works for you?"

Gila: [silence]

T. Betson: "Does it work for you?"

Gila: [silence]

T. Betson: "Can you nod to indicate that you can hear me?"

Gila: [nods faintly]

T. Betson: "Okay, that's a start. We need to close things up a little, we're running out of time. I need to know that you can be okay when you leave here."

Gila: [sits up a little] "Okay."

T. Betson: "Okay, what?"

Gila: "I don't want you to be getting anxious. You sound anxious."

T. Betson: [smiles] "I guess I do, don't I? You can still read other people, huh, even given where you're at? That's really something. I *am* anxious, yes, I'm wor –"

Gila: "Okay. It's okay. I'll be...don't worry. Thank you."

T. Betson: "Okay? That's good. I guess. But, do you want to tell me how you're going to manage, so I have a sense of –"

Gila: "No."

T. Betson: "No? Hm. Do you know what you're feeling right now?"

Gila: "No. I need to go."

T. Betson: "You look very sad. Very small and very sad."

Gila: [silence]

T. Betson: "Gila?"

Gila: "I'm sorry."

T. Betson: "It's not an accusation, please, it's just the opposite. I'm sorry you can't hear it that way."

Gila: [silence]

T. Betson: "We're going to need to end. I'm sorry about that."

Gila: "I know. I'm sorry. I...it's just..." [tries to hold back tears]

T. Betson: "What is it? Tell me."

Gila: "It's hard to get up and leave."

T. Betson: "That's okay. We can take an extra minute."

Gila: [silence]

T. Betson: [silence]

Gila: "Tell me what to do, please."

T. Betson: "You're going to get up in a minute or two and head back home. You're going to be okay, try to keep things together as you have been doing so far. And then, you're going to come back in here next week, at the same time. I have the same time available."

Gila: [silence]

T. Betson: "How does that sound?"

Gila: [shakes her head]

T. Betson: "No?"

Gila: "I don't know *anything*."

T. Betson: "I know. That's why we're going to just keep talking."

Gila: [shakes her head]

T. Betson: "Why are you shaking your head?"

Gila: "I *can't*."

T. Betson: "I know."

Gila: "But, I can't. Keep going."

T. Betson: "I hear that. You have been through so much already. But, we don't have to understand everything right away, okay? You're very strong, really, even though I know you don't feel that way now. It's clear that you are and I think, I really do, that, in spite of everything, there is a part of you that really wants to figure this out."

Gila: "I can't. I *tried*."

T. Betson: "I know."

Gila: "I *tried*. I can't. Again."

T. Betson: "But, you need to, Gila. You need –"

Gila: "I don't. That's the difference now. I *don't. Need. To do anything*. It's *over*. The game is over."

T. Betson: [silence]

Gila: "It's over."

T. Betson: "There's a part of you that wants something better for yourself, I believe that. Okay? And, frankly, if there isn't, we're going to have to take another approach, but I think there *is*. And, that's the part of you I'm talking to."

Gila: "My head hurts."

T. Betson: "I know. I see that."

Gila: [crying] "My head hurts me."

T. Betson: "I hear that, Gila, I do. We're going to keep things very simple. For now, all you have to do is get yourself back home and maybe eat something. Maybe take a warm bath. Do you think you can do that? You look so cold, you're shaking. I want you to try to take in what I'm saying to you. Can you hear my voice? Try to listen to me telling you what you need to do. Do you think that you can do that?"

I was a girl who thought I was a prince.

In the game we were playing, my father the king decreed and pleaded to bequeath me all his kingdom in its glory.

Yes, I said. Oh yes. A psalm this is by david. His voice is my shepherd I shall not want.

In situations of danger I hear him, in moments of crisis he tells me what to do. Although I walk in the valley of shadows I don't fear death for his voice is with me.

Your voice is my guide is my rod, leads the way.

Three women came, archangels in their leather jackets, grey black hair, punk fairy godmothers, ghostbusters all. They said where is the smart-ass girl who's pulsing under there? You ain't no humble shepherd boy, there's fire in those eyes, it's blaring. Ditch the lofty regal gig and play.
    I stared in awe. I told them nothing.

I listened anyway.

Oh Father if you are in heaven, *don't.*
    Being david didn't interfere with princely duties.

It was being king that interfered with being david.

You see. When it was time I tried to hear the girl inside, my head was quiet.

I looked everywhere. I offered everything. I sought out reinforcements. Specialists. People with expertise in coaxing kinderlach behind their papa's coattails, hiding.

It answered nothing.

I gave up looking when one day the kingdom fell, the palace burned, the boy had gone. A child was there, under the rubble, naked, howling.

Do you know why I didn't hear it burning? Father, can't you see? Your kingdom was on fire, *was* a fire, and when you left I wore the crown.

When yes I said, oh yes, I meant: becoming an exalted soldier.

You didn't warn me: orders would be needed and *I* would be the one to give them.

You didn't *say,*
    When I become the king, the girlchild vanishes.
    That being you meant I was banished.

I get it now.
    I needed someone – there was no one else to be.

There is no such thing as a prince david.

O. Rex took out his eyes when he realized how he got the throne.
    O what a futile plea, trying, crying, to un-see,
    with me it was becoming rex that blinded me.

Oh yes, I said, *hineni,* yes.
    And while I was him, no one was me.
    The way she always wanted things to be.

A David psalm.
    You dip my head in oil, my cup overflows.

Of course I said I can't let go.

Now my head wet, dripping with anointment, is breaking, no.

I was a girl who did not want –

I am the girl who didn't know I was king who did not know I was a girl.

brainstorm books

Acknowledgments

When, as a rising sophomore in college, I first wrote the phrase "forgive me father, for I have sinned," I had a lot of psychological conviction but very little writerly insight about what it meant. Later that summer, in my first experience in a writing workshop, Jim Miller asked me why I worded things that way, and when I said I had no idea he said, "well, whatever it is, I guess it's important to you. If you want to keep it, you should go figure that out." That relationship to writing was eye-opening to me: you could say something you meant and figure out what you meant later. In the same spirit of pedagogic generosity and amusement, Jim asked me if I was deliberately participating in the tradition of confessional autobiography and when the nineteen-year-old that I was said "what is confessional autobiography?" he shook his head and in some combination of disbelief and affection said, "start reading, kiddo, start with St. Augustine."

I met Phillip Lopate that same summer and he has been my primary and closest reader ever since. Every time I think I know what he's going to say or whether he will like or dislike something, he surprises me. His wisdom, knowledge, and aversion to "hysteria" is indispensable to me. We have our share of running disagreements but even when he's critical, I've never felt that he needs me to agree with him. That freedom is a true gift.

Elisabeth Young-Bruehl suggested I start writing some of the things I couldn't find a way to say. Although I sent her earlier versions of this book, I wish I could have shared how it turned out. I would love to know what she made of all this, especially my quarrel with psychoanalysis.

At Columbia, I am grateful to Leslie Jamison for her sensitivity, camaraderie, and conversations about therapy. Rivka Galchen offered guidance, insight, and practical advice when I needed it, in addition to doses of non-judgmental empathy that helped me through the pitching/publishing process. And Hilton Als has such a unique way of provoking openness that I was repeatedly disarmed; his deep and abiding commitment to psychological complexity gave me courage to say things on paper that until then I had only ever said in my head.

I want to thank Eileen Joy and Vincent W.J. van Gerven Oei at punctum books for believing in this project, and moreover, for doing the hard work with me of formatting a project that is, in large part, an attempt at wrestling with form. I am so grateful for their patience, enthusiasm, and good cheer.

And to Jonathan, who makes everything possible.

Made in the USA
Middletown, DE
25 September 2024

61435693R00186